T0155867

Lecture Notes in Computer Science 12670

More information about this subseries at http://www.springer.com/series/8637

Abdelkader Hameurlain ·
A Min Tjoa (Eds.)

Transactions on Large-Scale Data- and Knowledge-Centered Systems XLVIII

Special Issue In Memory of
Univ. Prof. Dr. Roland Wagner

 Springer

Editors-in-Chief
Abdelkader Hameurlain
IRIT, Paul Sabatier University
Toulouse, France

A Min Tjoa
IFS, Vienna University of Technology
Vienna, Austria

ISSN 0302-9743   ISSN 1611-3349   (electronic)
Lecture Notes in Computer Science
ISSN 1869-1994   ISSN 2510-4942   (electronic)
Transactions on Large-Scale Data- and Knowledge-Centered Systems
ISBN 978-3-662-63518-6   ISBN 978-3-662-63519-3   (eBook)
https://doi.org/10.1007/978-3-662-63519-3

This Springer imprint is published by the registered company Springer-Verlag GmbH, DE
part of Springer Nature
The registered company address is: Heidelberger Platz 3, 14197 Berlin, Germany

Preface

This special issue of our Transactions on Large-Scale Data- and Knowledge-Centered Systems (TLDKS) is dedicated to Roland Wagner, who passed away on January 3, 2020. His death was a tremendous loss to everyone who knew him and to the entire information, database, and knowledge systems community.

Roland Wagner (born in 1952) studied computer science at the University of Linz, where he also received his doctorate in 1979. In 1987 he was appointed professor for information systems at the Johannes Kepler University Linz (JKU). In 1990 he founded the Institute for Applied Oriented Knowledge Processing at JKU. In the same year, the idea to organize the DEXA conference on Database and Expert System Applications was born and realized with a few colleagues.

Roland was very excited and enthusiastic when, together with Mukesh Mohania, we planned an additional conference on Data Warehousing and Knowledge Discovery (DAWAK) to complement our DEXA conference, to bring these two communities together. Due to the success of DAWAK, which has established itself as one of the most important international scientific events on Big Data Analytics and Knowledge Discovery, it was again Roland who, together with Josef Küng and ourselves, initiated the idea of publishing the most relevant articles in this important area as a Lecture Notes in Computer Science (LNCS) journal. The idea of TLDKS was born. In 2009, the inaugural LNCS journal Transactions on Large-Scale Data and Knowledge-Centered System was published by Springer.

Roland Wagner was a very special person and scientist. He was literally driven by the spirit to make the world a better place through scientific work in his field. All of his actions were derived from this spirit. The creation and organization of conferences, the establishment of excellent centers, the cooperation with developing countries, and, last but not least, his commitment to people with special needs testify to this spirit and this driving force. With his commitment and enthusiasm, he triggered a large number of projects, initiatives, and innovations that are very well recognized in Austria and internationally. He received the Humanity Medal of Upper Austria (2003), the First Class Medal of the Prague Czech Technical University (2002), and the Upper Austrian Silver Decoration of Honor (2011). The Roland Wagner Award, founded in his honor, is presented every two years by the Austrian Computer Society at the International Conference on Computers Helping People with Special Needs (under the auspices of UNESCO) for achievements by scientists or organizations that have groundbreaking effects on the lives of people with disabilities.

Roland Wagner was a wonderful colleague who wholeheartedly supported our community. He inspired many of us immensely, and we can best honor him through our work as researchers in developing contributions that will ultimately lead to applications for a world where "no one should be left behind". Roland is bitterly missed, but his legacy will be kept alive through the many initiatives he established, the many collaborations he instigated, and the many students and researchers he mentored throughout the world.

This special issue includes eight invited papers addressing a range of relevant and hot topics: Distributed Database Systems, NewSQL, Scalable Transaction Management, Caches, Strong Consistency, Data Warehouse, ETL, Reinforcement Learning, Stochastic Approximation, Multi-Agent Systems, Ontology, Requirements Engineering, Model-Driven Development, Organizational Modelling, Digital Government, New Institutional Economics, and Data Governance.

The paper *"Roland Wagner - Scientist with a Big Heart"*, which appears in the front matter, synthesizes in a remarkable way the multi-faceted career and the trajectory of Roland Wagner: his main scientific contributions, the creation of the Institute for Applied Oriented Knowledge Processing at JKU, the foundation, with his friend A Min Tjoa, of the International Conference on Database and Expert Systems Applications (DEXA), the launch of this international journal TLDKS, and the establishment of bridges between several public and private institutes. These links between research and development highlight his commitment, his valuable contributions, and his interest in improving economic and societal aspects through information technology.

In the first research paper, *"Distributed Database Systems: The Case for NewSQL"*, the authors make the case for NewSQL, which is the latest technology in the big data management landscape. They describe in detail the main characteristics of NewSQL database systems, where the main objective is to combine the scalability and availability of NoSQL with the consistency and usability of classical SQL database systems. The authors illustrate the introduced principles with the Spanner and LeanXcale systems.

In the second research paper, *"Boosting OLTP Performance Using Write-Back Client-Side Caches"*, the authors present a comprehensive evaluation of client-side caches to enhance the performance of MySQL for online transaction processing (OLTP) workloads. They focus on the TPC-C benchmark and the write-back policy of the client-side cache. The authors extend the cache with a transaction processing storage manager (Berkeley DB) to minimize its amount of required memory, quantifying its impact on TPC-C's tpm-C.

The third scientific contribution is focused on *"pygrametl: A Powerful Programming Framework for Easy Creation and Testing of ETL Flows"*. Here, the authors present an overview of the latest version of pygrametl, an open source Python-based framework for ETL programmers. They describe how pygrametl offers a novel approach to ETL programming by providing a framework that abstracts over the data warehouse tables while still allowing the user to use the full power of Python.

In the fourth paper, entitled *"A Data Warehouse of Wi-Fi Sessions for Contact Tracing and Outbreak Investigation"*, the authors seek to leverage the availability of common existing digital infrastructure, such as the increasingly ubiquitous Wi-Fi networks, that can be readily activated to assist in large-scale contact tracing. Then, they describe and discuss the design, implementation, and deployment of a data warehouse of Wi-Fi sessions for contact tracing and disease outbreak investigation. Finally, the authors present the case where the data warehouse of Wi-Fi sessions is experimentally deployed at full scale on a large local university campus in Singapore.

The fifth paper addresses *"Convergence Proof for Actor-Critic Methods Applied to PPO and RUDDER"*. The authors prove under commonly used assumptions the convergence of actor-critic reinforcement learning algorithms. Their framework shows convergence of the well-known Proximal Policy Optimization (PPO) algorithm and of the recently introduced Return Decomposition for Delayed Rewards (RUDDER) algorithm.

In the sixth paper, entitled *"Revival of MAS Technologies in Industry"*, the authors introduce a new MAS Platform – the Cluster 4.0 Integration Platform. It utilizes (1) semantics to explicitly describe products, production, and resources for their easier integration and exploitation and (2) OPC-UA to connect software agents to physical machines.

In the seventh paper, entitled *"From Strategy to Code: Achieving Strategical Alignment in Software Development Projects Through Conceptual Modelling"*, the authors propose S2C, a strategy-to-code methodological approach to integrate organizational, business process, and information system modelling levels to support strategic alignment in software development. They discuss how their model-driven approach not only supports strategic alignment, but fosters the elicitation of business process performance measurement requirements.

In the last paper of this special issue, entitled *"On State-Level Architecture of Digital Government Ecosystems: From ICT-Driven to Data-Centric"*, the authors systematically approach the state-level architecture of digital government ecosystems. They establish the notion of data governance architecture, which links data assets with accountable organizations. Finally, the authors describe how the proposed framework perfectly fits the current discussion on moving from ICT-driven to data-centric digital government.

We strongly hope that this special issue, dedicated to the memory of our friend and colleague Roland Wagner, presents a broad spectrum of interesting developments relating to data management systems.

We would like to sincerely thank the authors who spontaneously accepted our invitation to contribute to this special issue and without taking into account their strong constraints and their commitments elsewhere.

Our special thanks also go to Gabriela Wagner, who has always perfectly managed all the volumes of the TLDKS journal since its creation and launch in March 2009, for her efforts and availability.

April 2021

Abdelkader Hameurlain
A Min Tjoa

Organization

Editors-in-Chief

Abdelkader Hameurlain   Paul Sabatier University, France
A Min Tjoa   Technical University of Vienna, Austria

Editorial Board

Reza Akbarinia   Inria, France
Dagmar Auer   FAW, Austria
Djamal Benslimane   Lyon 1 University, France
Stéphane Bressan   National University of Singapore, Singapore
Mirel Cosulschi   University of Craiova, Romania
Dirk Draheim   University of Innsbruck, Austria
Johann Eder   Alpen Adria University Klagenfurt, Austria
Anastasios Gounaris   Aristotle University of Thessaloniki, Greece
Theo Härder   Technical University of Kaiserslautern, Germany
Sergio Ilarri   University of Zaragoza, Spain
Petar Jovanovic   Universitat Politècnica de Catalunya, Spain
Aida Kamišalić Latifić   University of Maribor, Slovenia
Dieter Kranzlmüller   Ludwig-Maximilians-Universität München, Germany
Philippe Lamarre   INSA Lyon, France
Lenka Lhotská   Technical University of Prague, Czech Republic
Vladimir Marik   Technical University of Prague, Czech Republic
Jorge Martinez Gil   Software Competence Center Hagenberg, Austria
Franck Morvan   Paul Sabatier University, France
Torben Bach Pedersen   Aalborg University, Denmark
Günther Pernul   University of Regensburg, Germany
Soror Sahri   Paris Descartes University, France
Shaoyi Yin   Paul Sabatier University, France
Feng "George" Yu   Youngstown State University, USA

Message from Bruno Buchberger: Roland Wagner - Scientist with a Big Heart

Bruno Buchberger

Research Institute for Symbolic Computation, Johannes Kepler University, Linz,
Austria
bruno.buchberger@jku.at

In 1974, I had just joined the Johannes Kepler University (JKU) as a young professor for computer mathematics and gave my first course on "Introduction to Theoretical Computer Science". I will never forget two students who attended this course: A Min Tjoa and Roland Wagner. They behaved so differently from most of the other students. They would stay in the institute, sometimes just in the seminar room, until late in the evening and on weekends. They worked on their own ideas and very early started to write papers. They were excited about science and research and, by intrinsic motivation, without any external persuasion, apparently understood the fascination of university life and an academic career.

Their topics of interest were different from mine and, for some years, I lost track of their careers until, in 1989, I had moved my Research Institute for Symbolic Computation (RISC) to the renovated Castle of Hagenberg – about 20 km off the JKU main campus - with the intention to build up what I called a "Softwarepark", i.e. a place where research and teaching institutions would grow in close interaction with start-up companies and established companies. For a quick growth, I wanted to convince a couple of my JKU colleagues to open up branches of their JKU institutes in the frame of the new Softwarepark Hagenberg.

This turned out to be not so easy because, at that time, only very few professors, in addition to doing research, wanted to work with companies on applied projects and neither wanted to think about supporting start-up companies and creating IT jobs. In this situation, Roland, who was an associate professor in the meantime, phoned me and said "super, I want to join you with my group". And this word "super" is my main and dear memory about Roland. In the coming years, I heard "super" many times from him. Whatever new idea or plan I had to expand the growing Softwarepark, Roland said "super" and I knew I could rely on him to get it on track.

At the beginning, I had nothing to offer to him than a first small grant from the Upper Austrian Government and a room in the castle, which later, when I had raised private money for erecting more and more buildings in the Softwarepark, became the castle restaurant.

We shared rooms and we shared the pioneering spirit of just working for research and, at the same time, for very practical company projects. We were proud to show my RISC and his institute FAW (Research Institute for Application-oriented Knowledge Processing) to visitors, politicians, companies, students, and potential co-workers and, quickly, the Softwarepark started to grow. More and more companies joined and also (very few) other JKU institutes, notably Peter Klement's FLLL (Fuzzy Logic Laboratory Linz) and Gustav Pomberger's Software Engineering Group. As a team of four JKU institutes, we then founded a couple of other, grant-based, research institutions as, for example, the new FH Hagenberg (University of Applied Sciences, Faculty of Informatics), the Software Competence Center Hagenberg, the High School for Communication, and others.

And every time some new ideas and initiatives came to our mind, Roland said "super" and embarked on them with full energy and optimism.

Also, Roland invented and realized quite some projects, institutions, and initiatives on his own, which showed not only his strength as an internationally renowned and recognized researcher and scientist but also his interest and engagement for the societal and economic implications of IT and his big heart, in particular, for those who need support and special attention. Thus, together with his Ph.D. student and later professor Klaus Miesenberger, he initiated a project for helping visually impaired students, which grew into the "Institut Integriert Studieren". He also was a driving force behind the International Conference on Computers Helping People with Special Needs. Together with the Mayor of Hagenberg, Rudolf Fischlehner, we also made it possible to host a company in the frame of the Softwarepark that employs exclusively people with special needs, who feel completely integrated into the vibrating life of a technology park.

The days of joint work are over but Roland's spirit will stay forever with us. When I visited him in the hospital and just felt a little disappointed about everyday problems in the Softwarepark he reminded me that we had a "super" time together and that our spirit should always strive for a "super" positive attitude. Roland, I feel very grateful for what you did for the community and for me personally and I will always remember you as the "super" man!

Contents

Distributed Database Systems: The Case for NewSQL

Patrick Valduriez[1]([✉]), Ricardo Jimenez-Peris[2], and M. Tamer Özsu[3]

[1] Inria, University of Montpellier, CNRS, LIRMM, Montpellier, France
Patrick.Valduriez@inria.fr
[2] LeanXcale, Madrid, Spain
rjimenez@leanxcale.com
[3] University of Waterloo, Waterloo, Canada
tamer.ozsu@uwaterloo.ca

Abstract. Until a decade ago, the database world was all SQL, distributed, sometimes replicated, and fully consistent. Then, web and cloud applications emerged that need to deal with complex big data, and NoSQL came in to address their requirements, trading consistency for scalability and availability. NewSQL has been the latest technology in the big data management landscape, combining the scalability and availability of NoSQL with the consistency and usability of SQL. By blending capabilities only available in different kinds of database systems such as fast data ingestion and SQL queries and by providing online analytics over operational data, NewSQL opens up new opportunities in many application domains where real-time decisions are critical. NewSQL may also simplify data management, by removing the traditional separation between NoSQL and SQL (ingest data fast, query it with SQL), as well as between operational database and data warehouse/data lake (no more ETLs!). However, a hard problem is scaling out transactions in mixed operational and analytical (HTAP) workloads over big data, possibly coming from different data stores (HDFS, SQL, NoSQL). Today, only a few NewSQL systems have solved this problem. In this paper, wne make the case for NewSQL, introducing their basic principles from distributed database systems and illustrating with Spanner and LeanXcale, two of the most advanced systems in terms of scalable transaction management.

Keywords: Distributed database · Database system · DBMS · SQL · NoSQL · NewSQL · Polystore · Scalable transaction management

1 Introduction

The first edition of the book Principles of Distributed Database Systems [10] appeared in 1991 when the technology was new and there were not too many products. In the Preface to the first edition, we had quoted Michael Stonebraker who claimed in 1988 that in the following 10 years, centralized DBMSs would be an "antique curiosity" and most organizations would move towards distributed DBMSs. That prediction has certainly proved to be correct, and most systems in use today are either distributed or

© Springer-Verlag GmbH Germany, part of Springer Nature 2021
A. Hameurlain and A Min Tjoa (Eds.): TLDKS XLVIII, LNCS 12670, pp. 1–15, 2021.
https://doi.org/10.1007/978-3-662-63519-3_1

parallel. The fourth edition of this classic textbook [11] includes the latest developments, in particular, big data, NoSQL and NewSQL.

NewSQL is the latest technology in the big data management landscape, enjoying a rapid growth in the database system and business intelligence (BI) markets. NewSQL combines the scalability and availability of NoSQL with the consistency and usability of SQL (SQL here refers to SQL database systems, which is the common term used for relational database systems). By providing online analytics over operational data, NewSQL opens up new opportunities in many application domains where real-time decisions are critical. Important use cases are IT performance monitoring, proximity marketing, e-advertising, risk monitoring, real-time pricing, real-time fraud detection, internet-of-things (IoT), etc.

NewSQL may also simplify data management, by removing the traditional separation between NoSQL and SQL (ingest data fast, query it with SQL), as well as between the operational database and data warehouse or data lake (no more complex data extraction tools such as ETLs or ELTs!). However, a hard problem is scaling transactions in mixed operational and analytical (HTAP) workloads over big data, possibly coming from different data stores (HDFS files, NoSQL databases, SQL databases). Currently, only a few NewSQL database systems have solved this problem, e.g., the LeanXcale NewSQL database system that includes a highly scalable transaction manager [9] and a polystore [6].

NewSQL database systems have different flavors and architectures. However, we can identify the following common features: support of the relational data model and standard SQL; ACID transactions; scalability using data partitioning in shared-nothing clusters; and high availability using data replication. We gave a first in-depth presentation of NewSQL in a tutorial at the IEEE Big Data 2019 conference [15], where we provide a taxonomy of NewSQL database systems based on major dimensions including targeted workloads, capabilities and implementation techniques.

In this paper, we make the case for NewSQL. First, we briefly recall the principles of distributed database systems (Sect. 2), which are at the core of NewSQL systems. Then, we briefly introduce SQL systems (Sect. 3) and NoSQL systems (Sect. 4). In Sect. 5, we present in more details our case for NewSQL. Finally, Sect. 6 concludes and discusses research directions in NewSQL.

2   Principles of Distributed Database Systems

The current computing environment is largely distributed, with computers connected to Internet to form a worldwide distributed system. With cluster and cloud computing, organizations can have geographically distributed and interconnected data centers, each with hundreds or thousands of computers connected with high-speed networks. Within this environment, the amount of data that is captured has increased dramatically, creating the big data boom. Thus, there is a need to provide high-level data management capabilities, as with database systems, on these widely distributed data in order to ease application development, maintenance and evolution. This is the scope of distributed database systems [11], which have moved from a small part of the worldwide computing environment a few decades ago to mainstream today.

A distributed database is a collection of multiple, logically interrelated databases located at the nodes of a distributed system. A distributed database system is then defined as the system that manages the distributed database and makes the distribution transparent to the users, providing major capabilities such as data integration, query processing, transaction management, replication, reliability, etc.

There are two types of distributed database systems: geo-distributed and single location (or single site). In the former, the sites are interconnected by wide area networks that are characterized by long message latencies and higher error rates. The latter consist of systems where the nodes are located in close proximity allowing much faster exchanges leading to much shorter message latencies and very low error rates. Single location distributed database systems are typically characterized by computer clusters in one data center and are commonly known as parallel database systems [4] emphasizing the use of parallelism to increase performance as well as availability. In the context of the cloud, it is now quite common to find distributed database systems made of multiple single site clusters interconnected by wide area networks, leading to hybrid, multisite systems.

In a distributed environment, it is possible to accommodate increasing database sizes and bigger workloads. System expansion can usually be handled by adding processing and storage power to the network. Obviously, it may not be possible to obtain a linear increase in "power" since this also depends on the overhead of distribution. However, significant improvements are still possible. That is why distributed database systems have gained much interest in scale-out architectures in the context of cluster and cloud computing. Scale-out (also called horizontal scaling) should be contrasted with the most commonly used scale-up (also called vertical scaling), which refers to adding more power to a server, e.g., more processors and memory, and thus gets limited by the maximum size of the server. Horizontal scaling refers to adding more servers, called "scale-out servers" in a loosely coupled fashion, to scale almost infinitely. By making it easy to add new component database servers, a distributed database system can provide horizontal scaling, in addition to vertical scaling.

In the context of the cloud, there is also the need to support elasticity, which is different from scalability, in order to adapt to workload changes and be able to process higher (or lower) transaction rates. Elasticity requires dynamically provisioning (or de-provisioning) of servers to increase (or decrease) the global capacity and live data migration [1], e.g., moving or replicating a data partition from an overloaded server to another, while the system is running transactions.

In observing the changes that have taken place since the first edition of the book [14], which focused on distribution in relational databases, what has struck us is that the fundamental principles of distributed data management still hold, and distributed data management can still be characterized along three dimensions: distribution, heterogeneity and autonomy of the data sources (see Fig. 1). This characterization has been useful for all subsequent editions, to include the new developments in many topics, which are reflected in Fig. 1, which identifies four main categories: the early client-server database systems, with limited distribution; the recent distributed and parallel systems, including NoSQL and NewSQL with high distribution; the P2P systems with high distribution and autonomy; and the multidatabase systems and polystores with high distribution, autonomy and heterogeneity.

What has changed much since the first edition of the book and made the problems much harder, is the scale of the dimensions: very large-scale distribution in the context of cluster, P2P, and cloud; very high heterogeneity in the context of web and big data; and high autonomy in the context of web and P2P. It is also interesting to note that the fundamental principles of data partitioning, data integration, transaction management, replication and SQL query processing have stood the test of time. In particular, new techniques and algorithms (NoSQL, NewSQL) can be presented as extensions of earlier material, using relational concepts.

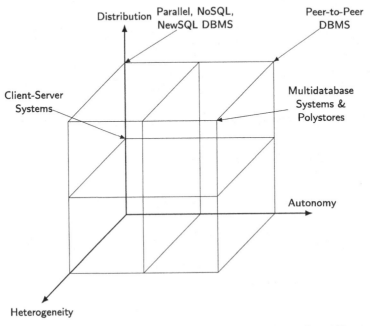

Fig. 1. Distributed database system dimensions (modified after [10]).

3 SQL Database Systems

SQL (relational) database systems are at the heart of any information system. The fundamental principle behind relational data management is data independence, which enables applications and users to deal with the data at a high conceptual level while ignoring implementation details. The major innovation of SQL database systems has been to allow data manipulation through queries expressed in a high-level (declarative) language such as SQL. Queries can then be automatically translated into optimized query plans that take advantage of underlying access methods and indices. Many other advanced capabilities have been made possible by data independence: data modeling, schema management, consistency through integrity rules and triggers, ACID transaction support, etc.

The fact that SQL has been an industry standard language has had a major impact on the data analysis tool industry, making it easy for tool vendors to provide support for reporting, BI and data visualization on top of all major SQL database systems. This trend has also fostered fierce competition among tool vendors, which has led to high-quality tools for specialized applications.

The data independence principle has also enabled SQL database systems to contin-uously integrate new advanced capabilities such as object and document support and to adapt to all kinds of hardware/software platforms from very small devices to very large computers (NUMA multiprocessor, cluster, etc.) in distributed environments. In particular, distribution transparency supports the data independence principle.

SQL database systems come in two main variants, operational and analytical, which have been around for more than three decades. The two variants are complementary and data from operational databases have to be uploaded and pre-processed first so it can be queried.

Operational database systems have been designed for OLTP workloads. They excel at updating data in real-time and keeping it consistent in the advent of failures and con-current accesses by means of ACID transactions. But they have a hard time in answering large analytical queries and do not scale well. We can distinguish two kinds of systems with respect to scalability: systems that scale up (typically in a NUMA mainframe) but do not scale out and systems that scale out, but only to a few nodes using a shared-disk architecture. Figure 2 illustrates the SQL shared-disk architecture, with multiple DB servers accessing the shared disk units. Within a DB server, all SQL functionality is implemented in a tightly coupled fashion. The reason for such tight coupling is to maxi-mize performance, which, in the early days of databases, was the only practical solution. Shared-disk requires disks to be globally accessible by the nodes, which requires a stor-age area network (SAN) that uses a block-based protocol. Since different servers can access the same block in conflicting update modes, global cache consistency is needed. This is typically achieved using a distributed lock manager, which is complex to imple-ment and introduces significant contention. In the case of OLTP workloads, shared-disk has remained the preferred option as it makes load balancing easy and efficient, but scalability is heavily limited by the distributed locking that causes severe contention.

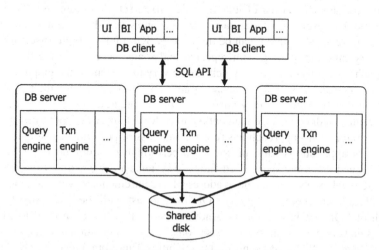

Fig. 2. SQL shared-disk architecture.

Analytical database systems have been designed for data warehouses and OLAP workloads. They exploit parallel processing, in particular, intraquery parallelism, to reduce the response times of large analytical queries in read-intensive applications. Unlike operational database systems that use shared-disk, they use a shared-nothing architecture. The term "shared-nothing" was proposed by Michael Stonebraker [12] to better contrast with two other popular architectures, shared-memory and shared-disk. In the 1980's, shared-nothing was just emerging (with pioneers like Teradata) and shared-memory was the dominant architecture.

A shared-nothing architecture is simply a distributed architecture, i.e., the server nodes do not share either memory or disk and have their own copy of the operating system. Today, shared-nothing clusters are cost-effective as servers can be off-the-shelf components (multicore processor, memory and disk) connected by a low-latency network such as Infiniband or Myrinet. Shared-nothing provides excellent scalability, through scale-out, unlike shared-memory and shared-disk. However, it requires careful partitioning of the data on multiple disk nodes. Furthermore, the addition of new nodes in the system presumably requires reorganizing and repartitioning the database to deal with the load balancing issues. Finally, fault-tolerance is more difficult than with shared-disk as a failed node will make its data on disk unavailable, thus requiring data replication. However, it is for its scalability advantage that shared-nothing has been first adopted for OLAP workloads, as it is easier to parallelize read-only queries. For the same reason, it has been adopted for big data systems, which are typically read-intensive.

4 NoSQL Database Systems

SQL databases, whether operational or analytical, are inefficient for complex data. The rigid schema is the problem. For instance, creating a schema for rows that have optional or structured fields (like a list of items), with a fixed set of columns is difficult, and querying the data even more. Maintainability becomes very hard. Graph data is also difficult to manage. Although it can be modeled in SQL tables, graph-traversal queries may be very time consuming, with repeated and sparse accesses to the database (to mimic graph traversals on tables), which can be very inefficient, if the graph is large.

About a decade ago, SQL database systems were criticized for their "One Size Fits All" approach. Although they have been able to integrate support for all kinds of data (e.g., multimedia objects, documents) and code (e.g., user-defined functions, user-defined oeprators), this approach has resulted in a loss of performance, simplicity, and flexibility for applications with specific, tight performance requirements. Therefore, it has been argued that more specialized database systems are needed.

NoSQL database systems came to address the requirements of web and cloud applications, NoSQL meaning "Not Only SQL" to contrast with the "One Size Fits All" approach of SQL database systems. Another reason that has been used to motivate NoSQL is that supporting strong database consistency as operational database systems do, i.e., through ACID transactions, hurts scalability. Therefore, most NoSQL database systems have relaxed strong database consistency in favor of scalability. An argument to support this approach has been the famous CAP theorem from distributed systems theory [5], which states that a distributed system with replication can only provide two out of the following three properties: (C) consistency, (A) availability, and (P) partition tolerance. However, the argument is simply wrong as the CAP theorem has nothing to do with database scalability: it is related to replica consistency (i.e., strong mutual consistency) in the presence of network partitioning. Thus, a weaker form of consistency that is typically provided is eventual consistency, which allows replica values to diverge for some time until the update activity ceases so the values eventually become identical (and mutually consistent).

As an alternative to SQL, different NoSQL database systems support different data models and query languages/APIs other than standard SQL. They typically emphasize one or more of the following features: scalability, fault-tolerance, availability, sometimes at the expense of atomicity, strong consistency, flexible schemas, and practical APIs for programming complex data-intensive applications. This is obtained by relaxing features found in SQL database systems such as full SQL support, ACID transactions, in particular, atomicity and consistency, which become weaker (e.g., atomicity only for some operations, eventual consistency) and strong schema support.

There are four main categories of NoSQL database systems based on the underlying data model, i.e., key-value, wide column, document, and graph. Within each category, we can find different variations of the data model, as there is just no standard (unlike the relational data model), and different query languages or APIs. For document database systems, JSON is becoming the de facto standard, as opposed to older, more complex XML. There are also multi-model systems, to combine multiple data models, typically document and graph, in one system.

To provide scalability, NoSQL database systems typically use a scale-out approach in a shared-nothing cluster. They also rely on replication and failover to provide high availability. NoSQL database systems are very diverse as there is just no standard. However, we can illustrate the architecture of key-value database systems that is more uniform and quite popular (see Fig. 3) and the basis for many variations. A major difference with the SQL architecture, which is client-server, is distribution by design to take full advantage of a shared-nothing cluster. In particular, it supports the popular master–worker model for executing parallel tasks, with master nodes coordinating the activities of the worker nodes, by sending them tasks and data and receiving back notifications of tasks done.

This key-value (KV) database system architecture has two loosely-coupled layers: KV engine and data store. The KV engine is accessed by KV clients, with a simple KV API that is specific to each system, but with typical operations such as put, get and scan (enables to perform a simple range query). Such API eases integration with code libraries and applications. The functionality provided by a KV engine corresponds to the low-level part of an SQL system: i.e., operation processing using indexes, replication, fault-tolerance and high availability. But there is no such thing as query engine or transaction engine. The data store is in many cases a distributed, fault-tolerant file system, such as HDFS, and in other cases a custom storage engine running on top of the local file system providing caching facilities and basic operations for reading and updating data.

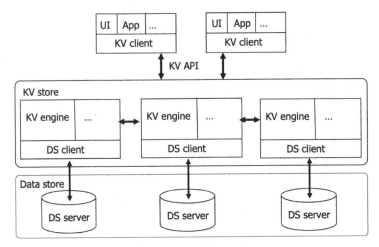

Fig. 3. NoSQL key-value architecture.

Key-value database systems, e.g., DynamoDB and Cassandra, are schemaless so they are totally flexible with the stored data. They are in most cases scalable to large number of nodes. And they are very efficient at ingesting data. Wide column database systems, e.g., BigTable and HBase, enable vertical partitioning of the tables, while providing a key-value interface and sharing many features with key-value database systems. They provide some more functionality such as range scans and the possibility of defining a schema. Document database systems, e.g., MongoDB and CouchBase, use a flexible data representation, such as JSON or XML, and provide an API to access these data or sometimes a query language. Graph database systems, e.g., Neo4J and OrientDB, are specialized in storing and querying graphs efficiently. They are very efficient when the graph database can be centralized at one machine, and replicated at others. But if the database is big and needs to be distributed and partitioned, efficiency is lost.

5   The Case for NewSQL

NewSQL is a new class of database system that seeks to combine the advantages of NoSQL (scalability, availability) and SQL (ACID consistency and usability) systems. The main objective is to address the requirements of enterprise information systems, which have been supported by SQL database systems. But there is also the need to be able to scale out in a shared-nothing cluster in order to support big data, as characterized by the famous 3 big V's (Volume, Velocity, Variety). Examples of popular NewSQL database systems are LeanXcale, Spanner, CockroachDB, EsgynDB, SAP HANA, MemSQL, NuoDB, and Splice Machine. In the rest of this section, we present NewSQL in more detail, and illustrate with two of the most advanced systems in terms of scalable transaction management: Spanner and LeanXcale.

5.1 NewSQL Database Systems

NewSQL database systems come in different flavors, each targeted at different workloads and usages. Our taxonomy in [13] is useful to understand NewSQL database systems based on major dimensions including targeted workloads (OLTP, OLAP, HTAP), features and implementation techniques. The main new features are: scalable ACID transactions, in-memory support, polystore, and HTAP support. Each of these features can be mapped into one of the 3 V's of big data. NewSQL database systems typically support more than one feature, but are often characterized by the one feature in which they excel, e.g., scalable ACID transactions. Note that some systems with some of the features have existed long before the term NewSQL was coined, e.g., main memory database systems.

Scalable ACID transactions are provided for big OLTP workloads using a distributed transaction manager that can scale out to large numbers of nodes. ACID properties of transactions are fully provided, with isolation levels such as serializability or snapshot isolation. The few systems that have solved this hard problem are LeanXcale [9] and Spanner [3], through horizontal scalability in a shared-nothing cluster typically on top of a key-value data store.

Scaling transaction execution to achieve high transaction throughput in a distributed or parallel system has been a topic of interest for a long time. In recent years solutions have started to emerge; we discuss two approaches in the next sections as embodied in the Spanner and LeanXcale database systems. Both of them implement the ACID properties in a scalable and composable manner. In both approaches, a new technique is proposed to serialize transactions that can support very high throughput rates (millions or even a billion transactions-per-second). Both approaches have a way to timestamp the commit of transactions and use this commit timestamp to serialize transactions. Spanner uses real time to timestamp transactions, while LeanXcale uses logical time. Real time has the advantage that it does not require any communication, but requires high accuracy and a highly reliable realtime infrastructure. The idea is to use real time as timestamp and wait for the accuracy to elapse to make the result visible to transactions. LeanXcale adopts an approach in which transactions are timestamped with a logical time and committed transactions are made visible progressively as gaps in the serialization order are filled by newly committed transactions. Logical time avoids having to rely on creating a real-time infrastructure.

Main memory database systems, such as MemDB, SAP HANA and VoltDB, keep all data in memory, which enables processing queries at the speed of memory without being limited by the I/O bandwidth and latency. They come in two flavors, analytical and operational. The main memory analytical database systems are very fast. But the main limitation is that the entire database, the auxiliary data, and all intermediate results must fit in memory.

Polystores, also called multistore systems [2], provide integrated access to a number of different data stores, such as HDFS files, SQL and NoSQL databases, through one or more query languages. They are typically restricted to read-only queries, as supporting distributed transactions across heterogeneous data stores is a hard problem. They are reminiscent of multidatabase systems (see Database Integration Chapter in [11]), using a query engine with the capability of querying different data stores in realtime, without storing the data themselves. However, they can support data sources with much more heterogeneity, e.g., key-value, document and graph data. Polystores come in different flavors, depending on the level of coupling with the underlying data stores: loosely-coupled (as web data integration systems), tightly-coupled (typically in the context of data lakes), and hybrid.

HTAP (Hybrid Transactional Analytical Processing) systems are able to perform OLAP and OLTP on the same data. HTAP allows performing real-time analysis on operational data, thus avoiding the traditional separation between operational database and data warehouse and the complexity of dealing with ETLs. HTAP systems exploit multiversioning to avoid conflicts between long analytical queries and updates. However, multiversioning by itself is not enough, in particular, to make both OLAP and OLTP efficient, which is very hard.

NewSQL database systems can have one or more of these features and/or technologies, e.g., scalable operational, HTAP and main memory, or for the most advanced systems, HTAP with scalable transactions and polystore capabilities. The architecture of the most advanced NewSQL database systems is interesting, typically using a key-value store to provide a first level of scalability (see Fig. 4). This approach can provide the ability of the NewSQL database system to support a key-value API, in addition to plain SQL, in order to allow for fast and simple programmatic access to rows. Although appealing, this approach makes it complex for application developers since the key-value store typically does not know that the stored data is relational, how it is organized and how metadata is kept. Atop a key-value store layer, the SQL engine can also be made scalable. Thus, we can have a fully distributed architecture, as shown below, where the three layers (key-value store, transaction engine and SQL query engine) can scale out independently in a shared-nothing cluster.

Such a distributed architecture provides many opportunities to perform optimal resource allocation to the workload (OLAP vs OLTP). To scale out query processing, traditional parallel techniques from SQL analytical database systems are reused. However, within such an architecture, the SQL query engine should exploit the key-value data store, by pushing down within execution plans the operations that can be more efficiently performed close to the data, e.g., filter and aggregate. Scaling out transaction management is much harder and very few NewSQL database systems have been able to achieve it.

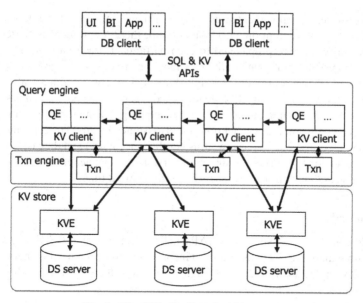

Fig. 4. NewSQL distributed architecture.

5.2 Spanner

Spanner [3] is an advanced NewSQL database system with full SQL and scalable ACID transactions. It was initially developed by Google to support the e-advertising AdWords application, which is update intensive with millions of suppliers monitoring their maximum cost-per-click bids.

Spanner uses traditional locking and 2PC and provides serializability as isolation level. Since locking results in high contention between large queries and update transactions, Spanner also implements multiversioning, which avoids the conflicts between reads and writes and thus the contention stemming from these conflicts. However, multiversioning does not provide scalability. In order to avoid the bottleneck of centralized certification, updated data items are assigned timestamps (using real time) upon commit. For this purpose, Spanner implements an internal service called TrueTime that provides the current time and its current accuracy. In order to make the TrueTime service reliable and accurate, it uses both atomic clocks and GPS since they have different failures modes that can compensate each other. For instance, atomic clocks have a continuous drift, while GPS loses accuracy in some meteorological conditions, when the antenna gets broken, etc. The current time obtained through TrueTime is used to timestamp transactions that are going to be committed. The reported accuracy is used to compensate during timestamp assignment: after obtaining the local time, there is a wait time for the length of the inaccuracy, typically around 10 ms. To deal with deadlocks, Spanner adopts deadlock avoidance using a wound-and-wait approach thereby eliminating the bottleneck of deadlock detection. Storage management in Spanner is made scalable by leveraging Bigtable, a wide column data store.

Multiversioning is implemented as follows. Private versions of the data items are kept at each site until commitment. Upon commit, the 2PC protocol is started during which buffered writes are propagated to each participant. Each participant sets locks on the updated data items. Once all locks have been acquired, it assigns a commit timestamp larger than any previously assigned timestamp. The coordinator also acquires the write locks. Upon acquiring all write locks and receiving the prepared message from all participants, the coordinator chooses a timestamp larger than the current time plus the inaccuracy, and bigger than any other timestamps assigned locally. The coordinator waits for the assigned timestamp to pass (waiting for the inaccuracy) and then communicates the commit decision to the client. Using multiversioning, Spanner also implements read-only transactions that read over the snapshot at the current time.

5.3 LeanXcale

LeanXcale is an advanced NewSQL HTAP database system with full SQL and polystore support with scalable ACID transactions. It incorporates three main components: storage engine, query engine and transactional engine – all three distributed and highly scalable (i.e., to hundreds of nodes).

LeanXcale provides full SQL functionality over relational tables with JSON columns. Clients can access LeanXcale with any analytics tool using a JDBC or ODBC driver. An important capability of LeanXcale is polystore access using the scripting mechanism of the CloudMdsQL query language [6, 7]. The data stores that can be accessed range from distributed raw data files (e.g., HDFS through parallel SQL queries) to NoSQL database systems (e.g., MongoDB, where queries can be expressed as JavaScript programs).

The storage engine is a proprietary relational key-value store, KiVi, which allows for efficient horizontal partitioning of tables and indexes, based on the primary key or index key. Each table is stored as a KiVi table, where the key corresponds to the primary key of the LeanXcale table and all the columns are stored as they are in KiVi columns. Indexes are also stored as KiVi tables, where the index keys are mapped to the corresponding primary keys. This model enables high scalability of the storage layer by partitioning tables and indexes across KiVi data nodes. KiVi provides the typical put and get operations of key-value stores as well as all single table operations such as predicate-based selection, aggregation, grouping, and sorting, i.e., any algebraic operator but join. Multitable operations, i.e., joins, are performed by the query engine and any algebraic operator above the join in the query plan. Thus, all algebraic operators below a join are pushed down to the KiVi storage engine where they are executed entirely locally.

The query engine processes OLAP workloads over operational data, so that analytical queries are answered over real-time (fresh) data. The parallel implementation of the query engine follows the single-program multiple data (SPMD) approach, which combines intra-query and intra-operator parallelism. With SPMD, multiple symmetric workers (threads) on different query instances execute the same query/operator, but each of them deals with different portions of the data.

The query engine optimizes queries using two-step optimization. As queries are received, query plans are broadcast and processed by all workers. For parallel execution, an optimization step is added, which transforms a generated sequential query plan into a parallel one. This transformation involves replacing table scans with parallel table scans, and adding shuffle operators to make sure that, in stateful operators (such as group by, or join), related rows (i.e., rows to be joined or grouped together) are handled by the same worker. Parallel table scans combined with pushed down filtering, aggregation and sorting divide the rows from the base tables among all workers, i.e., each worker will retrieve a disjoint subset of the rows during table scan. This is done by dividing the rows and scheduling the obtained subsets to the different query engine instances. Each worker then processes the rows obtained from subsets scheduled to its query engine instance, exchanging rows with other workers as determined by the shuffle operators added to the query plan. To process joins, the query engine supports two strategies for data exchange (shuffle and broadcast) and various join methods (hash, nested loop, etc.), performed locally at each worker after the data exchange takes place.

The query engine is designed to integrate with arbitrary data stores, where data resides in its natural format and can be retrieved (in parallel) by running specific scripts or declarative queries. This makes it a powerful polystore that can process data from its original format, taking full advantage of both expressive scripting and massive parallelism. Moreover, joins across any native datasets, such as HDFS or MongoDB, including LeanXcale tables, can be applied, exploiting efficient parallel join algorithms [8]. To enable ad-hoc querying of an arbitrary data set, the query engine processes queries in the CloudMdsQL query language, where scripts are wrapped as native subqueries.

LeanXcale scales out transactional management [9] by decomposing the ACID properties and scaling each of them independently but in a composable manner. First, it uses logical time to timestamp transactions and to set visibility over committed data. Second, it provides snapshot isolation. Third, all the functions that are intensive in resource usage such as concurrency control, logging, storage and query processing, are fully distributed and parallel, without any coordination. The transactional engine provides strong consistency with snapshot isolation. Thus, reads are not blocked by writes, using multiversion concurrency control. The distributed algorithm for providing transactional consistency is able to commit transactions fully in parallel without any coordination by making a smart separation of concerns, i.e., the visibility of the committed data is separated from the commit processing. In this way, commit processing can adopt a fully parallel approach without compromising consistency that is regulated by the visibility of the committed updates. Thus, commits happen in parallel, and whenever there is a longer prefix of committed transactions without gaps the current snapshot is advanced to that point. For logical time, LeanXcale uses two services: the commit sequencer and the snapshot server. The commit sequencer distributes commit timestamps and the snapshot server regulates the visibility of committed data by advancing the snapshot visible to transactions.

In addition to scalability, in the context of the cloud, LeanXcale supports non-intrusive elasticity and can move data partitions without affecting transaction processing. This is based on an algorithm that guarantees snapshot isolation across data partitions being moved without actually affecting the processing over the data partitions.

6 Conclusion

In this paper, we made the case for NewSQL, which is enjoying a fast growth in the database system and BI markets in the context of big data. NewSQL combines the scalability and availability of NoSQL with the consistency and usability of SQL. NewSQL systems come in different flavors, each targeted at different workloads and usages. However, they all rely on the principles of distributed database systems, in particular, data partitioning, query processing, replication and transaction management, which have stood the test of time.

We characterized NewSQL systems by their main new features, which are: scalable ACID transactions, main memory support, polystore, and HTAP support. NewSQL database systems typically support more than one feature, but are often characterized by the one feature in which they excel, e.g., scalable ACID transactions.

By blending capabilities only available in different kinds of database systems such as fast data ingestion and SQL queries and by providing online analytics over operation-al data, NewSQL opens up new opportunities in many application domains where real-time decision is critical. Important use cases are IT performance monitoring, proximity marketing, e-advertising (e.g., Google AdWords), risk monitoring, real-time pricing, real-time fraud detection, IoT, etc. Before NewSQL, these applications could be developed, but using multiple systems and typically at a very high price. NewSQL may also simplify data management, by removing the traditional separation between NoSQL and SQL (ingest data fast, query it with SQL), as well as between operational database and data warehouse/data lake (no more ETLs!).

A hard problem is scaling out transactions in mixed operational and analytical (HTAP) workloads over big data, possibly coming from different data stores (HDFS, SQL, NoSQL). Today, only a few NewSQL systems have solved this problem, e.g., Spanner and LeanXcale, which we described in more details. Both of them implement the ACID properties in a scalable and composable manner, with a new technique to serialize transactions that can support very high throughput rates (millions or even a billion transactions-per-second). Both approaches have a way to timestamp the commit of transactions and use this commit timestamp to serialize transactions. Spanner uses real time to timestamp transactions, while LeanXcale uses logical time, which avoids having to rely on a complex real-time infrastructure. Furthermore, in addition to scalable transactions, LeanXcale provides polytore support, to access multiple data stores such as HDFS and NoSQL, and non-intrusive elasticity.

NewSQL is relatively new, and there is much room for research. Examples of research directions include: JSON and SQL integration, to seamlessly access both relational and JSON data, and thus combine the advantages of SQL and NoSQL with one database system; streaming SQL to combine data streams and NewSQL data; integration with popular big data frameworks such as Spark to perform analytics and machine learning; and defining specific NewSQL HTAP benchmarks.

References

1. Agrawal, D., Das, S., El Abbadi, A.: Data Management in the Cloud: Challenges and Opportunities. Synthesis Lectures on Data Management. Morgan & Claypool Publishers (2012)
2. Bondiombouy, C., Valduriez, P.: Query processing in multistore systems: an overview. Int. J. Cloud Comput. **5**(4), 309–346 (2016)
3. Corbett, J.C., et al.: Spanner: Google's globally-distributed database. In: Proceedings of the USENIX Symposium on Operating Systems Design and Implementation, pp. 251–264 (2012)
4. DeWitt, D., Gray, J.: Parallel database systems: the future of high-performance database systems. Commun. ACM **35**(6), 85–98 (1992)
5. Gilbert, S., Lynch, N.A.: Brewer's conjecture and the feasibility of consistent, available, partition-tolerant web services. SIGACT News **33**(2), 51–59 (2002)
6. Kolev, B., Valduriez, P., Bondiombouy, C., Jimenez-Peris, R., Pau, R., Pereira, J.: CloudMdsQL: Querying Heterogeneous Cloud Data Stores with a Common Language. Distrib. Parallel Databases **34**(4), 463–503 (2016). https://doi.org/10.1007/s10619-015-7185-y
7. Kolev, B., Valduriez, P., Bondiombouy, C., Jimenez-Peris, R., Pau, R., Pereira, J.: The Cloud-MdsQL multistore system. In: Proceedings of the ACM SIGMOD Conference, pp. 2113–2116 (2016)
8. Kolev, B., et al.: Parallel polyglot query processing on heterogeneous cloud data stores with LeanXcale. In: Proceedings of the IEEE BigData Conference, pp. 1757–1766 (2018)
9. Jimenez-Peris, R., Patiño-Martinez, M.: System and method for highly scalable decentralized and low contention transactional processing. European patent #EP2780832, US patent #US9,760,597 (2011)
10. Özsu, M.T., Valduriez, P.: Principles of Distributed Database Systems, 1st edn. Prentice-Hall (1991)
11. Özsu, M.T., Valduriez, P.: Principles of Distributed Database Systems, 4th edn. Springer (2020). https://doi.org/10.1007/978-3-030-26253-2
12. Stonebraker, M.: The case for shared nothing. IEEE Database Eng. Bull. **9**(1), 4–9 (1986)
13. Stonebraker, M., Weisberg, A.: The VoltDB main memory DBMS. IEEE Data Eng. Bull. **36**(2), 21–27 (2013)
14. Valduriez, P.: Principles of distributed data management in 2020? In: Hameurlain, A., Liddle, S.W., Schewe, K.-D., Zhou, X. (eds.) DEXA 2011. LNCS, vol. 6860, pp. 1–11. Springer, Heidelberg (2011). https://doi.org/10.1007/978-3-642-23088-2_1
15. Valduriez, P., Jimenez-Peris, R.: NewSQL: principles, systems and current trends. Tutorial, IEEE Big Data Conference (2019). https://www.leanxcale.com/scientific-articles

Boosting OLTP Performance Using Write-Back Client-Side Caches

Shahram Ghandeharizadeh$^{(\boxtimes)}$, Haoyu Huang, and Hieu Nguyen

Computer Science Department, University of Southern California, Los Angeles, USA
{shahram,haoyuhua,hieun}@usc.edu

Abstract. We present a comprehensive evaluation of client-side caches to enhance the performance of MySQL for online transaction processing (OLTP) workloads. We focus on TPC-C benchmark and the write-back policy of the client-side cache. With this policy, the cache processes all application writes and propagates them to its data store asynchronously. We observe with 1 TPC-C warehouse, the cache enhances performance of MySQL InnoDB by 70%. The cache scales horizontally as a function of the number of warehouses and servers to boost TPC-C's tpm-C by factors as high as 25 folds with 100 warehouses and 20 servers. The main limitation of the cache is its requirement for an abundant amount of memory. We extend the cache with a transaction processing storage manager (Berkeley DB, BDB) to minimize its amount of required memory, quantifying its impact on TPC-C's tpm-C. We detail two variants, Async-BDB and Sync-BDB. The slowest variant, Sync-BDB, continues to scale horizontally to boost TPC-C performance by more than 13 folds with 100 TPC-C warehouses.

1 Introduction

Client-side caches such as memcached [4], Redis [33], and Ignite [3] are used by popular Internet destinations such as Facebook [31]. They complement a data store to expedite processing of workloads that exhibit a high read to write ratios. An application uses a client-side cache to minimize the number of references to the data store. This study explores the use of these caches to enhance the performance of write-heavy online transaction processing (OLTP) workloads. Examples include e-commerce, order-entry, and financial applications.

OLTP workloads require ACID (atomic, consistent, isolated, and durable) transactions that enable a system designer to reason about system behavior [20]. Client-side caches are non-transparent to an application developer, empowering them to author cache entries optimized to meet the requirements of an application [2,31]. Moreover, a developer may author customized logic in the form of read and write *sessions* [18] that consist of (a) one data store transaction and (b) read and/or write of one or more cache entries[1]. A session implements ACID semantics across both the data store and the client-side cache [18].

---

[1] Section 2.2 provides a formal definition of session.

© Springer-Verlag GmbH Germany, part of Springer Nature 2021
A. Hameurlain and A Min Tjoa (Eds.): TLDKS XLVIII, LNCS 12670, pp. 16–44, 2021.
https://doi.org/10.1007/978-3-662-63519-3_2

This study uses client-side caches in combination with in-application logic to enhance the overall performance of write-heavy OLTP workloads. The key insight is to process both read and write sessions using the cache, minimizing the number of references to the data store (the slowest component of an architecture). With writes, we use the write-back policy [15] of client-side caches. It buffers writes in the cache and propagates them to the data store asynchronously. This design stores the latest value of a data item in the caching layer, causing the corresponding copy in the data store to become stale. It raises the following fundamental challenge. OLTP workloads insert new data and subsequently issue queries that reference this data. With a relational data store, queries may join multiple tables together, fusing potentially stale and up-to-date rows together. It is not possible to cache the result of future unknown queries that observe a cache miss and may reference stale data in the data store. Hence, the challenge is how to process such future cache misses efficiently while preserving strong consistency requirement of OLTP workloads.

To address this challenge, we introduce the concept of Query Result Change, QRC, that maintains changes to the result of a data store query. A write session identifies those queries whose cached result sets are impacted by its database transaction, generating a QRC for each impacted query. A cache miss for one such query must issue the query to the data store for a result set and apply relevant QRCs to it to compute its latest value. We use leases [18,19] to serialize this read with concurrent write sessions that may be generating new QRCs for a query result. A scalable design and implementation of QRCs is the novel contribution of this study.

We use the TPC-C benchmark [35] to quantify benefits of our proposed concepts. TPC-C models an order-entry environment. Its five transactions include entering a new order, delivering orders, recording payments, checking the status of orders, and monitoring the level of stock at the warehouses. Its tpm-C metric is the number of New-Order transactions executed per minute. It is a write-heavy workload consisting of 92% write transactions. We detail the implementation of these transactions using client-side caches. We present results showing that the client-side cache enhances tpm-C of MySQL InnoDB with one warehouse by 70%. Our implementation scales horizontally as a function of the number of warehouses. With 100 warehouses and 20 nodes in the caching layer, our technique boosts TPC-C's tpm-C more than 15 folds when compared with MySQL.

A limitation of using write-back in combination with QRCs is their requirement for an abundant amount of memory. We extend Twemcached with a transactional storage manager, Berkeley DB [32,34] (BDB), to implement a persistent cache. This introduces three variants of the cache manager: in-memory Twemcached without BDB (X-Twemcached), Twemcached with BDB transactions performed synchronously (Sync-BDB), and Twemcached with BDB transactions performed asynchronously (Async-BDB).

We detail how one implements durability of transactions using X-Twemcached and Async-BDB. In addition, we describe the use of replication to enhance availability of the caching layer in the presence of failures. We quantify the memory overhead of each using TPC-C.

Our contributions include:

- Primitives to implement a write-back policy while preserving strong consistency. These primitives include session objects, mapping objects, queues, leases, and QRCs. We use range leases similar to range locks to provide strong consistency and prevent the phantom problem. (Sect. 2).
- An implementation of the TPC-C benchmark using the write-back primitives. (Sect. 3).
- An in-memory (X-Twemcached) and persistent implementations (Async-BDB and Sync-BDB) of primitives that scale horizontally. (Sect. 4).
- An evaluation of alternative implementations using MySQL. A summary of our finidings are as follows:
  - X-Twemcached requires an abundant amount of memory and enhances the performance of MySQL in all our experiments. (Sect. 4.4).
  - Sync-BDB requires the least amount of memory. It does not enhance performance of MySQL with a few TPC-C warehouses. In our experiments, Sync-BDB enhanced performance of MySQL beyond 20 TPC-C warehouses. (Figs. 7, 9, 10 in Sect. 4).
  - Async-BDB requires less memory than X-Twemcached. Whether it enhances performance of MySQL depends on the amount of memory and the number of warehouses. (Fig. 12 of Sect. 4).

The rest of this paper is organized as follows. Section 2 presents the client-side cache and its write-back primitives. Section 3 presents the implementation detail of TPC-C using these primitives. Section 4 presents an evaluation of MySQL by itself and once extended with the variants of client-side cache. We present related work in Sect. 5. Brief future research directions are presented in Sect. 6.

2   Extended Cache Manager

This section presents the client-side primitives, use of leases to implement sessions with ACID semantics, support for range predicates and QRCs, and background threads (BGTs) to propagate writes buffered in the cache to the data store. It ends with a discussion of the implementation details to enhance performance and provide durability.

2.1   An Architecture

Figure 1 shows the architecture of a client-side cache. A load balancer directs user requests to different application servers. Each application server consists of either one or several AppNode instances serving user requests. A Dendrite implements caching of range predicate result sets, indexing of QRCs, and range leases for consistency. The AppNode and its Dendrite have access to client components to communicate with the persistent data store (e.g., JDBC with SQL systems)

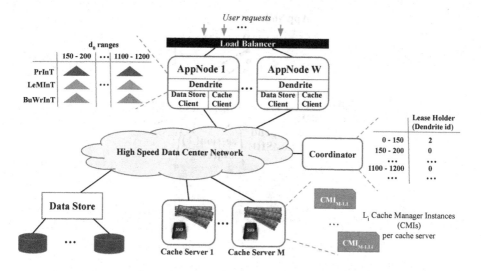

Fig. 1. A data store extended with a client-side cache.

and the cache (e.g., Whalin Client with memcached). We assume a transactional data store with ACID semantics such as PostgreSQL [21], MySQL's InnoDB [30], Mongo DB 4.0 [29], etc.

Multiple cache manager instances (CMIs) may be deployed on a cache server. Example CMIs include an in-memory key-value store such as *memcached* [4] or *Redis* [33]. AppNodes communicate with CMIs via message passing. These key-value caches provide simple interfaces such as `get`, `set`, `append` and `delete`.

Definition 1. *A cache entry is represented as a key-value pair (k_i, v_i) where k_i identifies the entry and v_i is the value of the entry. Both k_i and v_i are application specific and authored by a developer.*

A key-value pair (k_i, v_i) represents the results of a query or a block of software that embodies one or more queries. A developer extends the application logic, AppNode of Fig. 1, to look up the value of a key k_i prior to executing its corresponding query or software block. If a value v_i is found, a cache hit, the application logic proceeds to consume the value. Reads benefit from the cache because result look-up is much faster than query processing using the data store [17, 31].

Figure 2 shows the write-back policy for processing writes. An application write updates its impacted key-value pairs using a refill technique such as an incremental update (append, prepend, increment, etc.) or read-modify-write (RMW) ①. Next, it constructs a *session object* containing the sequence of changes that must be applied as a transaction to the data store and inserts it in a CMI ②. It appends id of this session (SID) in a *mapping* object of the cache entries impacted by this write ③. The key of the mapping object is a cache entry k_M and its value is SID. Finally, the session appends its SID to a

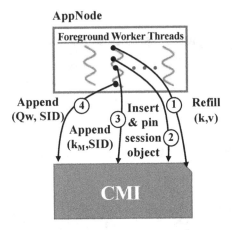

Fig. 2. A write session without QRCs.

queue ④. This queue is used by Background Threads, BGTs, to discover sessions and apply their session objects to the data store in the same serial order that they commit. Below, we formalize these concepts.

Definition 2. *A session object consists of a sequence of changes to the data store as described by the transaction that constitutes the session. It may identify one or more query result changes, QRCs.*

The definition of a *change* is specific to the data store's data model. It is different for the relational data model (SQL) when compared with the document data model, e.g., MongoDB.

Session objects enable a client-side cache to implement a write-back policy [15]. A challenge is how to process references for a missing cache entry with stale data in the data store, i.e., pending QRCs corresponding to different session objects. In [15], we describe *mappings* that identify session objects (pending writes in the cache) for a cache entry. A cache miss applies the session objects to the data store first. Subsequently, it queries the data store for the missing cache entry and populates the cache with this entry. This approach works well with read-heavy workloads. However, its performance with write-heavy workloads is inferior to a data store by itself. Below, we provide a formal definition of mapping. Subsequently, we address performance limitations of write-heavy workloads by introducing the concept of QRC.

Definition 3. *A mapping is a key-value pair that uniquely identifies a cache entry and the sequence of session ids that impact the value of this cache entry.*

Ideally, a cache miss should be processed with one data store transaction. The concept of mapping fails to realize this objective because a mapping my identify several pending session objects that must be applied as transactions to the data store. To realize our objective, we introduce and use the concept of Query Result

Change, QRC. A write transaction generates a QRC and associates it with its session object and the data in the data store. A miss for a cache entry must query the data store and apply the QRCs to the obtained results to compute the missing cache entry. Thus, a cache miss results in at most one data store transaction using QRCs.

Definition 4. *A query result change, QRC, consists of a sequence of changes to the result of a data store query. It is generated by a write session.*

Section 2.3 details a write session that generates QRCs.

Definition 5. *A queue consists of a sequence of session ids pertaining to the serial order in which they commit.*

A queue maintains the order in which session objects must be applied to the data store. It is used by background threads to discover session objects and apply them to the data store.

It is possible to have two or more queues, each queue is responsible for a mutually exclusive set of data items in the data store. For example, with TPC-C, one may have a queue per warehouse, its districts, orders, suppliers, and customers. With W warehouses, there are W queues.

A write session such as TPC-C's New-Order may write data items assigned to different queues (where a queue corresponds to a TPC-C warehouse). In this case, the id of this session is registered with the relevant queues.

The session object, its associated QRC (if any), mappings, and the queue are collectively termed *client-side primitives.* They are represented as key-value pairs and pinned in a CMI to prevent the cache replacement technique from evicting them. BGTs delete session objects and QRCs as a session is applied to the data store. They garbage collect session ids from mappings and queues periodically.

2.2 ACID Semantics: Sessions and Leases

We use the concept of a session to provide ACID semantics for the application's operations. It is implemented by an AppNode and builds on the concept of a transaction [20].

Definition 6. *A session identified by a unique id SID. It consists of one data store transaction and may read or write one or more cache entries. The data store transaction may be multi-statement, consisting of one or more data store operations.*

To illustrate a session and without loss of generality, with SQL, a data store read may be a SQL select statement and a data store write may be a SQL DML command (insert, delete, and update). A session may look up the result of one or more SQL select statements in the cache, issuing a SQL statement to the data store only when its result is missing from the cache. A session may represent the result of a multi-statement SQL command as one cache entry. Moreover, a SQL DML command may either generate a new value for a cache entry (potentially over-writing its existing value) or update an existing cache entry.

Concurrent sessions use S and X leases to implement the isolation property of ACID. Prior to reading a key-value pair, a session must obtain a Shared (S) lease on it. If the session intends to write a key-value pair, then it must obtain an eXclusive (X) lease on it[2].

Table 1. S and X lease compatibility.

Requested lease	Existing lease	
	S	X
S	Grant S lease	Abort and Retry
X	Grant X and void S lease	Abort and Retry

The S and X leases are different than read and write locks in several ways. First, S and X leases are non-blocking. As shown in the compatibility Table 1, when a session T_r requests a S lease on a key-value pair with an existing X lease, it aborts and retries. Second, when a session T_r requests an X lease on a data item with an existing S lease granted to session T_h, T_r wounds T_h by voiding its S lease. At its commit point, T_h is notified to abort and restart. This prevents write sessions from starving. Third, leases have a finite lifetime in the order of hundreds of milliseconds. Once a lease on a key-value pair expires, its referenced key-value pair is deleted. This is suitable for a distributed environment where an application node fails causing its sessions holding leases to be lost. These leases expire after some time to make their referenced data items available again.

All changes by a write session (X-lease holder) of a key-value pair are applied to a copy of this key-value pair, leaving the original unchanged. This copy is discarded should the session abort.

After executing its last statement, a session validates itself. This ensures all its leases are valid. Moreover, the session's S leases become golden. This means they may no longer be voided by an X lease. An X lease that encounters a golden S lease [5] is forced to abort and retry.

After validating itself and prior to committing, a write session generates its session object. Next, it obtains an X lease on queue(s) and inserts its identity in it (them). It obtains an X lease on the mapping of each of its referenced cache entries and appends its identity to each. It is possible for a session's X lease request on a queue (or a mapping object) to conflict with another concurrently executing session's X lease, causing the session to abort. An AppNode retries an aborted session several times prior to reporting an error.

---

[2] A write may be in the form of a read-modify-write or incremental update such as append, decrement, etc.

Once the session commits, the participating CMIs release the leases obtained by the session and make its modified cache entries permanent, i.e., replace the original with their modified copies.

Different components of an architecture may implement the write-back policy and its session objects, QRCs, mappings and queues. For example, they may be implemented by the application instances, CMIs, or a middleware between the application instances and CMIs, or a hybrid of these. This paper describes an implementation using AppNode instances, see Fig. 1.

2.3   Range Predicates and QRCs

We use the client-side caching solution of [13] for processing range predicates, e.g., Stock-Level transaction of TPC-C as detailed in Sect. 3.2. Its Dendrite (see Fig. 1) looks up results of range predicates in the cache and indexes QRCs. A dendrite is extensible and allows a software developer to implement the interfaces for insert, delete, and modify that impact the cached result sets of a range predicate. It employs an order-preserving in-memory interval tree [23] to implement a Predicate Interval Tree (PrInT), a Lease Manager Interval Tree (LeMInT), and a Buffered Write Interval Tree (BuWrInT).

PrInT indexes the cached predicates and their result sets. The lower and upper bounds of a predicate identify an interval. It is associated with the key of the cached result-set. PrInT stores this pairing by indexing the interval, facilitating fast lookups when the predicate is issued again. Given a predicate, PrInT may identify other cached entries that either overlap or contain this predicate. These can be used to compute the results of a predicate.

BuWrInT associates the interval impacted by a write with the key of a QRC stored in the cache. The write transaction must generate this QRC, e.g., the New-Order transaction of TPC-C. An AppNode uses BuWrInT to process a predicate that observes a cache miss as follows. It uses the interval referenced by the predicate to identify the QRCs that overlap it. Next, it queries the data store for a result set, applies the identified QRCs to it to compute its latest value. Finally, it inserts this value in the cache for future references and produces it as output.

With concurrent threads, a Dendrite uses the concept of range locks to pre-server consistency of the cached entries. Its implementation uses a Lease Manager Interval Tree, LeMInT. This tree maintains leases on ranges that are read and written. The maximum number of entries in LeMInT is dictated by the number of concurrent threads processing predicates.

Figure 3 shows how a write session generates and indexes a QRC. First, the session uses PrInT to look up all the cached entries that overlap its impacted range interval ①. It updates every entry that is cache resident ②, ignoring those missing from the cache. Next, it generates the session object containing its change, inserts and pins it in a CMI ③. It appends its changes for each impacted QRC ④ and associates the key of the QRC with the impacted range in BuWrInT ⑤. This write session also generates mappings and inserts its id in a

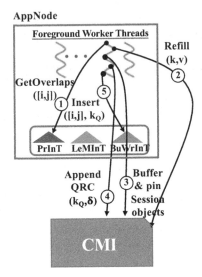

Fig. 3. A write session with QRC.

queue. These steps are similar to those of Fig. 2. They are not shown to simplify Fig. 3.

To tolerate failure of an AppNode, sessions that insert and delete entries in PrInT and BuWrInT generate log records that are stored in the caching layer. When a Dendrite starts for the first time, it looks up the CMIs for the relevant log records to re-construct its PrInT and BuWrInT interval trees.

2.4   Background Worker Threads, BGTs

There is one background thread, BGT, per queue. It applies the sessions in that queue to the data store in a first-in-first-out manner. This ensures serial execution of data store transactions in the same order as the write sessions updated the cache entries and generated session objects.

A BGT obtains an X lease on a queue, reads q sessions from it, and releases its lease. This allows concurrent write sessions to append their session id to the queue. The BGT applies these q sessions one after another. To apply a session, the BGT obtains an X lease on its session object and fetches it from the cache to obtain its list of changes. One or more of a session's changes may be **non-idempotent**. For example, a change may increment the number of deliveries by one (with Delivery transaction of TPC-C). To prevent repeated application of these changes in the presence of arbitrary BGT failures, we detect when a change has been applied to the data store and do not apply it again. The idea is as follows. When a BGT applies changes of a session to the data store, it first checks a table (collection) named Applied-Sessions for the SID. If the SID is found then the transaction commits without executing its other instructions. Otherwise, the transaction executes the pending changes and its last statement appends SID to Applied-Sessions. Using atomicity property of transactions, if a SID is found in Applied-Sessions then it is not applied a second time. After the data store executes the transaction, the BGT deletes the session's changes and its session object from the cache.

Periodically, a BGT garbage collects sessions from the Applied-Sessions table, queues, and mappings. It does so by maintaining a list of sessions it has applied to the data store. A session is considered garbage if it has no session object in the cache. The existence of a garbage session id in queues and mappings causes a BGT to observe a cache miss for its session object. In turn, the BGT adds this session id to be garbage collected.

It is possible for a session to belong to multiple queues. In this case, a BGT checks to verify the session is at the head of each queue. This step requires the BGT to obtain an X lease on all queues. Once it does so and its verification succeeds then it proceeds to apply the session to the data store, removes the session from the queues, and releases its lease. The BGT may conflict with other BGTs (namely a different BGT that owns one of the queues) when requesting its X lease. In this case, it releases its leases and backs off (sleeps) for an expo-nentially increasing time. Once the BGT obtains an X lease on all queues, if the session is not at the head of all queues then, once again, it releases all its leases and backs off for an exponentially increasing time. This synchronization ensures a global serial order among transactions impacting different warehouses, preserving Isolation property of ACID semantics across sessions. With TPC-C implementation of Sect. 3, it is used to implement those New-Order transactions that consist of items from different warehouses.

2.5   Discussion

To enhance performance, the number of round-trips between the application and the participating CMIs must be minimized. Cache managers such as memcached and Redis support multi-get commands that enable the application to fetch the value of multiple keys with one command. We develop equivalent commands for insert, append and swap. With multi-set/append/swap, the application specifies a sequence of $\{k_i, v_i\}$ pairings. With multi-set/append, for each specified pairing, the server sets/appends the provided v_i to the value of key k_i. Similarly, with multi-swap, the server overwrites the value of the specified key k_i with v_i. A session uses multi-append to append its session id to both the queue and map-pings of the cache entries that it updates. It uses multi-swap to overwrite the value of cache entries that it updates. A BGT uses multi-set to update the value of multiple QRCs. The result of each command is a sequence of STORED or NOT-STORED per specified pairing.

For writes to be durable, client-side primitives must be available until they are applied to the data store. Their loss is not acceptable because the system already acknowledged their successful processing. We replicate primitives on three different cache servers on different racks to enhance availability in the presence of cache server failures. A write is not acknowledged until all replicas return success in pinning the primitives. Replication causes additional overhead by requiring memory and utilizing network bandwidth, as quantified in Sect. 4.3.

Replication by itself is not enough to survive data center power failure. In this case, primitives may be stored on non-volatile memory such as NVDIMM-N[1] that detects server failure and flushes its DRAM content to flash for persistence.

3   TPC-C Implementation

Tables 2, 3, 4, 5 and 6 show the five transactions that constitute the TPC-C workload. Column 1 of these tables shows the SQL query and DML commands that constitute each transaction. Column 2 identifies the SQL statement as either a query (Read) or a DML command (Write). For each SQL query, the 3rd column identifies the key that is looked up in the cache. If a value is found (a cache hit) then no query is issued to the data store. Otherwise (a cache miss), the query is issued to the data store, a cache entry is computed and inserted in the cache. For each SQL DML, the 4th column identifies the key updated by the write session. For each SQL query, the 5th column identifies its mapping in case of a cache miss. Column 6 shows the mapping updated by a DML command. Order-Status and Stock-level do not have Columns "Key written" and "Updated Mapping" because they are read-only transactions, i.e., no DML command.

New-Order and Stock-Level transactions are interesting. New-Order produces QRCs as detailed in Sect. 3.2 and illustrated in Fig. 4. Stock-Level consumes QRCs when it encounters a cache miss, see discussion of Query 2.2 of Sect. 3.2. A BGT deletes a session object and its QRCs (if any) after applying the session object to the data store. This means at an instance in time, concurrent threads may compete for a QRC. We use leases to synchronize them to ensure either (1) a QRC is applied to the result of a query before its corresponding session object is propagated to the data store, or (2) a QRC is discarded if its corresponding session object has been applied to the data store.

Below, we detail New-Order and Stock-Level transactions in turn. Subsequently, we present the implementation of BGT.

3.1   New-Order Transaction

The New-Order transaction enters a customer order as one database transaction. The number of items in an order is randomly selected from 5 to 15, [5,15]. On average, ten items constitute an order. The average quantity of each item is randomly selected from 1 to 10, [1,10]. For a given terminal, the warehouse id is a constant. The district number (D_ID) is randomly selected from 1 to 10, [1,10]. Subsequently, it selects a non-uniform random customer number (C_ID) belonging to this warehouse and district.

With client-side caches, the interesting part of the New-Order transaction is its iteration on the items to adjust their warehouse quantity, see last row of Table 2 sub-divided using dashed lines. With OLTP-Bench implementation, this

Table 2. New-Order transaction, w is warehouse id, d is district number, c is customer id, o is order-line number, i is item id, T is item quantity.

SQL statement	Read or write	Key look up	Key written	Mapping	Updated mapping
SELECT C_DISCOUNT, C_LAST, C_CREDIT, W_TAX FROM Customer, Warehouse WHERE W_ID = w AND C_W_ID = w AND C_D_ID = d AND C_ID = c	R	CustWhse_w_d_c			
SELECT D_NEXT_O_ID, D_TAX FROM District WHERE D_W_ID = w AND D_ID = d FOR UPDATE	R	Dist_w_d		DISTRICT_w_d	
UPDATE District SET D_NEXT_O_ID = D_NEXT_O_ID + 1 WHERE D_W_ID = w AND D_ID = d	W		Dist_w_d		DISTRICT_w_d
INSERT INTO NewOrder (NO_O_ID, NO_D_ID, NO_W_ID) VALUES (o, d, w)	W		NewOrderIds_w_d		NEW_ORDER_w_d
INSERT INTO Order (O_ID, O_D_ID, O_W_ID, O_C_ID, O_ENTRY_D, O_OL_CNT, O_ALL_LOCAL) VALUES (o, d, w, c, ?, ?, ?)	W		CustomerIDOrder_w_d_o, OIAmount_w_d_o, LastOrder_w_d_c		ORDER_w_d
Per item do: SELECT I_PRICE, I_NAME, I_DATA FROM Item WHERE I_ID = i	R	Item_i			
SELECT S_QUANTITY, S_DATA, S_DIST_01, S_DIST_02, S_DIST_03, S_DIST_04, S_DIST_05, S_DIST_06, S_DIST_07, S_DIST_08, S_DIST_09, S_DIST_10 FROM Stock WHERE S_I_ID = i AND S_W_ID = w FOR UPDATE	R	Stk_w_i		STOCK_w_i	
UPDATE Stock SET S_QUANTITY = ? , S_YTD = S_YTD + ?, S_ORDER_CNT = S_ORDER_CNT + 1, S_REMOTE_CNT = S_REMOTE_CNT + ? WHERE S_I_ID = i AND S_W_ID = w	W		Stk_w_i, StkItemsEqQty_w_T		STOCK_w_i
INSERT INTO OrderLine (OL_O_ID, OL_D_ID, OL_W_ID, OL_NUMBER, OL_I_ID, OL_SUPPLY_W_ID, OL_QUANTITY, OL_AMOUNT, OL_DIST_INFO) VALUES (o,d,w,?,?,?,?,?,?)	W		OrderLine_w_d_o, Last200rdersItemIds_w_d		ORDER_LINE_w_d_o

is realized using a for loop that issues the two SQL DML commands in the last row of Table 2. (The entire for loop is one transaction.)

The insert and update DML commands in the "per item loop" produce session objects, see Table 2. The session executing these commands generates one

Table 3. Payment transaction, w is warehouse id, d is district number, c is customer id, ln is customer last name.

SQL statement	Read or write	Key look up	Key written	Mapping	Updated mapping
UPDATE Warehouse SET W_YTD = W_YTD + ? WHERE W_ID = w	W			WAREHOUSE_w	WAREHOUSE_w
SELECT W_STREET_1, W_STREET_2, W_CITY, W_STATE, W_ZIP, W_NAME FROM Warehouse WHERE W_ID = w	R	Whse_w			
SELECT D_STREET_1, D_STREET_2, D_CITY, D_STATE, D_ZIP, D_NAME FROM District WHERE D_W_ID = w AND D_ID = d	R	Dist2_w_d			DISTRICT_w_d
If customer with last name: SELECT C_ID FROM Customer WHERE C_W_ID = w AND C_D_ID = d AND C_LAST = ln End If	R	CustIds_w_d_ln			
SELECT C_FIRST, C_MIDDLE, C_LAST, C_STREET_1, C_STREET_2, C_CITY, C_STATE, C_ZIP, C_PHONE, C_CREDIT, C_CREDIT_LIM, C_DISCOUNT, C_BALANCE, C_YTD_PAYMENT, C_PAYMENT_CNT, C_SINCE FROM Customer WHERE C_W_ID = w AND C_D_ID = d AND C_ID = c	R	Customer_w_d_c		CUSTOMER_w_d_c	
SELECT C_DATA FROM Customer WHERE C_W_ID = w AND C_D_ID = d AND C_ID = c	R	CData_w_d_c		CUSTOMER_w_d_c	
UPDATE Customer SET C_BALANCE = ?, C_YTD_PAYMENT = ?, C_PAYMENT_CNT = ?, C_DATA = ? WHERE C_W_ID = w AND C_D_ID = d AND C_ID = c	W		Customer_w_d_c CData_w_d_c		CUSTOMER_w_d_c
UPDATE Customer SET C_BALANCE = ?, C_YTD_PAYMENT = ?, C_PAYMENT_CNT = ? WHERE C_W_ID = w AND C_D_ID = d AND C_ID = c	W		Customer_w_d_c		CUSTOMER_w_d_c
INSERT INTO History (H_C_D_ID, H_C_W_ID, H_C_ID, H_D_ID, H_W_ID, H_DATE, H_AMOUNT, H_DATA) VALUES (?,?,c,d,w,?,?,?)	W				HISTORY_w_d_c

session object to be applied to the data store by a BGT asynchronously. Each iteration has the old and the new quantity of an item. The client-side implementation obtains an X lease on ranges [old,old] and [new,new] using a Dendrite's LeMInT. (A range may correspond to a single value, e.g., [20,20].) We remove the item from the cache entry associated with [old,old] and insert it in the cache entry

Table 4. Delivery transaction, w is warehouse id, d is district id, c is customer id, o is order id.

SQL statement	Read or write	Key look up	Key written	Mapping	Updated mapping
For each district in 10 Districts: SELECT NO_O_ID FROM NewOrder WHERE NO_D_ID = d AND NO_W_ID = w ORDER BY NO_O_ID ASC LIMIT 1	R	NewOrderIds_w_d		NEW_ORDER_w_d	
DELETE FROM NewOrder WHERE NO_O_ID = o AND NO_D_ID = d AND NO_W_ID = w	W		NewOrderIds_w_d		NEW_ORDER_w_d
SELECT O_C_ID FROM Order WHERE O_ID = o AND O_D_ID = d AND O_W_ID = w	R	CIDOrder_w_d_o		ORDER_w_d	
UPDATE Order SET O_CARRIER_ID = ? WHERE O_ID = o AND O_D_ID = d AND O_W_ID = w	W		LastOrder_w_d_c		ORDER_w_d
UPDATE OrderLine SET OL_DELIVERY_D = ? WHERE OL_O_ID = o AND OL_D_ID = d AND OL_W_ID = w	W	OrderLine_w_d_o			ORDER_LINE_w_d_o
SELECT SUM(OL_AMOUNT) AS OL_TOTAL FROM OrderLine WHERE OL_O_ID = o AND OL_D_ID = d AND OL_W_ID = w	R	OlAmount_w_d_o		ORDERLINE_w_d_o	
UPDATE Customer SET C_BALANCE = C_BALANCE + ?, C_DELIVERY_CNT = C_DELIVERY_CNT + 1 WHERE C_W_ID = w AND C_D_ID = d AND C_ID = c	W		Customer_w_d_c		CUSTOMER_w_d_c

Table 5. Order-Status transaction, w is warehouse id, d is district id, c is customer id, o is order id.

SQL statement	Read or write	Key look up	Mapping
SELECT C_FIRST, C_MIDDLE, C_LAST, C_STREET_1, C_STREET_2, C_CITY, C_STATE, C_ZIP, C_PHONE, C_CREDIT, C_CREDIT_LIM, C_DISCOUNT, C_BALANCE, C_YTD_PAYMENT, C_PAYMENT_CNT, C_SINCE FROM Customer WHERE C_W_ID = w AND C_D_ID = d AND C_ID = c	R	Customer_w_d_c	CUSTOMER_w_d_c
SELECT O_ID, O_CARRIER_ID, O_ENTRY_D FROM Order WHERE O_W_ID = w AND O_D_ID = d AND O_C_ID = c ORDER BY O_ID DESC LIMIT 1	R	LastOrder_w_d_c	ORDER_w_d
SELECT OL_NUMBER , OL_I_ID, OL_SUPPLY_W_ID, OL_QUANTITY, OL_AMOUNT, OL_DELIVERY_D FROM OrderLine WHERE OL_O_ID = o AND OL_D_ID = d AND OL_W_ID = w	R	OrderLine_w_d_o	ORDERLINE_w_d_o

associated with [new,new]. These entries are identified by PrInT. We construct the following changes and store them in the cache: (key = qrc-wid-old, value = {$pull: {session id, item id}}), (key = qrc-wid-new, value = {$add: {session id, item id}}). We index their keys in BuWrInt. Note that these changes are to be

Table 6. Stock-Level transaction, w is warehouse id, d is district id, o is order id, i is item id, T is item quantity.

SQL statement	Read or write	Key look up	Mapping
`SELECT D_NEXT_O_ID FROM DISTRICT WHERE D_W_ID = w AND D_ID = d`	R	`Dist_w_d`	`DISTRICT_w_d`
`SELECT OL_I_ID, OL_O_ID FROM OrderLine WHERE OL_W_ID = w AND OL_D_ID = d AND OL_O_ID < latestOrderId AND OL_O_ID >= latestOrderId - 20`	R	`Last20OrdersItemIds_w_d`	`ORDERLINE_w_d_o`
`SELECT S_I_ID FROM Stock WHERE S_W_ID = w AND S_QUANTITY >= 0 AND S_QUANTITY < Threshold`	R	`StkItemsEqQty_w_T` for $0 \leq T < Threshold$	`STOCK_w_i`

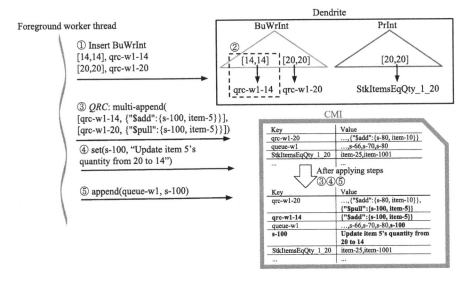

Fig. 4. A New-Order transaction updates item 5's quantity from 20 to 14. Its session id is s-100 in warehouse 1.

applied to the result of Query 2.2 of Stock-Level transaction and independent of the changes associated with the session object.

Example 3.1. *Assume the BuWrInt contains a range [20, 20] and is associated with a QRC entry qrc-w1-20. Assume the PrInt contains a range [20, 20] and points to a cache entry that contains item-25 and item-1001. Figure 4 shows an execution of a New-Order transaction that updates item 5's quantity from 20 to 14 in warehouse 1. The transaction's session id is s-100.*

The New-Order transaction first inserts two ranges [14, 14] and [20, 20] into BuWrInt ①. Insert [20, 20] has no impact because it already exists in the

BuWrInt ②. Next, it constructs the QRCs; it appends { $add: {s-100, item-5}} to qrc-w1-14 and appends { $pull: {s-100, item-5}} to qrc-w1-20. It then inserts the session object with the change "Update item 5's quantity from 20 to 14" in the cache. The session id s-100 identifies this session object. Lastly, the transaction appends the session id s-100 to warehouse 1's queue, queue-w1.

3.2 Stock-Level Transaction

The Stock-Level transaction computes the number of recently sold items that have a stock level below a specified threshold. Its input are a warehouse id (w), district id (d), and a threshold of minimum quantity in stock selected at random within [10,20]. Its output is a single value, count of items that have a stock level below the threshold T. This read transaction constitutes 4% of the workload and its OLTP-Bench implementation consists of the following two queries:

1. Fetch the last order id for the specified warehouse and district:

```
01 | SELECT D_NEXT_O_ID
02 | FROM DISTRICT
03 | WHERE D_W_ID = w AND D_ID = d;
```

2. Count distinct items in the last 20 orders of a district with warehouse quantity less than the threshold:

```
01 | SELECT COUNT(DISTINCT (S_I_ID)) AS STOCK_COUNT
02 | FROM ORDER_LINE , STOCK
03 | WHERE OL_W_ID = w AND OL_D_ID = d AND OL_O_ID <
        D_NEXT_O_ID AND OL_O_ID >= D_NEXT_O_ID - 20 AND
        S_W_ID = w AND  S_I_ID = OL_I_ID AND S_QUANTITY < T;
```

We represent the result of the first query as a cache entry and maintain it up to date as a new order transaction impacts its value, see Table 2. The second query is more complex. We represent it as two queries:

2.1 Compute distinct items in the last twenty orders for the specified warehouse and district:

```
01 | SELECT DISTINCT(OL_I_ID) , OL_O_ID
02 | FROM OrderLine
03 | WHERE OL_W_ID = w AND OL_D_ID = d AND OL_O_ID <
        D_NEXT_O_ID AND OL_O_ID >= D_NEXT_O_ID - 20;
```

2.2 Compute distinct items in the input warehouse with quantity less than the specified threshold:

```
01 | SELECT S_I_ID , S_QUANTITY
02 | FROM Stock
03 | WHERE S_W_ID = w AND S_QUANTITY < T;
```

We count items common in the result set of these two queries, i.e., item ids that are at the intersection of both result sets. The resulting value is the output of Stock-Level transaction.

Result of Query 2.1 for each warehouse and district combination is represented as a cache entry `Last20OrdersItemIds_w_d`. The value of this cache entry is a list of item id, order id for its last twenty orders. (It does not require the range predicate processing of Sect. 2.3 even though its qualification list consists of a range predicate.) New order transactions impact the value of this cache entry. They append the item ids of their order to its value and remove item ids of the oldest order, i.e., those with oldest < current - 20. They are able to remove these items because order id is attached to each item id. This processing is implemented in the application using Read-Modify-Write.

We process Query 2.2 as follows. We use PrInT (predicate interval tree of Sect. 2.3) to maintain a collection of closed intervals representing points: [0,0], [1,1], [2,2], ..., [T-1,T-1]. These points correspond to the threshold values for Query 2.2. Each identifies the key of a QRC in the cache. The value of a QRC is either a list of item ids or an empty set. (Note that the empty set is a value and does not imply a cache miss.) The session obtains a S lease from LeMInT on the interval of Query 2.2, [0,T]. Next, it issues a multi-get for keys in PrInT that fall in [0,T]. The set of item ids is the result of this query.

Both Stock-Level and New-Order transactions may observe a cache miss for a key-value pair of a point [p,p] in PrInT. They issues the query to the data store:

```
01 |  SELECT S_I_ID
02 |  FROM Stock
03 |  WHERE S_W_ID=? AND S_QUANTITY=p;
```

Subsequently, they look up BuWrInT with interval [p,p] to obtain a list of removed and inserted item ids. After applying each change to the obtained query result, they proceed to consume the results.

Example 3.2. *Assume the BuWrInt contains two ranges [14, 14] and [20, 20]. Assume the PrInt contains one range [20, 20]. Figure 5 shows an execution of a Stock-Level transaction that reads items that have quantity from 0 to 15.*

The Stock-Level transaction looks up [0,15) in PrInt and observes a miss ①. It then looks up [0,15) in BuWrInt and finds qrc-w1-14 ②. qrc-w1-14 identifies a query result change that adds item 5 to the range [14,14] in District 14 of warehouse 1 ③. Next, the session issues Query 2.2. to the data store. The data store produces a table consisting of items item-1 and item-2 with the same quantity 12 as its output ④. It adds item 5 to the query result ⑤ and represents the result as two entries: {key=StkItemsEqQty_1_12, value= "item-1,item2"} and {key=StkItemsEqQty_1_14, value= "item-5"} ⑥. It follows to insert these two

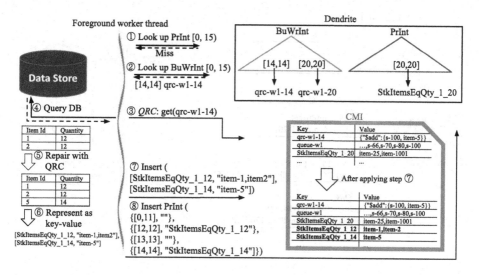

Fig. 5. Stock-Level reads items with quantity from [0, 15].

*entries in the cache and four ranges into PrInt for future lookups. The four
ranges include [0, 11], [12, 12], [13, 13], and [14, 14]. The values of ranges [12,
12] and [14, 14] are StkItemsEqQty_1_12 and StkItemsEqQty_1_14, respectively.
The values of ranges [0,11] and [13,13] are empty since there are no items with
quantity that falls within these two ranges.*

3.3   BGTs

A BGT that applies session objects to the data store performs the following
operations. First, it constructs the impacted intervals by this session, i.e., a set
of {[old,old]} and a set of {[new,new]}. Next, for each interval, it acquires an
X lease on it, identifies changes (either remove or insert) associated with this
session, and deletes these changes from the respective QRCs.

Example 3.3. *Assume the session object s-100 is at the head of the session
queue of warehouse 1, queue-w1. Assume the cache contains two QRC entries:
qrc-w1-20 and qrc-w1-14. It also contains one session object for the New-Order
session s-100 with the value "Update item 5's quantity from 20 to 14". Figure 6
shows an execution of a background worker that applies s-100 to the data store.*

*The BGT reads the list of session objects, s-100, s-104,..., from the session
queue of warehouse 1, queue-w1 ①. It then applies the change by each session
object. The value of session object s-100 is "Update item 5's quantity from 20
to 14" ②. Note that 14 and 20 identify two QRC entries. The BGT translates*

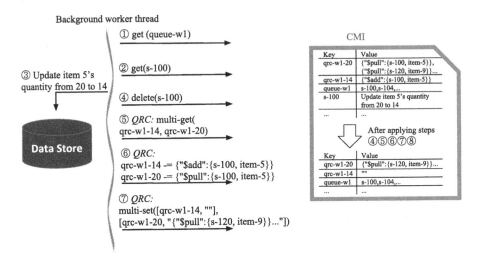

Fig. 6. Execution of a BGT.

the change into a transaction and applies it to the data store ③. Next, it deletes s-100 ④. Finally, it removes s-100 from qrc-w1-14 and qrc-w1-20 ⑤- ⑦.

3.4 Persistent Cache

We extended IQ-Twemcache with Berkeley Database (BDB) to implement a transactional persistent cache. The objective of this implementation are two folds. First, to minimize the amount of memory required by the client-side primitives. Second, to persist client-side primitives in the presence of failures. We analyze two variants: Async-BDB, and Sync-BDB. Sync-BDB realizes both objectives. Async-BDB realizes only the first objective using BDB. To tolerate failures with Async-BDB, we replicate client-side primitives across multiple instances of Async-BDB on different servers. Both Async-BDB and Sync-BDB configure the BDB database to be transactional providing ACID semantics. Below, we provide details of Async-BDB and Sync-BDB in turn.

With Async-BDB, a *put* inserts its entry in IQ-Twemcache first. If an entry is a client-side primitive and is larger than a pre-specified threshold, we write the entry to BDB and free its memory space in IQ-Twemcache. If a put inserts an application key into IQ-Twemcache successfully then we delete it from BDB. A background thread reads a session queue to identify session objects, writes these session objects to BDB, and unpins them in IQ-Twemcache. It prioritizes evicting a client-side primitive. When Async-BDB evicts an entry, it writes it to BDB.

A *get* for an application key looks up the key in IQ-Twemcache. If it observes a cache miss then it looks up the key in BDB. If it observes a miss in BDB then it returns a cache miss. With Async-BDB, a get for a client-side primitive looks up BDB first. If not found then it looks up the cache.

Sync-BDB writes a client-side primitive to BDB synchronously. A *put* for an application key inserts the key in IQ-Twemcache and deletes it from BDB. A *get* for a client-side primitive always looks up BDB. Sync-BDB processes the following in the same way as Async-BDB: (1) a get for an application key and (2) an IQ-Twemcache eviction.

4   Evaluation

This section uses the TPC-C benchmark to evaluate the performance of MySQL InnoDB by itself, and MySQL InnoDB augmented with either an in-memory implementation of client-side primitives using Twemcached with leases, Async-BDB, and Sync-BDB (See Sect. 3.4 for a description of the last two.) These configurations are labeled MySQL, X-Twemcached, Async-BDB, and Sync-BDB for short. With all configurations, MySQL is configured with a 48 GB buffer pool and a 2 GB log file size.

Our experiments were conducted on a cluster of *emulab* [37] nodes. Each node has two 2.4 GHz 64-bit 8-Core (32 virtual cores) E5-2630 Haswell processors, 8.0 GT/s bus speed, 20 MB cache, 64 GB of RAM, connects to the network using 10 Gigabits networking card and runs Ubuntu OS version 16.04 (kernel 4.10.0). Each experiment ran for 5 min and the cache was fully warmed up prior to starting an experiment. With abundant amount of memory, cache hit rate is 100%.

All results are obtained using OLTP-Bench [12] implementation of TPC-C extended with sessions and leases for strong consistency.

The main lessons of this section are as follows:

1. With 1 server and 1 warehouse, X-Twemcached and Async-BDB outperform MySQL by more than 70%. This holds true with a high number of terminals (50), even though X-Twemcached and Async-BDB abort and retry more than 90% of sessions. See Sect. 4.1.
2. X-Twemcached, Async-BDB, and Sync-BDB scale horizontally as a function of the number of warehouses to outperform MySQL by several orders of magnitude. See Sect. 4.2.
3. One may replicate session objects, mappings, and queues of write-back with X-Twemcached and Async-BDB to enhance their durability in the presence of failures. Its overhead reduces overall throughput (tpm-C) by 10% to 25%. When Asyc-BDB is configured with 3 replicas, Sync-BDB with 1 replica is a superior alternative. (Sync-BDB persists session objects, mappings, and queues to its SSD and does not require replication.) See Sect. 4.3.
4. X-Twemcached and Async-BDB require abundant am ount of memory. With limited memory, X-Twemcached is inferior to MySQL independent of the number of warehouses and the number of servers. Async-BDB, on the other hand, is superior to MySQL with a large number of warehouses and nodes. See Sects. 4.4 and 4.5.

Below, we present the experiments that embody these lessons in turn.

4.1   One Warehouse: Vertical Scalability

Figure 7 shows the tpm-C and vertical scalability of MySQL, MySQL with X-Twemcached, MySQL with Async-BDB, and MySQL with Sync-BDB as a function of the number of terminals issuing requests. (To make the figures readable, labels identify a caching technique without repeating MySQL as the data store name.) These numbers are gathered from a configuration consisting of two physical servers. One server hosts either MySQL by itself or MySQL with one of the cache managers. A second server hosts OLTP-Bench that generates transactions pertaining to TPC-C workload.

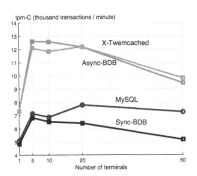
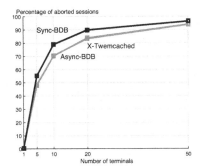

Fig. 7. 1 warehouse.   **Fig. 8.** Aborted sessions.

Both X-Twemcached and Async-BDB outperform MySQL by a wide margin. With 5 terminals, their tpm-C is more than 70% higher. A CMI is configured with 48 GB of memory and there are no evictions. Hence, X-Twemcached and Async-BDB provide comparable tpm-C.

Sync-BDB provides the lowest performance and is inferior to MySQL. It stores session objects, mappings, and the queue of sessions in BDB and implements modifications to each as a transaction. A BDB transaction produces log records that are flushed to SSD prior to transaction commit. These SSD writes are in the critical path of performing operations and cause Sync-BDB to be inferior to MySQL by itself.

The rate at which the data store, MySQL, processes transactions dictates how many sessions are propagated from the caching layer to the data store. At the end of the experiment, X-Twemcached and Async-BDB apply 30,000 and 25,000 sessions to MySQL, respectively. X-Twemcached propagates a higher number of sessions because its BGTs do not incur the overhead of fetching data from the persistent BDB. For example, with 5 threads, BGTs of Async-BDB perform more than 110,000 BDB put operations and 147,000 BDB dequeue operations in the background. X-Twemcached BGTs perform these operations using in-memory key-value pair.

By writing to BDB, Async-BDB requires less memory than X-Twemcached. We quantify this in Sect. 4.4.

The tpm-C with MySQL drops from 20 to 50 terminals due to contention for locks that causes different terminals to wait on one another. We see the same with both X-Twemcached and Async-BDB with an increasing percentage of sessions aborting and re-trying as a function of the number of terminals. Figure 8 shows more than 90% of sessions abort and re-try with 50 terminals. This percentage is higher with Sync-BDB because it holds leases for a longer time interval since its writes to BDB are in the critical path of requests. Delivery sessions constitute more than 90% of the aborted[3] sessions because each delivery is for ten orders.

4.2 Multiple Warehouses: Horizontal Scalability

Experiments of this section show the write-back primitives scale horizontally. These experiments vary the number of servers in the caching tier as a function of the number of warehouses. All experiments are conducted with 5 terminals issuing transactions to a warehouse. (Each terminal is an OLTP-Bench thread.) Hence, five warehouses are assigned to each cache server. In all experiments, one server hosts MySQL. Each cache server hosts 5 CMIs, one CMI per warehouse. As we increase the number of warehouses to 100, the number of cache servers increases to 20.

The large system configuration with 100 warehouses supports a high tpm-C. A single OLTP-Bench process cannot generate requests fast enough. We use multiple OLTP-Bench processes with each issuing transactions to different warehouses. In all reported results, we ensured the OLTP-Bench servers do not become fully utilized to limit tpm-C of a configuration.

Figure 9a shows tpm-C as a function of the number of warehouses. Figure 9b shows scalability relative to 1 warehouse. We report the performance of MySQL running on one server by itself to quantify the performance enhancement observed by the write back policy. It scales up to 20 warehouses. Subsequently, it levels off as the SSD of its server becomes fully utilized. Its tpm-C drops as we increase the number of warehouses and terminals due to a higher number of random I/Os reducing SSD efficiency.

X-Twemcached, Async-BDB, and Sync-BDB scale almost linearly, see Fig. 9b. However, Sync-BDB degrades performance of MySQL with 1 and 10 warehouses. Beyond 20 warehouses, while Sync-BDB enhances performance of MySQL, its enhancement is lower than both X-Twemcached and Async-BDB, see Fig. 9a. In these experiments, Sync-BDB employs multiple SSDs on different cache servers to process its writes. With 100 warehouses, it uses 20 servers with 20 SSDs compared to 1 server with 1 SSD with MySQL, enhancing MySQL performance significantly. X-Twemcached and Async-BDB outperform Sync-BDB by removing SSD writes from the critical path of processing requests.

---

[3] We minimize the impact of these aborts on the observed performance by requiring a session to generate its session objects, QRCs, and mapping at its commit time. This overhead is not incurred if the session aborts.

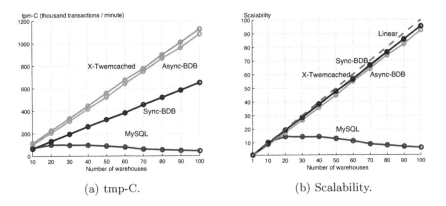

(a) tmp-C.   (b) Scalability.

Fig. 9. Horizontal scalability, 5 terminals per warehouse.

In sum, X-Twemcached and Async-BDB enhance tpm-C of MySQL by several orders of magnitude. Sync-BDB's improvements are negative with 1 and 10 warehouses (−0.28% and −8.68%, respectively). Beyond 20 warehouses, it also enhances MySQL performance by a wide margin.

4.3   Replication for Durability

With X-Twemcached and Async-BDB, one may replicate session objects, mappings, and the queues to minimize their loss in the presence of cache server failures. This replication imposes an overhead that reduces the performance enhancements of write-back. This section quantifies this overhead.

Figure 10 shows the normalized throughput of X-Twemcached, Async-BDB, Sync-BDB relative to MySQL. We show MySQL relative to itself with 1.0 as the baseline. With X-Twemcached and Async-BDB, we present numbers with 1 replica and 3 replicas[4]. We do not report this with Sync-BDB because it persists session objects, mappings, and the queue to tolerate cache server failures.

Figure 10 shows X-Twemcached, Async-BDB, and Sync-BDB improve tpm-C of MySQL more than 13 folds with 100 warehouses. X-Twemcached outperforms the other alternatives because it is in-memory. In general, performance enhancements of X-Twemcached and Async-BDB decrease by 10% to 25% with 3 replicas when compared with 1 replica.

---

[4] With 1 and 10 warehouse experiments of Fig. 10, we launched 3 cache servers and ensured the CMIs that participate in a replica-set are assigned to 3 different cache servers.

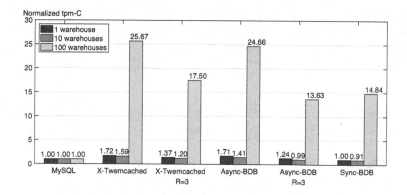

Fig. 10. Normalized tpm-C, 5 terminals per warehouse.

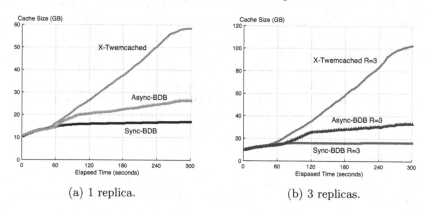

(a) 1 replica.   (b) 3 replicas.

Fig. 11. 100 warehouses, 1 terminal per warehouse.

4.4 Memory Requirement

Figure 11 quantifies the memory requirement of X-Twemcached, Sync-BDB and Async-BDB. The experiments are configured with 100 warehouses. We run two experiments: one with 1 replica (Fig. 11a), and another with 3 replicas (Fig. 11b) for session objects, mappings, and the queue of sessions. Each figure shows the amount of required memory as a function of 1 terminal issuing transactions to 1 warehouse. Both provide similar observations. Sync-BDB requires a lower amount of memory compared with X-Twemcached and Async-BDB by persisting session objects, queues, QRCs to BDB.

Async-BDB requires a lower amount of memory when compared with X-Twemcached by persisting session objects, mappings and the queues to BDB asynchronously. Once a cache entry is persisted, Async-BDB frees its assigned memory by inserting it in the free queue so that it can be reused for the next inserted key-value pair.

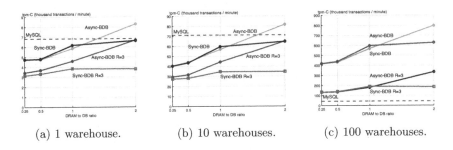

| (a) 1 warehouse. | (b) 10 warehouses. | (c) 100 warehouses. |

Fig. 12. TPC-C with limited memory, 5 terminals per warehouse.

With Async-BDB and X-Twemcached, the foreground threads generate session objects, mappings, and queue elements continuously, increasing their required memory footprint significantly over time. Sync-BDB stores session objects in BDB, causing its required memory size to stabilize during the experiment. After 5 min, Async-BDB uses twice the amount of memory compared with Sync-BDB, while it is 4x (6x) with X-Twemcached 1 (3) replicas.

The New-Order transaction generates new cache entries. This explains why the amount of memory required by Sync-BDB increases as a function of time in Fig. 11. The next section considers the impact of limited memory.

4.5   Limited Memory

With a limited amount of memory, whether a caching technique enhances performance of MySQL depends on the number of warehouses. Figure 12 highlights this by reporting tpm-C as a function of the amount of memory (DRAM) to the database ratio with 1, 10, and 100 warehouses. We do not show X-Twemcached because it reverts to write-through with limited memory and it degrades performance of MySQL for all reported warehouses.

Figure 12 shows tpm-C with both 1 replica and 3 replicas. With Sync-BDB, we consider three replicas to enhance availability in the presence of cache server failures. The replicas with Async-BDB are for both durability and availability.

With 1 warehouse, DRAM must be twice the database size in order for Async-BDB to enhance performance of MySQL. Even then, it degrades MySQL performance with 3 replicas. The same observation holds true with 10 warehouses. With 100 warehouses, Async-BDB and Sync-BDB enhance MySQL performance. They use the bandwidth of 20 SSDs (attached to 20 different servers) to complement the bandwidth of 1 SSD with MySQL. This holds true even when the available memory is 25% of the database size.

The results of this section highlight the importance of persistent caches, both Async-BDB and Sync-BDB. Without persistence (i.e., X-Twemcached), the limited memory prevents the use of write-back to improve performance even with 100 warehouses.

5   Related Work

Host-side caches enhance the performance of OLTP workload by staging disk
blocks from a hard disk drive (HDD) onto solid state disk (SSD) [6,10,22,25].
These *transparent* caches are different than our client-side caches in that they
manage disk blocks and require no additional software from an application developer. Our proposed client-side cache complements host-side caches to further
enhances their performance. To illustrate, Fig. 13 shows tpm-C of MySQL with
HDD (MySQL:HDD) and SSD (MySQL:SSD). Performance of MySQL with a
host-side cache named FlashCache, MySQL:HDD+FlashCache, falls somewhere
in between the two. Relative to MySQL:HDD, it provides the highest gains with
1 to 10 terminals. X-Twemcached complements the use of FlashCache to enhance
tpm-C an additional 70%.

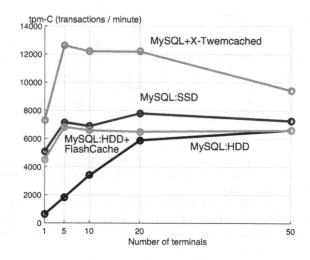

Fig. 13. tpm-C of host-side and client-side caches.

This study is inspired by in-memory DBMS architectures [8,11,24,27,28,
36]. Anti-Caching [8] presents TPC-C results showing MySQL with a write-
through memcached is inferior to MySQL by itself. This is consistent with our
evaluation using the write-through policy (results are not presented due to lack of
space). Our client-side cache uses the write-back policy to enhance performance
of MySQL by itself. To realize the reported performance benefits, it is important
to use multi-set/append/swap commands to minimize the number of network
round-trip times between AppNodes and CMIs. These concepts along with the
write-back policy are absent from the evaluation of [8].

6   Future Research

A relational data store such as MySQL is a building block of applications with
write intensive workloads. Once an application exhausts the processing capabil-

ity of the data store, a system architect may either augment the data store with a cache [14,16–18,31], switch to a data store with a data model more amenable to scale for the application workload [7,9,26], or switch to an in-memory relational data store [8,11,24,27,28,36,38]. The cache augmented approach is the only approach that does not require data migration using an extract-transform-load tool. It complements the existing database and its data store, requiring the application software to be extended with the write-back primitives described in this study. The other approaches offer their own advantages. A future research direction is to articulate both the qualitative and quantitative differences between these alternatives, providing insights to practitioners.

References

1. NVDIMM: Changes are Here So What's Next (2016). https://www.imcsummit. org/2016/videos-and-slides/nvdimm-changes-are-here-so-whats-next/
2. Annamalai, M., et al.: Sharding the shards: managing datastore locality at scale with Akkio. In: 13th USENIX Symposium on Operating Systems Design and Implementation (OSDI 2018), Carlsbad, CA, pp. 445–460 (2018). USENIX Association
3. Apache: Ignite - In-Memory Data Fabric (2016). https://ignite.apache.org/
4. Six Apart: Memcached Specification (2019). http://code.sixapart.com/svn/ memcached/trunk/server/doc/protocol.txt
5. Astrahan, M.M., et al.: System R: relational approach to database management. ACM Trans. Database Syst. 1(2):97–137 (1976)
6. Byan, S., et al.: Mercury: host-side flash caching for the data center. In: IEEE 28th Symposium on Mass Storage Systems and Technologies (MSST), San Diego, CA, pp. 1–12. IEEE, April 2012
7. Cattell, R.: Scalable SQL and NoSQL data stores. SIGMOD Rec. 39, 12–27 (2011)
8. DeBrabant, J., Pavlo, A., Tu, S., Stonebraker, M., Zdonik, S.B.: Anti-caching: a new approach to database management system architecture. PVLDB 6(14), 1942–1953 (2013)
9. Decandia, G., et al.: Dynamo: Amazon's highly available key-value store. In: Proceedings of Twenty-First ACM SIGOPS Symposium on Operating Systems Principles, SOSP 2007, pp. 205–220. ACM Press (2007)
10. DELL: Dell Fluid Cache for Storage Area Networks (2014). http://www.dell.com/ learn/us/en/04/solutions/fluid-cache-san
11. Diaconu, C., et al.: Hekaton: SQL server's memory-optimized OLTP engine. In: Proceedings of the 2013 ACM SIGMOD International Conference on Management of Data, SIGMOD 2013, pp. 1243–1254. ACM, New York (2013)
12. Difallah, D.E., Pavlo, A., Curino, C., Cudré-Mauroux, P.: OLTP-bench: an extensible testbed for benchmarking relational databases. PVLDB 7(4), 277–288 (2013)
13. Ghandeharizadeh, S., Alabdulkarim, Y., Nguyen, H.: CPR: client-side processing of range predicates. In: Da Silva, D., Wang, Q., Zhang, L.-J. (eds.) CLOUD 2019. LNCS, vol. 11513, pp. 340–354. Springer, Cham (2019). https://doi.org/10.1007/978-3-030-23502-4_24
14. Ghandeharizadeh, S., Irani, S., Lam, J., Yap, J.: CAMP: a cost adaptive multiqueue eviction policy for key-value stores. In: Middleware (2014)
15. Ghandeharizadeh, S., Nguyen, H.: Design, implementation, and evaluation of writeback policy with cache augmented data stores. PVLDB 12(8), 836–849 (2019)

16. Ghandeharizadeh, S., Yap, J.: Gumball: a race condition prevention technique for cache augmented SQL database management systems. In: ACM SIGMOD DBSocial Workshop (2012)

17. Ghandeharizadeh, S., Yap, J.: Cache augmented database management systems. In: Proceedings of the ACM SIGMOD Workshop on Databases and Social Networks, DBSocial 2013, pp. 31–36. ACM, New York (2013)

18. Ghandeharizadeh, S., Yap, J., Nguyen, H.: Strong consistency in cache augmented SQL systems. In: Proceedings of the 15th International Middleware Conference, Middleware 2014, pp. 181–192. ACM, New York (2014)

19. Gray, C., Cheriton, D.: Leases: an efficient fault-tolerant mechanism for distributed file cache consistency. In: Proceedings of the Twelfth ACM Symposium on Operating Systems Principles, SOSP 1989, pp. 202–210. Association for Computing Machinery, New York (1989)

20. Gray, J.N.: Notes on data base operating systems. In: Bayer, R., Graham, R.M., Seegmüller, G. (eds.) Operating Systems. LNCS, vol. 60, pp. 393–481. Springer, Heidelberg (1978). https://doi.org/10.1007/3-540-08755-9_9

21. T. P. G. D. Group: PostgreSQL: The World's Most Advanced Open Source Relational Database (2020). https://www.postgresql.org/

22. Holland, D.A., Angelino, E., Wald, G., Seltzer, M.I.: Flash caching on the storage client. In: Presented as Part of the 2013 USENIX Annual Technical Conference (USENIX ATC 2013), San Jose, CA, pp. 127–138. USENIX (2013)

23. Jagadish, H.V.: On indexing line segments. In: Proceedings of the 16th International Conference on Very Large Data Bases, VLDB 1990, San Francisco, CA, USA, pp. 614–625. Morgan Kaufmann Publishers Inc. (1990)

24. Kallman, R., et al.: H-store: a high-performance, distributed main memory transaction processing system. Proc. VLDB Endow. 1(2), 1496–1499 (2008)

25. Kim, H., et al.: Flash-conscious cache population for enterprise database workloads. In: International Workshop on Accelerating Data Management Systems Using Modern Processor and Storage Architectures - ADMS 2014, Hangzhou, China, 1 Sept 2014, pp. 45–56. VLDB (2014)

26. Lakshman, A., Malik, P.: Cassandra: a decentralized structured storage system. SIGOPS Oper. Syst. Rev. 44(2), 35–40 (2010)

27. Larson, P.-A., Levandoski, J.: Modern main-memory database systems. Proc. VLDB Endow. 9(13), 1609–1610 (2016)

28. Ma, L., et al.: Larger-than-memory data management on modern storage hardware for in-memory oltp database systems. In: Proceedings of the 12th International Workshop on Data Management on New Hardware, DaMoN 2016, pp. 9:1–9:7. ACM, New York (2016)

29. MongoDB Inc.: MongoDB https://www.mongodb.com/

30. MySQL: Designing and implementing scalable applications with Memcached and MySQL, A MySQL White Paper, June 2008. http://www.mysql.com/why-mysql/memcached/

31. Nishtala, R., et al.: Scaling Memcache at Facebook. In: Presented as Part of the 10th USENIX Symposium on Networked Systems Design and Implementation (NSDI 2013), Lombard, IL, pp. 385–398. USENIX (2013)

32. Oracle Inc.: Berkeley DB (2019). http://download.oracle.com/otn/berkeley-db/db-18.1.25.tar.gz

33. RedisLabs: Redis (2019). https://redis.io/

34. Seltzer, M.I.: Beyond relational databases. Commun. ACM 51(7), 52–58 (2008)

35. TPC Corp.: TPC-C Benchmark (2019). http://www.tpc.org/tpcc/

36. Tu, S., Zheng, W., Kohler, E., Liskov, B., Madden, S.: Speedy transactions in multicore in-memory databases. In: Proceedings of the Twenty-Fourth ACM Symposium on Operating Systems Principles, SOSP 2013, pp. 18–32. ACM, New York (2013)

37. White, B., et al.: An integrated experimental environment for distributed systems and networks. SIGOPS Oper. Syst. Rev. **36**(SI):255–270 (2002)

38. Zamanian, E., Shun, J., Binnig, C., Kraska, T.: Chiller: contention-centric transaction execution and data partitioning for modern networks. In: Proceedings of the 2020 ACM SIGMOD International Conference on Management of Data, SIGMOD 2020, pp. 511–526. Association for Computing Machinery, New York (2020)

pygrametl: A Powerful Programming Framework for Easy Creation and Testing of ETL Flows

Søren Kejser Jensen[1]([⊠]) [iD], Christian Thomsen[1] [iD], Torben Bach Pedersen[1] [iD], and Ove Andersen[2] [iD]

[1] Department of Computer Science, Aalborg University, Aalborg, Denmark
`{skj,chr,tbp}@cs.aau.dk`
[2] Danish Geodata Agency, Nørresundby, Denmark
`ovand@gst.dk`

Abstract. Extract-Transform-Load (ETL) flows are used to extract data, transform it, and load it into data warehouses (DWs). The dominating ETL tools use graphical user interfaces (GUIs) where users must manually place steps/components on a canvas and manually connect them using lines. This provides an easy to understand overview of the ETL flow but can also be rather tedious and require much trivial work for simple things. We, therefore, challenge this approach and propose to develop ETL flows by writing code. To make the programming easy, we proposed the Python-based ETL framework `pygrametl` in 2009. We have extended `pygrametl` significantly since the original release, and in this paper, we present an up-to-date overview of the framework. `pygrametl` offers commonly used functionality for programmatic ETL development and enables the user to efficiently create effective ETL flows with the full power of programming. Each dimension is represented by a dimension object that manages the underlying table or tables in the case of a snowflaked dimension. Thus, filling a slowly changing or snowflaked dimension only requires a single method call per row as `pygrametl` performs all of the required lookups, insertions, and assignment of surrogate keys. Similarly to dimensions, fact tables are each represented by a fact table object. Our latest addition to `pygrametl`, Drawn Table Testing (DTT), simplifies testing ETL flows by making it easy to define both preconditions (i.e., the state of the database before the ETL flow is run) and postconditions (i.e., the expected state after the ETL flow has run) into a test. DTT can also be used to test ETL flows created in other ETL tools. `pygrametl` also provides a set of commonly used functions for transforming rows, classes that help users parallelize their ETL flows using simple abstractions, and editor support for working with DTT. We present an evaluation that shows that `pygrametl` provides high programmer productivity and that the created ETL flows have good run-time performance. Last, we present a case study from a company using `pygrametl` in production and consider some of the lessons we learned during the development of `pygrametl` as an open source framework.

O. Andersen—The work was done while employed at Aalborg University and FlexDanmark.

The original version of this chapter was revised: affiliation, email address of the last author and ref. 17 have been updated. The correction to this chapter is available at https://doi.org/10.1007/978-3-662-63519-3_9

A. Hameurlain and A Min Tjoa (Eds.): TLDKS XLVIII, LNCS 12670, pp. 45–84, 2021.
https://doi.org/10.1007/978-3-662-63519-3_3

1   Introduction

The Extract-Transform-Load (ETL) flow is a crucial part of a data warehouse (DW) project. The task of an ETL flow is to extract data from possibly heterogeneous data sources, perform transformations (e.g., conversions and cleaning of data), and finally load the transformed data into a DW. It is well-known in the DW community that it is both very time-consuming and difficult to get the ETL right due to its high complexity [24]. It is often estimated that up to 80% of the time in a DW project is spent on the ETL.

Many commercial and open source tools support users in implementing ETL flows [4,55]. The leading ETL tools provide graphical user interfaces (GUIs) in which the users define the flow of data visually. While these are easy to use and inherently provide an overview of the ETL flow, they also have disadvantages. For example, users might require a component that is not provided by the graphical ETL tool. Instead, users must create solutions based on (often complicated) combinations of the provided components or by integrating custom-coded components into the ETL flow. Both are very time-consuming solutions.

In an ETL project, non-technical staff is often involved as advisors, decision makers, etc. but the core development is (in our experience) done by skilled ETL specialists. As trained specialists often can use textual interfaces efficiently while non-specialists use GUIs, it is attractive to consider alternatives to graphical ETL tools. In relation to this, one can recall the high expectations of Computer Aided Software Engineering (CASE) systems in the eighties. It was expected that non-programmers could take part in software development by specifying (not programming) characteristics in a CASE system that would then generate the code. Needless to say, these expectations were not fulfilled. It can be argued that forcing all ETL development into GUIs is a step back to the CASE idea.

We acknowledge that graphical ETL tools can be useful, but we also claim that for many ETL projects, a code-based solution is the right choice. Often it is simply much faster to express the desired operations in a few lines of code instead of placing components on a canvas and setting properties in dialog boxes. However, many parts of code-based ETL programs are redundant if each is written from scratch. To remedy this, a framework with common functionality is needed.

In this paper, we present an overview of the latest version of *pygrametl* (version 2.7), an open source Python-based framework for ETL programmers we first proposed in 2009 [56]. The framework provides common functionality for ETL development and while it is easy to get an overview of and start using, it is still very powerful. pygrametl offers a novel approach to ETL programming by providing a framework that abstracts over the DW tables while still allowing the user to use the full power of Python. For example, it is very easy to create (relational or non-relational) data sources as they are just iterable objects that produce *rows*. Thus, using a simple loop users can insert data into dimension and fact tables while only iterating over the source data once. Dimensions and fact tables are each represented by a *single object* which manages the underlying

DW tables. For example, use of snowflaked dimensions is very easy as the user only operates on *one* dimension object for the entire snowflake while **pygrametl** automatically manages all of the tables in the snowflake. Thus, filling a snowflaked dimension only requires a single method call per row. Users who prefer the inherent structure provided by graphical ETL tools can also optionally create their ETL flows using connected step objects.

For testing, **pygrametl** provides DTT that makes it simple to define a self-contained test that sets the state of a DW before a test is run (the precondition) and verifies it has a certain state afterward (the postcondition). DTT can, e.g., be used to create unit tests for each component of an ETL flow during development or to create integration tests that ensure the components work together. Exploiting parallelism to improve the performance of an ETL flow is also simple with **pygrametl**, e.g., transformations implemented as functions can be parallelized with only one line of code. In general, **pygrametl** utilizes functional and object-oriented programming to make ETL development easy. **pygrametl** is thus similar to other special-purpose frameworks that provide commonly used functionality like, e.g., the web frameworks Django [8] and Ruby on Rails [45] where development is done in Python and Ruby code, respectively. Our evaluation in Sect. 10 shows that **pygrametl** provides high programmer productivity and that the programmatically created ETL flows have good run-time performance when compared to a leading open source graphical ETL tool.

The paper is an extended version of [52] and is structured as follows: Sect. 2 presents an ETL scenario we use as a running example. Section 3 gives an overview of **pygrametl**. Sections 4–8 present the functionality and classes provided by **pygrametl** to support *data sources*, *dimensions*, *fact tables*, *flows*, and *testing*, respectively. Section 9 provides a short overview of the supporting functionality provided by **pygrametl** including helper functions, support for parallelism, and editor support. Section 10 evaluates **pygrametl** on the running example. Section 11 presents a case-study of a company using **pygrametl**. Section 12 documents our experience with publishing **pygrametl** as open source. Section 13 presents related work. Section 14 concludes and points to future work.

2   Example Scenario

We now describe an ETL scenario which we use as a running example. The example considers a DW where test results for tests of web pages are stored. This is inspired by work we did in the European Internet Accessibility Observatory (EIAO) project [53] but it has been simplified here for the sake of brevity.

In the system, there is a web crawler that downloads web pages. Each downloaded page is stored in a local file. The crawler stores data about the downloaded files in a log which is a tab-separated file with the fields shown in Table 1(a). Afterward, another program performs a number of different tests on the pages. These tests could, e.g., test if the pages are *accessible* (i.e., usable for disabled people) or conform to certain standards. Each test is applied to all pages, and the test outputs the number of errors detected. The results of the tests are written to a tab-separated file with the fields shown in Table 1(b).

Table 1. The source data format for the running example.

Field	Explanation
localfile	Name of local file where the page was stored
url	URL from which the page was downloaded
server	HTTP header's Server field
size	Byte size of the page
downloaddate	When the page was downloaded
lastmoddate	When the page was modified

(a) DownloadLog.csv

Field	Explanation
localfile	Name of local file where the page was stored
test	Name of the test that was applied to the page
errors	Number of errors found by the test on the page

(b) TestResults.csv

After all tests are performed, the data from the two files are loaded into a DW by an ETL flow. The schema of the DW is shown in Fig. 1. The schema has three dimensions: The test dimension holds information about each of the tests that are applied. This dimension is static and prefilled. The date dimension is filled by the ETL on-demand. The page dimension is *snowflaked* and spans several tables. It holds information about the downloaded pages including both static aspects (the URL and domain) and dynamic aspects (size, server, etc.) that may change between two downloads. The page dimension is also filled on-demand by the ETL. The page dimension is a *type 2 slowly changing dimension* (SCD) [23] where information about different *versions* of a given page is stored.

Each dimension has a surrogate key (with a name ending in *id*) and one or more attributes. The individual attributes have self-explanatory names and will not be described in further detail here. There is one fact table that has a foreign key to each of the dimensions and a single measure holding the number of errors found for a certain test on a certain page on a certain date.

3   Overview of the Framework

Unlike many commercial ETL tools which can move data from sources to a variety of targets, the purpose of `pygrametl` is only to make it easy to load data into dimensional DWs [23] managed by RDBMSs. Focusing on RDBMSs as the target for `pygrametl` keeps the design simple as it allows us to create good solutions that are specialized for this domain instead of thinking in very general *data integration terms*. The data sources, however, do *not* have to be relational.

When using `pygrametl`, the programmer writes code that controls the flow, the extraction (the E in ETL) from source systems, the transformations (the T

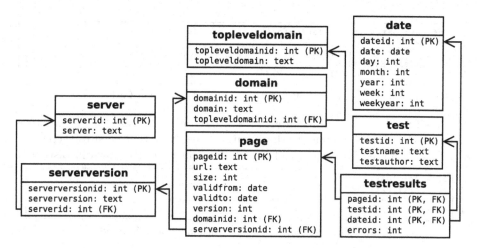

Fig. 1. The schema for the running example.

in ETL) of the source data, and the loading (the L in ETL) of the transformed data. For the flow control, extraction, and load, **pygrametl** offers components that support the user and makes it easy to create additional components. For the transformations, the user benefits heavily from being able to use Python.

Loading data into a DW is particularly easy with **pygrametl**. The general idea is that the user creates *objects* for each *fact table* and *dimension* (different kinds are supported) in the DW. An object representing a dimension offers convenient methods like **insert**, **lookup**, etc. that hide details of key assignment, SQL insertion, caching, etc. In particular, it should be noted that a snowflaked dimension is also treated in this way such that a single object can represent the entire dimension although the data is inserted into several tables in the database.

The dimension object's methods take *rows* as arguments. A row in **pygrametl** is a mapping from names to values. Based on our experiences with other tools, we found it important that **pygrametl** does not try to validate that all rows given to a dimension object have the same attributes or the same attribute types. If the user wants such checks, they can write code for that. It is then, e.g., possible to have additional attributes in a row or on purpose leave out certain attributes. **pygrametl** only raises an error if attributes required for an operation are missing. For example, all values to be inserted into a DW must exist when the insertion is done as **pygrametl** does not try to guess missing values. However, **pygrametl** has functionality for setting default values and/or on-demand callback of user-defined functions to compute the missing values. So, while some tools enforce uniformity of rows, **pygrametl** is designed to make it easy for the users to do what they want instead of what the tool *thinks* they want.

While **pygrametl** is written in Python [44] other languages could have been used. We chose Python due to its focus on programmer productivity and its large selection of libraries. Also, Python is dynamically typed (the type of a variable is checked at run-time) and strongly typed (a variable holding an integer cannot be used as a string). Consider, e.g., the Python function in Listing 1.

```
1  def getfloat(value, default=None):
2      try:
3          return float(value)
4      except Exception:
5          return default
```

Listing 1. Function that casts value to a float and returns default otherwise.

This function converts its input to a **float** or, if the conversion fails, to a value which defaults to **None**, Python's **null** value. Note that no static types are specified. The function can be called with different types as shown in Listing 2.

```
1  f1 = getfloat(10)
2  f2 = getfloat('1e1')
3  f3 = getfloat('A string', 10.0)
4  f4 = getfloat(['A', 'list'], 'Not a float!')
```

Listing 2. Using getFloat with and without a default value.

After executing the code, the value of **f1**, **f2**, and **f3** will 10.0 while the value of **f4** will be the string **Not a float!**. Thus, the expression **f1 + f2** will succeed, while **f3 + f4** will fail as a float and a string cannot be added together.

Python is predominantly object-oriented but to some degree also supports functional programming, e.g., by allowing use of functions or lambda expressions as arguments. This makes it very easy to customize behavior. **pygrametl**, for example, exploits this to support compute of missing values on-demand (see Sect. 5). Using Python's support for default arguments, **pygrametl** also provides reasonable defaults when possible to spare the user for unnecessary typing.

4   Data Source Support

pygrametl supports a large selection of data sources and makes it easy to add more. As explained in Sect. 3, data is moved around in *rows* in **pygrametl**. Instead of implementing a row class, we use Python's built-in dictionaries (**dict**) as it provides efficient mappings between keys (i.e., attribute names) and values (i.e., attribute values). The only requirement of data sources in **pygrametl** is that they are iterable (i.e., they must define the **__iter__** method) and produce **dict**s. Thus, it does not require a lot of programming to create new data sources. Of course, the complexity of the code that extracts the data heavily depends on the source format. **pygrametl** includes the following data sources.

SQLSource is a data source that returns the rows of an SQL query. The query, the database connection to use, and optionally new names for the result columns and initializing SQL are given when the data source is created.

CSVSource is a data source that returns the lines of a delimiter separated file as rows. This class is implemented in **pygrametl** as a reference to the class **csv.DictReader** in Python's standard library. In the running example, we have two tab-separated files and an instance of **CSVSource** should be created for each of them to load the data. For TestResults.csv, this is done as shown in Listing 3.

```
1   testresults = CSVSource(open('TestResults.csv', 'r'), delimiter='\t')
```

Listing 3. Reading a CSV file using the CSVSource data source.

TypedCSVSource functions like CSVSource but can also performs type casting of its input. In Listing 4 values from the field size are cast to ints.

```
1   testresults = TypedCSVSource(open('TestResults.csv', 'r'),
2                                casts={'size':int}, delimiter='\t')
```

Listing 4. Reading a CSV file using the TypedCSVSource data source.

PandasSource wraps a Pandas DataFrame [33] so it can be used as a data source as shown in Listing 5. Thus, Pandas can be used to extract and transform data before pygrametl loads it.

```
1   df = pandas.read_parquet("TestResults.parquet")
2   df = df.dropna()
3   testresults = PandasSource(df)
```

Listing 5. Using a Pandas DataFrame as a data source through PandasSource.

The above data sources take external data as input, while the following data sources take data sources as input to combine them or perform transformations.

MappingSource generalizes the cast concept from TypedCSVSource. For each row from a data source it executes arbitrary functions on its attribute values.

Both TypedCSVSource and MappingSource apply transformations to attribute values. TransformingSource in contrast applies transformations to rows, and can thus, e.g., add or remove attributes. For these three data sources, Python's support for functional programming is used as functions are passed as arguments.

MergeJoiningSource is a data source that equijoins rows from two other data sources. Thus, it must be given two data sources (which must deliver rows in sorted order) and the attributes to join on. Both of the data sources in the running example have the field localfile so an equijoin can be done as shown in Listing 6 where testresults and downloadlog are CSVSources.

```
1   inputdata = MergeJoiningSource(testresults, 'localfile',
2                                  downloadlog, 'localfile')
```

Listing 6. Joining the rows from two data source using MergeJoiningSource.

HashJoiningSource is a data source that equijoins rows from two other data sources using a hash map. Thus, the input data sources need not be sorted.

UnionSource and RoundRobinSource union rows from data sources together. UnionSource returns all rows from a data source before using the next, while RoundRobinSource switches after a user-defined number of rows are taken. A DynamicForEachSource automatically creates multiple data sources but presents them as one data source. This is, e.g., useful for a directory containing many CSV files. The user must provide a function that when called with an argument returns a data source and a sequence of arguments for it as shown in Listing 7.

```
1   srcs = DynamicForEachSource([... sequence of the names of the files ...],
2                           lambda f: CSVSource(open(f, 'r')))
3   for row in srcs: # will iterate over all rows from all the files;
4       ...             # the user can transform and load each row here
```

Listing 7. Reading a sequence of CSV files using DynamicForEachSource.

Last, CrossTabbingSource can pivot data from another data source, while data from another data source can be filtered using FilteringSource.

5   Dimension Support

The classes pygrametl uses for representing dimensions in a DW are shown in Fig. 2. Only public methods and their required arguments are shown. Note that SnowflakedDimension does not inherit from Dimension but offers the same interface and can be used as if it were a Dimension due to Python's duck typing.

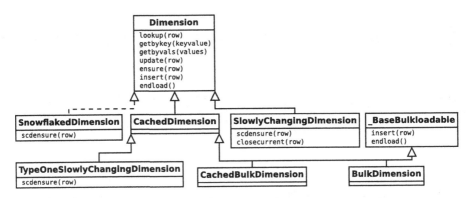

Fig. 2. Class hierarchy for the dimension supporting classes.

5.1   Basic Dimension Support

Dimension is the most basic class for representing a DW dimension in pygrametl. It is used for a dimension that has exactly one table in the DW. When an instance is created, the name of the represented dimension (i.e., the name of the table in DW), the name of the key column (we assume that a dimension has a non-composite key), and a list of attributes (the underlying table may have more attributes but pygrametl will then not manage them) must be given. By default, all of the none-key attributes are used for looking up the key value. To only use a subset of the attributes, a list of *lookup attributes* (lookupatts) can be given. In the running example, the test dimension has a surrogate key testid but in the CSV files, each is identified by testname. Thus, the value of the key must be found based on the test name and not all of test's attributes.

When the dimension object is given a row to insert into the table (explained below), the row need not contain a value for the dimension's key. If the key is not present, a method (called **idfinder**) is called with the row as an argument. Thus, when creating a **Dimension** instance, the **idfinder** method can also be set. If not set explicitly, it defaults to a method that assumes that the key is numeric and returns the current maximum value for the key incremented by one.

A default key value for non-existing dimension members can also be set (**defaultidvalue**). If a lookup does not succeed, this default key value is returned. This is used if new members should not be inserted into the dimension, but facts should still be recorded. By using a default key value, the facts would then reference a prefilled member representing that information is missing. In the running example, test is a prefilled dimension that should not be changed by the ETL flow. If data from the file TestResults.csv refers to a test that is not represented in the test dimension, we do not want to disregard the data by not adding a fact. Instead, we set the default foreign key value for the test dimension to be −1 which is the key value for a preloaded dimension member with the value *Unknown test* for the testname attribute. This is shown in Listing 8.

```
1  testdim = Dimension(name='test',
2                      key='testid',
3                      defaultidvalue=-1,
4                      attributes=['testname', 'testauthor'],
5                      lookupatts=['testname'])
```

Listing 8. Representing the test dimension using **Dimension**.

Finally, the user can provide a function as the argument **rowexpander**. With such a function, it possible to add required fields on-demand to a row before it is inserted into the dimension (explained in detail below).

Many of the methods defined in the **Dimension** class accept an optional *name mapping* when called. This name mapping is used to map between attribute names in the rows (i.e., dictionaries) used in **pygrametl** and names in the tables in the DW. In the running example, the rows from the source file TestResults.csv contain the attribute test but the corresponding attribute in the DW's dimension table is called testname. When the **Dimension** instance for test in **pygrametl** is given a row r to insert into the DW, it will look for the value of the testname attribute in r. However, this value does not exist since it is called test in r. A name mapping $n = \{'testname':'test'\}$ can then be set up such that when **pygrametl** code looks for the attribute testname in r, test is actually used instead.

Dimension offers the method **lookup** which based on the lookup attributes for the dimension returns the key for the dimension member. As arguments, it takes a row (which at least must contain the lookup attributes) and optionally a name mapping. **Dimension** also offers the method **getbykey**. This method is the opposite of **lookup**: As argument, it takes a key value and it returns a row with all attributes for the dimension member with the given key value. Another method for looking up dimension members is offered by **Dimension**'s **getbyvals** method. This method takes a row holding a subset of the dimension's attributes and optionally a name mapping. Based on the subset of attributes, it finds the dimension members that have equal values for the subset of attributes and returns those (full) rows. For adding a new member to a dimension, `Dimension` offers the method `insert`. This method takes a row and optionally a name mapping as arguments. The row is added to the DW's dimension table. All attributes of the dimension must be present in the `pygrametl` row. The only exception to this is the key. If the key is missing, the `idfinder` method is applied to find the key value. The method `update` takes a row that must contain the key and one or more of the other attributes. The member with the given key value is updated to have the same values as the given attributes.

`Dimension` also offers a combination of lookup and insert: `ensure`. This method first tries to use `lookup` to find the key value for a member. If the member does not exist and no default key value has been set, `ensure` proceeds to use `insert` to create the member. In any case, `ensure` returns the key value of the member to the caller. If the `rowexpander` has been set, that function is called by `ensure` before `insert` is called. This makes it possible to add calculated fields before an insertion to the DW's dimension table is done. In the running example, the date dimension has several fields that can be computed from the date string in the source data. However, it should only be computed once for each date. By setting `rowexpander` to a function that calculates them from the date string, the dependent fields are only calculated the first time `ensure` is invoked for a date.

`CachedDimension` has the same interface and semantics as `Dimension`. However, it internally caches dimension members in memory to speed up lookup operations. The caching can be complete such that the entire dimension is held in memory or partial such that only the most recently used members are held in memory. A `CachedDimension` can also cache new members when added.

When an instance of `CachedDimension` is created, it is possible to provide the same arguments as for `Dimension`. Further, optional arguments can be used to set the size of the cache, whether the cache should be prefilled with rows from the DW or be filled on-the-fly, whether full rows should be cached or only the keys and lookup attributes, and finally whether inserted rows should be put in the cache. A `CachedDimension` for the test dimension is shown in Listing 9.

```
1  testdim = CachedDimension(name='test',
2                            key='testid',
3                            defaultidvalue=-1,
4                            attributes=['testname', 'testauthor'],
5                            lookupatts=['testname'],
6                            size=500,
7                            prefill=True,
8                            cachefullrows=True)
```

Listing 9. Representing the test dimension using `CachedDimension`.

5.2   Advanced Dimension Support

`SlowlyChangingDimension` provides support for type 2 changes in a SCD [23] and in addition to type 2 changes, type 1 changes are also supported for a subset of the dimension's attributes. When an instance of `SlowlyChangingDimension` is created, it takes the same arguments as a `Dimension` instance. Further, the name of the attribute that holds versioning information for type 2 changes in the DW's dimension table can be given. If given, the version of a row with the greatest value for this attribute is considered the newest row and **pygrametl** will automatically maintain the version number for newly added versions. If there is no such attribute with version information, the user can specify another attribute to be used for the ordering of row versions. A number of other things can optionally be configured. It is possible to set which attribute holds the *from date* telling from when the dimension member is valid. Likewise, it is possible to set which attribute holds the *to date* telling when a member becomes replaced. A default value for the *to date* for a new member can also be set, as well as a default value for the *from date* for the first version of a new member. Further, functions that, based on data in new rows, calculate the *to date* and *from date* can be given, but if they are not set, **pygrametl** defaults to use a function that returns the current date. **pygrametl** offers convenient functions for this functionality. It is possible not to set any of these date related attributes such that no validity date information is stored for the different versions. It is also possible to list a number of attributes that should have type 1 changes (overwrites) applied. **SlowlyChangingDimension** has built-in support for caching. Finally, it is possible to configure if rows should be sorted by the RDBMS such that **pygrametl** uses SQL's **ORDER BY** or if **pygrametl** instead should retrieve all versions of a row and sort them in Python. At least for one popular commercial RDBMS, it is significantly faster to do it in Python.

SlowlyChangingDimension offers the same methods as **Dimension**. **lookup** is, however, modified to return the key value for the *newest* version. To handle versioning, **SlowlyChangingDimension** offers the method **scdensure**. This method must be given a row (and optionally a name mapping). Like **ensure** it sees if the member is present in the dimension and, if not, inserts it. However, it does not only do a lookup. It also detects if any changes have occurred. If changes have occurred for attributes where type 1 changes should be used, it updates the existing versions of the member. If changes have occurred for other attributes, it creates a new version of the member and adds the new version to the dimension. Unlike the previously described methods, **scdensure** modifies the given row. Specifically, it adds the key and versioning values to the row so the user does not have to retrieve them afterward. The method **closecurrent** sets an end date for the current version without creating a new version.

In the running example, the web pages we test might be updated. To record this, we let the page dimension be a type 2 SCD. We lookup the page using the URL and detect changes by considering the other attributes. Using **SlowlyChangingDimension** to do so is shown in Listing 10.

In this example, the **fromfinder** argument is a method that extracts a *from date* from the source data when creating a new member. It is also possible to give a **tofinder** argument to find the *to date* for a version to be replaced. If not given, this defaults to the **fromfinder**. If the user wants a different behavior, (e.g., that the *to date* is set to the day before the new member's from date), **tofinder** can be set to a function that performs the necessary calculations.

```
1   pagedim = SlowlyChangingDimension(
2       name='page',
3       key='pageid',
4       attributes=['url', 'size', 'validfrom', 'validto',
5                   'version', 'domainid', 'serverversionid'],
6       lookupatts=['url'],
7       fromatt='validfrom',
8       fromfinder=pygrametl.datereader('lastmoddate'),
9       toatt='validto',
10      versionatt='version')
```

Listing 10. Representing the page dimension using `SlowlyChangingDimension`.

`TypeOneSlowlyChangingDimension` is similar to `SlowlyChaningDimension` but *only* supports type 1 changes where dimension members are updated (not versioned) [23]. `SlowlyChaningDimension` also supports using type 1 changes, but they cannot be used alone, only together with type 2 changes. Also, by only supporting type 1 `TypeOneSlowlyChangingDimension` can be optimized more.

`SnowflakedDimension` supports filling a dimension in a snowflake schema [23]. A snowflaked dimension is spread over more tables such that there is one table for each level in the dimension hierarchy. The fact table references one of these tables that itself references tables that may reference other tables etc. The member must thus be created by joining the tables in the snowflaked dimension together.

Normally, it can be a tedious task to create ETL logic for filling a snowflaked dimension. First, a lookup must be made on the *root table* which is the table referenced by the fact table. If the member is represented there, it is also represented in the dimension tables further away from the fact table (otherwise the root table could not reference these and thus not represent the member at the lowest level). If the member is not represented in the root table, it must be inserted but it is then necessary to make sure that the member is represented in the next level of tables such that the key values can be used in references. This process continues for all the levels until the leaves. It is also possible to do the lookups and insertions from the leaves towards the root but when going towards the leaves, it is possible to stop the search earlier if a part of the member is already present. While searching from the root is not difficult as such, it takes a lot of tedious coding which makes the risk of errors bigger. This is remedied with `pygrametl`'s `SnowflakedDimension` which takes care of the repeated ensures such that data is inserted where needed in the snowflaked dimension but such that the user only has to make one method call to add/find the member.

An instance of `SnowflakedDimension` is constructed from other `Dimension` instances. The user creates a `Dimension` instance for each table participating in the snowflaked dimension and passes these instances to the `SnowflakedDimension` instance when creating. In the running example, the page dimension is snowflaked. We can create a `SnowflakedDimension` instance for the page dimension as shown in Listing 11 (where the different `Dimension` instances are created beforehand).

```
1   pagesf = SnowflakedDimension([
2           (pagedim, [serverversiondim, domaindim]),
3           (serverversiondim, serverdim),
4           (domaindim, tlddim)])
```

Listing 11. Representing the page dimension using `SnowflakedDimension`.

The argument is a list of pairs where the first element in each pair references each of the dimensions in the second element (the second element may be a list). For example, it can be seen that **pagedim** references **serverversiondim** and **domaindim**. We require that if t's key is named k, then an attribute referencing t from another table must also be named k. We also require that the tables in a snowflaked dimension form a tree (where the table closest to the fact table is the root) when we consider tables as nodes and foreign keys as edges. We could avoid both of these requirements but doing so would make **SnowflakedDimension** much more complicated to use. If the snowflake does not form a tree, the user can make **SnowflakedDimension** consider a subgraph that is a tree and use the individual **Dimension** instances to handle the parts not handled by the **SnowflakedDimension**. Consider, for example, a snowflaked date dimension with the levels day, week, month, and year. A day belongs both to a certain week and a certain month, but the week and the month may belong to different years (a week has a week number between 1 and 53 which belongs to a year). In this case, the user could ignore the edge between week and year when creating the **SnowflakedDimension** and instead use a single method call to ensure that the week's year is represented as shown in Listing 12.

```
1   # Represent the week's year. Read the year from weekyear
2   row['weekyearid'] = yeardim.ensure(row, {'year':'weekyear'})
3   # Now let SnowflakedDimension take care of the rest
4   row['dateid'] = datesnowflake.ensure(row)
```

Listing 12. Ensuring that a row exists in a `SnowflakedDimension`

SnowflakedDimension's `lookup` method calls the `lookup` method on the **Dimension** object at the root of the tree of tables. It is assumed that the lookup attributes belong to the table that is closest to the fact table. If this is not the case, the programmer can use `lookup` or `ensure` on a **Dimension** further away from the root and use the returned key value(s) as lookup attributes for the **SnowflakedDimension**. The method `getbykey` takes an optional argument that decides if the full dimension member should be returned (i.e., a join between the tables of the snowflaked dimension is done) or only the part from the root. This also holds for `getbyvals`. `ensure` and `insert` work on the entire snowflaked dimension starting from the root and moving downwards as much as needed. These two methods use the same code. The only difference is that `insert`, to be consistent with the other classes, raises an exception if nothing is inserted (i.e., if all parts were already there). Algorithm 1 shows how the code *conceptually* works but we do not show details like how to track if an insertion did happen.

The algorithm is recursive and both `ensure` and `insert` first invoke it with *dimension* set to the root table. First a normal `lookup` is performed. If the key value is found, it is set in the row and returned (Lines 2–4). If not, the algorithm

---

Algorithm 1. ensure_helper(*dimension*, *row*)

1: *keyval* ← *dimension.lookup*(*row*)
2: **if** found **then**
3:     *row*[*dimension.key*] ← *keyval*
4:     **return** *keyval*
5: **for each** table *t* that is referenced by *dimension* **do**
6:     *keyval* ← *ensure_helper*(*t*, *row*)
7: **if** *dimension* uses the key of a referenced table as a lookup attribute **then**
8:     *keyval* ← *dimension.lookup*(*row*)
9:     **if** not found **then**
10:         *keyval* ← *dimension.insert*(*row*)
11: **else**
12:     *keyval* ← *dimension.insert*(*row*)
13: *row*[*dimension.key*] ← *keyval*
14: **return** *keyval*

---

is applied recursively on each of the tables that are referenced from the current table (Lines 5–6). As a side-effect of the recursive calls, key values are set for all referenced tables (Line 3). If the key of one of the referenced tables is used as a lookup attribute for *dimension*, it might just have had its value changed in one of the recursive calls, and a new attempt is made to look up the key in *dimension* (Lines 7–8). If this attempt fails, we insert (part of) *row* into *dimension* (Line 10). We can proceed directly to this insertion if no key of a referenced table is used as a lookup attribute in *dimension* (Lines 11–12).

SnowflakedDimension also offers an scdensure method. This method can be used when the root is a SlowlyChangingDimension. In the running example, we previously created pagedim as an instance of SlowlyChangingDimension. When pagedim is used as the root as in the definition of pagesf in Listing 11, we can use the SCD support on a snowflake. With a single call of scdensure, a full versioned dimension member can be added such that the relevant parts are added to the five different tables in the page dimension.

When using the graphical ETL tools such as SQL Server Integration Services (SSIS) or Pentaho Data Integration (PDI), the use of snowflakes requires the user to use several lookup/update steps. It is thus not easy to start looking up/inserting from the root as foreign key values might be missing. Instead, the user has to start from the leaves and go towards the root. In pygrametl, the user only has to call one method on a SnowflakedDimension instance. pygrametl starts at the root (to save lookups) and only if needed moves to the other levels.

BulkDimension is used in scenarios where a lot of data must be inserted into a dimension and it becomes too time-consuming to use traditional SQL INSERTs (like the previously described Dimension classes do). BulkDimension instead writes new dimension values to a temporary file which can be bulk loaded.

The exact way to bulkload varies from RDBMS to RDBMS. Therefore, we require that the user passes a function that does the bulk loading when creating an instance of BulkDimension. This function is invoked by pygrametl when the bulkload should take place. When using the database driver psycopg2 [37] and the RDBMS PostgreSQL [36], the function can be defined as shown in Listing 13. Functions for more drivers are available in pygrametl's documentation [41].

```
1  def pgbulkloader(name, attributes, fieldsep, rowsep, nullval, filehandle):
2      global connection # Opened outside this function
3      cursor = connection.cursor()
4      cursor.copy_from(file=filehandle, table=name, sep=fieldsep,
5                       null=nullval, columns=attributes)
```

Listing 13. A user-defined function for bulk-loading rows into PostgreSQL

The user can optionally define which separator and line-ending to use, which file to write the data to, and which string value to use for representing NULL.

To enable efficient lookups, **BulkDimension** caches all the dimension's data in memory. This is viable for most dimensions as modern computers have large amounts of memory. But if it is impossible and efficient bulk loading is desired **CachedBulkDimension** can be used. Like **CachedDimension**, the size of its cache can be configured, but it also supports bulk loading. To avoid code duplication, the code for bulk loading has been placed in the class **_BaseBulkloadable** which **BulkDimension** and **CachedBulkDimension** then both inherit from.

6   Fact Table Support

pygrametl provides four classes for representing fact tables. They all assume that a fact table has a number of key attributes that reference dimension tables. Further, the fact tables may also have a number of measure attributes.

FactTable provides a basic representation of a fact table. When an instance is created, the programmer must provide the fact table's name, the names of the key attributes, and optionally the names of the measure attributes if such exist.

FactTable provides the method **insert** which takes a row and inserts a fact into the DW's table. It also provides the method **lookup** which takes a row that holds values for the key attributes and returns a row with values for both key and measure attributes. Finally, it provides the method **ensure** which first tries to use **lookup**, and if a match is found, compares the measure values between the fact in the DW and the given row. It raises an error if these are different. If no match is found, it invokes **insert**. All the methods support name mappings.

BatchFactTable inherits from **FactTable** and provides the same methods. However, it caches inserted rows in memory until a user-configurable number of rows can be inserted together. This can significantly improve performance.

BulkFactTable provides a write-optimized representation of a fact table. It does offer the **insert** method but not **lookup** or **ensure**. When **insert** is called the data is written to a file, and when a user-configurable number of rows have been added to the file it is loaded into the fact table using code in **_BaseBulkloadable**. Like for **BulkDimension** and **CachedBulkDimension**, the user has to provide a function that performs the bulk-loading. For the running example, a **BulkFactTable** instance can be created as shown in Listing 14.

```
1  facttbl = BulkFactTable(name='testresults',
2                          measures=['errors'],
3                          keyrefs=['pageid', 'testid', 'dateid'],
4                          bulkloader=pgbulkloader,
5                          bulksize=5000000)
```

Listing 14. Representing the fact table (testresults) using `BulkFactTable`.

`AccumulatingSnapshotFactTable` provides a representation of a fact table where facts can be updated. In our example, a fact could be inserted when a test starts and then be updated with the result later. The users must specify the key attributes to use for lookup (`keyrefs`) and those that can be updated (`otherrefs`). The two sets must be disjoint. Updates are performed by `ensure` if a row with the same `keyrefs` exists, in which case the remaining attributes are set to the new row's values. A fact can also be explicitly updated using `update`.

7 Flow Support

A good aspect of graphical ETL tools is that it is easy to get an overview of an ETL flow. To make it easy to create small components with encapsulated functionality and connect such components, `pygrametl` provides support for *steps* and data flow. The user can, e.g., create a step for extracting data, a step for transforming data, and a step for loading the data into the DW's tables. The steps can be coded individually before the data flow between them is defined.

`Step` is the basic class for flow support. It can be used directly or as a base class for other step classes. For each `Step` the user can set a *worker function* which is applied to each row passing through the `Step`. If not set by the user, the method `defaultworker` (which does nothing) is used. Sub-classes of `Step` overrides `defaultworker`. The user can also determine to which `Step` rows by default should be sent after the current. That means that when the worker function finishes its work, the row is passed on to the next `Step` unless the user specifies otherwise. So if no default `Step` is set or if the user wants to send the row to a non-default `Step` (e.g., for error handling), there is the method `_redirect` which the user can use to explicitly direct the row to a specific `Step`. `Step` also provides the method `_inject` which injects a new row into the flow before the current row is sent. The new row can be sent to a specific target, otherwise, the default will be used. This gives the user a great degree of flexibility.

`Steps` can modify the rows they are given. For example, `DimensionStep` calls `ensure` on a `Dimension` instance for each row it receives and adds the returned key to the row. Another example is `MappingStep` which applies functions to attributes values in each row. A similar class is `ValueMappingStep` which performs mappings from one value set to another. Thus, it is easy to perform a mapping from, e.g., country codes like *DK* and *DE* to country names like *Denmark* and *Germany*. To enable conditional flow control, `ConditionalStep` is provided. A `ConditionalStep` is given a condition as a function. The function is applied to each row and if the result evaluates to `True`, the row is sent to the next default `Step`. In addition, another `Step` can optionally set as the target for rows where the condition evaluates to `False`. Otherwise, the row is silently discarded.

Steps can also perform aggregation. The base class for aggregating steps is `AggregatingStep`. Its `defaultworker` is called for each row it receives and must maintain the data needed to compute the final aggregate. This is done by the method `defaultfinalizer` which when given a row writes the aggregate to it.

All of this could be implemented without `Steps`. However, they are included for users who prefer connected components as provide by graphical ETL tools.

8 Testing Support

`pygrametl` provides *Drawn Table Testing (DTT)* to make testing of ETL flows easier. DTT simplifies defining tests where the state of the data sources and/or the DW (i.e., rows in tables of the database) must be taken into consideration. Currently, practitioners often store data in XML or CSV files separate from the tests and then add code to their tests that loads the data from these files into the test database, thus setting the test's *preconditions*. Likewise, the expected state is often also stored in text files and compared to the test database after the ETL flow has run, thus setting the test's *postconditions*. DTT makes it easy for users to define preconditions and postconditions as part of their tests as they can simply *draw* a table with rows using text shown in Listing 15. We call such a text-based representation of a database table a *Drawn Table (DT)*.

```
1  | testid:int (pk) | testname:text | testauthor:text |
2  | --------------- | ------------- | --------------- |
3  | -1              | Unknown       | Unknown         |
4  | 1               | Test1         | Søren           |
5  | 2               | Test2         | Christian       |
6  | 3               | Test3         | Torben          |
7  | 4               | Test4         | Ove             |
```

Listing 15. Example of a DT.

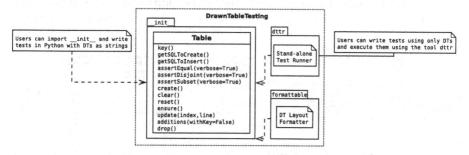

Fig. 3. Overview of the DTT package with public classes and intended use shown.

The DTT package consists of the DTT module and two command-line applications that use the module as shown in Fig. 3. By implementing the functionality of DTT as a module, interfaces for specific use-cases become easy to create.

Later, we will show how DTT can be used both from within Python (Sect. 8.5) and stand-alone using the test runner `dttr` (Sect. 8.6). `dttr` allows DTT to be used without the user has to write Python code. Also, while DTT is written in Python *it is not required* that users must implement their ETL flows in Python. Thus, the ETL flow can be implemented in another programming language or program (e.g., a graphical ETL tool).

8.1   Drawn Table (DT)

The DT in Listing 15 defines a table with three columns (of the shown types and of which `testid` is the primary key). The required syntax for a DT is as follows: the first row (called the *header*) contains `name:type` pairs for each column with each pair surrounded by vertical pipes. After a type, one or more constraints can be specified for the column as `(constraints)` with `(pk)` making the column (part of) the primary key. More information about constraints are provided in Sect. 8.2. If the table must hold any data, the header must be followed by a delimiter line containing only vertical pipes, spaces, and dashes (see Line 2) and then each row follows on a line of its own (see Line 3–7). Columns must be given in the same order as in the header and must be separated by pipes. For string values, any surrounding spaces are trimmed away. The syntax and types are checked by DTT's DT parser, while the constraints are checked by the RDBMS. A DT is also a valid table in GitHub Flavored Markdown [12].

How DTT tests an ETL flow using DTs is shown in Fig. 4. Before DTT can test the ETL flow, the user must create DTs that define the initial state of the test database (i.e., the preconditions) and/or DTs that define the expected state of the test database (i.e., the postconditions). Then DTT does the following: (i) Based on the DTs being set as preconditions, DTT automatically creates tables in a test database and loads the data from each DT into them. In this way, the initial state of the test database can easily be set without the user manually loading files or writing SQL. (ii) DTT then executes the user-defined ETL flow. (iii) Last, DTT verifies that the states of the postcondition DTs and the database tables they represent match. If they do not, DTT raises an informative error.

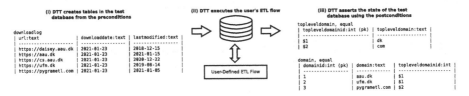

Fig. 4. Using DTT to test a user-defined ETL flow.

As an example, assume the DT in Listing 15 is the postcondition in a test, but that the ETL flow is not defined yet. Thus, the test will fail since the test DW is empty. To make the test pass, we implement the part of the ETL flow that extracts, transforms, and loads the data into the table represented by the DT. As we make progress with the implementation, we can run the test again and again until the implementation passes the test. Thus DTT also enables test-driven development for ETL flows. From this small example, it is clear how DTT makes it simple to test an ETL flow during development, which helps to catch mistakes early such that they can be fixed immediately at low cost [13].

By default, DTT uses an in-memory SQLite database to run all tests against as it is very fast and does not require any installation or configuration by the user. Both of these properties are important as testing will be neglected if running the test suite is too time-consuming, thus allowing problems to accumulate and become harder to correct as additional changes to the ETL flow are performed [3, 29]. The user can, however, optionally use any other RDBMS with a PEP 249 connector (e.g., to run the test using the RDBMS used in production).

8.2   Constraints

As shown in Listing 15 a column can be made part of the primary key by speci-fying (pk) as a constraint. The constraints unique and not null are also sup-ported and can be defined in the same manner. If multiple constraints are defined for one column, they must be separated by a comma. When representing multi-ple tables as DTs, foreign keys constraints are often required. In DTT, foreign keys must be specified as *fk target(att)* where *target* is the name of the referenced table and *att* is the referenced column. An example using foreign keys to connect test and testresults can be seen in Listing 16.

```
1   test
2   | testid:int (pk) | testname:text | testauthor:text |
3   | --------------- | ------------- | --------------- |
4   | -1              | Unknown       | Unknown         |
5   | 1               | Test1         | Søren           |
6   | 2               | Test2         | Christian       |
7   | 3               | Test3         | Torben          |
8   | 4               | Test4         | Ove             |
9
10  testresults
11  | testid:int (pk, fk test(testid)) | errors:int |
12  | -------------------------------- | ---------- |
13  | 1                                | 2          |
14  | 3                                | 0          |
```

Listing 16. Example of specifying foreign keys in a DT. Each table's name is above it. pageid and dateid are not shown to improve the examples readability.

8.3   Assertions

DTT can assert if a DT and a table in the test database are *equal, disjoint,* or if the DT is a *subset* of the table. As an example, assume that the user has specified that the DT in Listing 15 must be equal to the table in test database it represents. Thus, DTT verifies that the table in the test database contains the same rows as the DT (and only those) and if not, it raises an error and provides an easy-to-read explanation of why the test failed as shown in Listing 17.

```
1   AssertionError: test's rows differ from the rows in the database.
2   Drawn Table:
3    | testid:int (pk) | testname:text | testauthor:text |
4    | --------------- | ------------- | --------------- |
5    | -1              | Unknown       | Unknown         |
6    | 1               | Test1         | Søren           |
7    | 2               | Test2         | Christian       |
8    | 3               | Test3         | Torben          |
9    | 4               | Test4         | Ove             |
10
11  Database Table:
12   | testid:int (pk) | testname:text | testauthor:text |
13   | --------------- | ------------- | --------------- |
14   | 1               | Test1         | Søren           |
15   | 2               | Test2         | Christian       |
16   | 3               | Test3         | Torben          |
17   | 4               | Test2         | Christian       |
18   | -1              | Unknown       | Unknown         |
19
20  Violations:
21   | testid:int (pk) | testname:text | testauthor:text |
22   | --------------- | ------------- | --------------- |
23 E | 4               | Test4         | Ove             |
24   |                 |               |                 |
25 D | 4               | Test2         | Christian       |
```

Listing 17. Assert equal for a table in the test database and the DT in Listing 15

In this example, the part of the user's ETL flow loading the table contains a bug. The DT instance in Listing 15 specifies that the dimension should contain a row for unknown tests and four rows for tests written by different people (see the expected state at the top of the output). However, the user's ETL code added Test2 written by Christian a second time instead of Test4 written by Ove (see the middle table in the output). To help the user quickly identify what rows do not match, DTT prints the rows violating the assertion which for equality is the difference between the two relations (bottom). The expected rows (i.e., those in the DT) are prefixed by an E and the rows in the database are prefixed by a D. Note that the orders of the rows can differ without making the test fail.

Asserting that a table in the test database and a DT are disjoint, makes it easy to verify that something *is not* in the database table, e.g., to test a filter or to check for the absence of erroneous rows that previously fixed bugs wrongly added. Asserting that a DT is a subset of a table in the test database, makes it easy to define a sample of rows that can be compared to a table containing so many rows that it is infeasible to embed them in a test. For example, it is easy to test if the leap day 2020–02–29 exists in the date dimension.

When compared to a table in the database, a DT's instance does not have to contain all of the database table's columns. Only the state of the columns included in the DT is then compared. This is useful for excluding columns for which the user does not know the state or for which the state does not matter in the test, like a generated primary key or audit information such as a timestamp.

8.4   Variables

Cases can also occur where attribute values must be equal, but the exact values are unknown or do not matter. A prominent case is when foreign keys are used.

In DTT this is easy to state using *variables*. A variable has a name prefixed by $ (the prefix is user-configurable) and can be used instead of attribute values in a DT. DTT checks if variables with the same name represent the same values in the database and fail the test if not. Listing 18 shows an example of how to use variables to test that foreign keys are assigned correctly.

```
1    tld
2    | tldid:int (pk) | tld:text            |
3    | -------------- | ------------------- |
4    | $1             | dk                  |
5    | $2             | org                 |
6
7    domain
8    | domainid:int (pk) | domain:text     | tldid:int (fk tld(tldid)) |
9    | ----------------- | --------------- | ------------------------- |
10   | 1                 | aau.dk          | $1                        |
11   | 2                 | ufm.dk          | $1                        |
12   | 3                 | pygrametl.org   | $2                        |
```

Listing 18. Check foreign keys using variables. Each table's name is above it. `topleveldomain` is shortened to `tld` to improve the examples readability.

Here the user has stated that the **tldid** of **aau.dk** in **domain** must match the **tldid** of **dk** in **tld**, likewise for **ufm.dk**, while **pygrametl.org** must match the **tldid** of **org**. If they do not, DTT raises errors as shown in Listing 19.

```
1    ...
2    ValueError: Ambiguous values for $1; tld(row 0, column 0 tldid) is 1 and
        ↪   domain(row 0, column 2 tldid) is 2
3    ...
```

Listing 19. Excerpt from the output of a test with mismatching variables.

The error message is from the output of a test case where **domain** and **tld** have the IDs defined in two different orders. As such, the foreign key constraints were satisfied although **aau.dk** is referencing the topleveldomain **org**. This shows that variables can test parts of an ETL flow that cannot be verified by foreign keys as foreign keys only ensure that a value is present.

It is also possible to specify that an attribute value should not be included in the comparison. This is done with the special variable $_. When compared to any value, $_ is always considered to be equal. An example is shown in Listing 20 where the actual value of the primary key of the expected new row is not taken into consideration. $_! is a stricter version of $_ which disallows **NULL**.

```
1    | topleveldomainid:int (pk) | topleveldomain:text |
2    | ------------------------- | ------------------- |
3    | $_                        | dk                  |
4    | $_                        | org                 |
```

Listing 20. Example where a primary key value is ignored.

One limitation of variables is that a DT containing variables can only be used as a postcondition. The reason is of course that DTT does not know which values to insert into the database for the variables if the DT is used as a precondition.

8.5   Using Drawn Table Testing as a Python Package

DTT is easy to use as a Python package, i.e., as part of user-defined tests written in Python, e.g., using an existing testing framework like **unittest** or **pytest**.

The DT functionality is implemented by the **Table** class. To create an instance, a name for the table must be given as well as a string with a DT. An example of this is shown in Listing 21. Further, a string value representing **NULL** can optionally be given as well as an alternative prefix to be used for variables.

```
1   table = Table("test", """
2   | testid:int (pk) | testname:text | testauthor:text |
3   | --------------- | ------------- | --------------- |
4   | -1              | Unknown       | Unknown         |
5   | 1               | Test1         | Søren           |
6   | 2               | Test2         | Christian       |
7   | 3               | Test3         | Torben          |
8   | 4               | Test4         | Ove             |""")
9   table.ensure()
```

Listing 21. Example of creating and using a **Table** instance.

A DT's rows can also be loaded from an external source by providing either a path to a file containing a DT without a header or a data source to the constructor's **loadFrom** parameter. Data can thus be loaded from files, databases, etc., at the cost of the test not being self-contained. Users can of course represent multiple tables in the test database using multiple instances of **Table**.

After a **Table** instance is created, its **ensure** method can be executed. This will determine if a table with the same name and rows exists in the test database and otherwise create it (or raise an error if it contains other rows). If the user wants to create and fill the table even if it already exists, the **reset** method is provided. The **ensure** and **reset** methods raise an error if executed on a DT with variables as their values are unknown. The **create** method creates the table but does not load the rows. For users who prefer to create the table and insert the data represented by the DT themselves, the methods **getSQLToCreate** and **getSQLToInsert** are provided. DTT's asserts are implemented as the following methods: **assertEqual(verbose=True)**, **assertDisjoint(verbose=True)**, and **assertSubset(verbose=True)**. The detailed information they provide when a test fails (see Listing 17) can be disabled by executing them with the argument **False** for the parameter **verbose** (by default the argument is **True**).

Table instances are immutable. However, postconditions are often similar to preconditions except for a few added or updated rows. Therefore, we have made it simple to create a new **Table** instance from an existing one by appending or updating rows. Rows can be appended using the + operator, e.g., like **newTable = table + "| 5 | Test5 | Christian |" + "| 6 | Test6 | Ove |"**. The method **update(index, newrow)** creates a new instance with the values of the row at **index** changed to the values provided by **newrow**. For example, a copy of **table** with the first row changed, can be created as by **newTable = table.update(0, "| -1 | Unknown | N/A |")**. Note that a new instance of **Table** does not change the test database unless its **ensure**, **reset**, or **create** method is executed. By making **Table** instances immutable and creating new instances when they are modified, the user can very easily reuse the **Table** instance representing the precondition for multiple tests, and then as part of each test create a new instance with the postcondition based on it. After a number of additions and/or updates, it can be useful to get all modified rows. The user can then, e.g., make a test case where the ETL flow is executed for the new rows as shown in Listing 22.

```
1  def test_canInsertIntoTestDimensionTable(self):
2      expected = table + "| 5 | Test5 | Christian |" \
3                        + "| 6 | Test6 | Ove |"
4      newrows = expected.additions()
5      etl.executeETLFlow(newrows)
6      expected.assertEqual()
```

Listing 22. Example using the additions method.

In Listing 22, **expected** defines how the user expects the database state to become, but it is not the DTT package that puts the database in this state. The database is modified by the user's own ETL flow executed on Line 5. After the user's ETL flow have been executed, DTT verifies that the table in the test database and the DT are equal with **expected.assertEqual()** on Line 6.

A full example using DTT with Python's **unittest** module is shown in Listing 23. When using **unittest**, a class must be defined for each set of tests. We find it natural to group tests for a dimension into a class such that they can share DTs. A class using DTT to test the ETL flow for the test dimension is defined on Line 1. It inherits from **unittest.TestCase** as required by **unittest**. Two methods are then overridden: **setUpClass(cls)** and **setUp(self)**.

```
1   class TestStateTest(unittest.TestCase):
2       @classmethod
3       def setUpClass(cls):
4           cls.cw = dtt.connectionwrapper()
5           cls.initial = table = dtt.Table("test", """
6           | testid:int (pk) | testname:text | testauthor:text |
7           | --------------- | ------------- | --------------- |
8           | -1              | Unknown       | Unknown         |
9           | 1               | Test1         | Søren           |
10          | 2               | Test2         | Christian       |
11          | 3               | Test3         | Torben          |
12          | 4               | Test4         | Ove             |""")
13
14      def setUp(self):
15          self.initial.reset()
16
17      def test_insertNew(self):
18          expected = self.initial + "| 5 | Test5 | Christian |"
19          newrows = expected.additions()
20          etl.executeETLFlow(self.cw, newrows)
21          expected.assertEqual()
22
23      def test_insertExisting(self):
24          row = {testid:3, 'testname':'Test3', 'testauthor':'Torben'}
25          etl.executeETLFlow(self.cw, [row])
26          self.initial.assertEqual()
```

Listing 23. DTT tests for the test dimension.

The method `setUpClass(cls)` is executed before the tests are. The method requests a connection to a test database from DTT on Line 4 and defines a DT with the initial state of the dimension in Line 5. By creating them in `setUpClass(self)`, they are only initialized once and can be reused for each test. To ensure the tests do not affect each other, which would make the result depend on their execution order, the `test` table in the database is reset before each test by `setUp(self)`. On Line 17 and Line 23 the tests are implemented as methods prefixed by `test_`. `test_insertNew(self)` tests that a new row is inserted correctly, while `test_insertExisting(self)` tests that inserting an existing row does not create a duplicate. In this example, both of these tests execute the user's ETL flow by calling `executeETLFlow(connection, newrows)`.

8.6   Using Drawn Table Testing as a Stand-Alone Tool

The `dttr` (for DTT Runner) command-line application allows DTT to be used without doing any Python programming, i.e., with tests consisting only of DTs. Internally, `dttr` uses the DTT module and thus provides all of its functionality.

`dttr` uses *test files* (files with the suffix `.dtt`) to specify preconditions and/or postconditions. An example of a test file is given in Listing 24. Note that a test file does not contain any Python code. This file only contains one precondition (i.e., a DT with a name, but without an assert above it) on Line 1–4 and one postcondition (i.e., a DT with both a name and an assert above it) on Line 6–13). However, having both a precondition and a postcondition is not required, a `.dtt` file can contain any number of preconditions and/or postconditions. Users are free to structure their tests as they please. It is, e.g., possible to have a test file for the fact table and another test file for a dimension table and still ensure that an inserted fact's foreign key references a specific dimension member.

```
1   test
2   | testid:int (pk)  | testname:text  | testauthor:text  |
3   | --------------   | ------------   | --------------   |
4   | -1               | Unknown        | Unknown          |
5
6   test, equal
7   | testid:int (pk)  | testname:text  | testauthor:text  |
8   | --------------   | ------------   | --------------   |
9   | -1               | Unknown        | Unknown          |
10  | 1                | Test1          | Søren            |
11  | 2                | Test2          | Christian        |
12  | 3                | Test3          | Torben           |
13  | 4                | Test4          | Ove              |
```

Listing 24. Example of a `dttr` test file.

The syntax for a precondition in a test file is as follows. On the first line of a precondition, the name of the table must be given, it is `test` in Listing 24. The default test database is used when only the name of the table is given. Alternatively, users can specify a PEP 249 connection in a configuration file and append @ and the name of the connection to the table name, e.g., `test@targetdw`. After the table name, a DT must be specified (Lines 2–4). Preconditions and postconditions in a test file must be separated by an empty line (Line 5).

For a postcondition the name of the table must also be given first, followed by a comma and the assertion to use (Line 6). In the example, the table name is **test** like for the precondition, but they may be different. For example, the precondition could define the initial state for **inputdata@sourcedb** while the postcondition could define the expected state for **test@targetdw**. While the assertion **equal** is used in this example, DTT's other two assertions can also be used with: **disjoint** and **subset**. Then a DT is given like for the precondition (Lines 7–13). A DT used as part of a postcondition can contain variables.

For tests that require more data than what is feasible to embed in a DT, data from an external file or a database can be added to a DT by specifying a data source as its last line. For example, the line **csv DownloadLog.csv \t** adds the contents of DownloadLog.csv to the DT (using a tab the field separator) in addition to any rows drawn as part of the DT. By adding **sql oltp SELECT testid, testname, testauthor FROM test** as the last line, all rows of the table **test** from the PEP 249 connection **oltp** are added to the DT. This is user-extensible through a configuration file so users (or administrators) can add support for other sources of data, e.g., XML or a NoSQL DBMS like MongoDB.

dttr can be executed from the command-line as shown in Listing 25. Note that the ETL program to test and its arguments are given to **dttr** using **--etl**

```
1  dttr --etl "/Path/To/MyETLProgram --run MyFlow --loaddim test"
```

Listing 25. How to execute **dttr**.

When run, **dttr** by default looks for all **.dtt** files under the current working directory, but optional arguments allow the user to select which files to read. **dttr** then reads all these **.dtt** files. Then the preconditions from the files are set. This is done using **Table**'s **ensure** method. After the preconditions have been set, the user's ETL flow is executed. When the ETL flow has finished, all postconditions and variables are checked using **Table**'s **assert** methods.

9 Supporting Functionality

In addition to the modules and classes described in the previous sections (Sect. 4–8), **pygrametl** provides helpful supporting functionality that makes the modules and classes simpler to use and helps users parallelize their ETL flows.

9.1 Functions

pygrametl provides functions that operate on rows (e.g., to copy, rename, or project) and functions that convert types, but return a user-configurable default value if the conversion cannot be done (e.g., like **getfloat** shown in Listing 1).

Particularly for use with **SlowlyChangingDimension** and its support for time stamps on versions, **pygrametl** provides a number of functions for parsing strings to create date and time objects. Some of these functions use functional programming such that they dynamically create new functions based on their arguments. In this way, specialized functions for extracting time information can be created. For an example, refer to **pagedim** we defined in Listing 10. There we set **fromfinder** to a dynamically generated function that reads the attribute **lastmoddate** from each row and transforms the read text into a **date** object.

While the set of provided functions is relatively small, it is important to remember that the user has access to the many Python libraries that exist. Also, users can create private libraries with the functionality they often use.

9.2   Parallelism

ETL flows often have to handle large data volumes and parallelization is a natural way to achieve good performance. **pygrametl** has support for both task parallelism and data parallism [58]. The support was designed to preserve the simplicity of **pygrametl** programs. For example, extraction and transformation of data can run in another process using a **ProcessSource** as shown in Listing 26.

```
1  rawdata = CSVSource(open('DownloadLog.csv', 'r'))
2  transformeddata = TransformingSource(rawdata, transformation1,
   ↪ transformation2)
3  inputdata = ProcessSource(transformeddata)
```

Listing 26. Transforming rows in a separate process using **ProcessSource**.

The **ProcessSource** spawns a process that extracts the **rawdata** and transforms it into **transformeddata** before assigning it to the **inputdata** variable in the main process. Similarly, **Dimension** instances can also run in another process, by means of **DecoupledDimension** which has the same interface as **Dimension** but pushes all the work to a **Dimension** instance in another process. This instance is given to **DecoupledDimension** when it is created as shown in Listing 27.

```
1  pagedim = DecoupledDimension(SlowlyChangingDimension(name='page', ...))
```

Listing 27. Update a dimension in another process using **DecoupledDimension**.

Work on a **FactTable** instance can also be performed in another process by using **DecoupledFactTable** as shown in Listing 28. Decoupled instances can be defined to *consume* data from each other such that, e.g., **lookup** operations don't become blocking but rather return a placeholder value that a consuming instance will get without involvement from the user (or main process). For details, see [58].

```
1  facttbl = DecoupledFactTable(BulkFactTable(name='testresults', ...),
2                               consumes=[pagedim],
3                               returnvalues=False)
```

Listing 28. Update a fact table in another process using **DecoupledFactTable**.

Finally, **pygrametl** provides the **splitpoint** annotation which makes user-defined functions run in parallel with other tasks as shown in Listing 29.

```
1  @splitpoint(instances=2)
2  def myfunction(*args):
3      # Do some (possibly expensive) transformations here
```

Listing 29. Run a function in multiple processes using the `splitpoint`.

pygrametl uses processes instead of threads when running on CPython, the reference implementation of Python. The reason is that CPython cannot execute Python bytecode using multiple threads due to the global interpreter lock. However, pygrametl uses threads when running on Jython, an implementation of Python in Java, as the HotSpot JVM can execute multiple threads in parallel.

9.3   Editor Support

A key benefit of DTT is that users can easily understand the preconditions and postconditions of a test from the DTs. However, to gain the full benefit of DTs, their columns should be aligned across rows as they otherwise become very difficult to read. A very poorly formatted DT can be seen in Listing 30.

```
1  | testid:int (pk) | testname:text | testauthor:text |
2  | -------
3      | -1              | Unknown         | Unknown         |
4  | 1                   | Test1         | Søren         |
5              | 2 | Test2     | Christian     |
6  | 3                   | Test3         | Torben        |
7  | 4       | Test4         | Ove           |
```

Listing 30. Example of a very poorly formatted DT.

It is clear that poor formatting makes a DT harder to read. However, as properly formatting each DT can be tedious, DTT provides the `formattable` script which automates the task (see Fig. 3). It is designed to be used with extensible text editors so users can format a DT by placing the cursor on a DT and executing the script. Thus, integrating the script with the popular editors' Emacs and Vim requires only a few lines of Elisp and Vimscript, respectively.

10   Evaluation

To evaluate pygrametl and compare the development efforts for visual and code-based programming, an extended version of the original paper about pygrametl [57] presented an evaluation where the running example was implemented in both pygrametl and the graphical ETL tool PDI [34], a popular open source ETL tool. Ideally, the comparison should have included commercial ETL tools, but the license agreements of these tools (at least the ones we have read) explicitly forbid publishing any evaluation/performance results without the consent of the provider, so this was not possible. In this section, we present the findings of the evaluation. The implemented ETL flow and the data generator are available from pygrametl.org [43].

10.1 Productivity

It is obviously difficult to make a comparison of two such tools, and a full-scale test would require several teams of fully trained specialists, which is beyond our resources. We obviously know **pygrametl** well, but we also have significant experience with PDI from earlier projects. Each tool was used to create an identical solution twice. When creating the solution for the first time, we spent time on designing and implementing the ETL Flow. All the time we spent creating it again was *interaction time* (time spent on typing and clicking).

The **pygrametl**-based program was very easy to develop. It took a little less than an hour the first time, and 24 min the second time. The program consists of ~140 short lines, e.g., only one argument per line when creating **Dimension** objects. This strongly supports that it is easy to develop ETL programs using **pygrametl**. The main method of the ETL is shown in Listing 31.

```
1   def main():
2       for row in inputdata:
3           extractdomaininfo(row)
4           extractserverinfo(row)
5           row['size'] = pygrametl.getint(row['size'])
6           # Add the data to the dimension and fact tables
7           row['pageid'] = pagesf.scdensure(row)
8           row['dateid'] = datedim.ensure(row, {'date':'downloaddate'})
9           row['testid'] = testdim.lookup(row, {'testname':'test'})
10          facttbl.insert(row)
11      connection.commit()
```

Listing 31. Main method of the ETL flow made to measure development time.

The methods **extractdomaininfo** and **extractserverinfo** contain four lines of code to extract domain, top-level domain, and server name. Note that the page dimension is a SCD, where **scdensure** is an easy way to fill both a snowflaked and a SCD. The date dimension uses a **rowexpander** passed to the **datedim** object to (on demand) calculate the attribute values so **ensure** can find or insert a member. The test dimension is preloaded, and we only do lookups.

The PDI-based solution took us a little more than two hours to create the first time, and 28 min the second time. The flow is shown in Fig. 5.

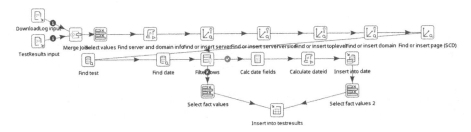

Fig. 5. Data flow in PDI-based solution.

We emulate the `rowexpander` feature of `pygrametl` by first looking up a date and then calculating the remaining date attributes in case there is no match. Note how we must fill the page snowflake from the leaves towards the root.

To summarize, `pygrametl` was faster to use than PDI. The first solution was much faster to create in `pygrametl` and we believe that it is far simpler to work out in `pygrametl` (compare the main method and Fig. 5). In addition, it was a little faster to create the solution a second time by typing code compared to click around in the GUI. So, while experienced PDI users may be able to create a solution as fast in PDI, we believe that `pygrametl` is simpler and easier to use.

10.2 Performance

The extended version of the original paper [57] also presented performance results for both PDI and `pygrametl` on the running example. In this paper, we provide new results for the same running example, but with newer versions of both PDI (version 7.1) and `pygrametl` (version 2.5) when executed on newer hardware.

To test the performance of the solutions, we generated data. The generator was configured to create results for 2,000 different domains each having 100 pages. Five tests were applied to each page. Thus, data for one month gave 1 million facts. To test the SCD support, a page could remain unchanged between two months with probability 0.5. For the first month, there were thus 200,000 page versions and for each following month, there were ~100,000 new page versions. We did the tests for 5, 10, 50, and 100 months, i.e., on data sets of realistic sizes. The solutions were tested on a virtual machine (we did not test PDI's support for distributed execution) with three virtual processors, and 16 GB of RAM (the CPUs were never completely used during the experiments and the amount of RAM was large enough to allow all of the dimension data to be cached). The virtual machine ran openSUSE Leap 42.2 Linux, pygrametl 2.5 on Python 3.6, PDI 7.1 on OpenJDK 8, and PostgreSQL 9.4. The virtual machine was running under VirtualBox 5.1 on Windows 10 on a host machine with 32 GB of RAM, SSD disk, and a 2.70 GHz Intel i7 CPU with 4 cores and hyperthreading.

We used a DW where the primary key constraints were declared but the foreign key constraints were not. The DW had an index on `page(url, version)`.

PDI was tested in two modes. One with a single connection to the DW such that the ETL is transactionally *safe* and one which uses a special component for bulk loading the facts into PostgreSQL. This special component makes its own connection to the DW. This makes the load faster but transactionally *unsafe* as a crash can leave the DW loaded with inconsistent data. The `pygrametl`-based solution uses bulk loading of facts (using `BulkFactTable`) but is always running in a *safe* transactional mode with a single connection to the DW. The solutions were configured to use caches without size limits. When PDI was tested, the maximum Java heap size was set to 12 GB.

Figure 6(a) shows the elapsed wall-clock time for the loads and Fig. 6(b) shows the spent CPU time. It can be seen that the amounts of time grow linearly for both PDI and `pygrametl`. It is however clear that `pygrametl` is significantly

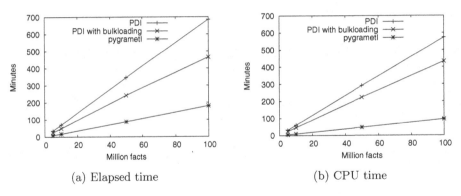

(a) Elapsed time   (b) CPU time

Fig. 6. Performance results.

faster than PDI in this experiment. When loading 100 million facts, the **pygram-etl**-based solution handles 9208 facts/s. PDI with a single connection handles 2433 and PDI with two connections handles 3584 facts/s. Also, while servers often have many CPUs/cores it is still desirable if the ETL uses little CPU time, so more CPU time is available for other purposes like processing queries. This is particularly relevant if the ETL is running on a virtualized server with contention for the CPUs. From Fig. 6(b), it can be seen that **pygrametl** also uses much less CPU time than PDI. For example, when loading the data set with 100 million facts, **pygrametl**'s CPU utilization is 53%. PDI's CPU utilization is 83% with one connection and 93% with two. It is clear to see that in terms of resource consumption; it is beneficial to create a light-weight specialized program instead of using a general feature-rich but heavy-weight ETL application.

11   Case Study

The company FlexDanmark handles demand-responsive transport in Denmark. For example, elderly people are picked up at home and driven to a hospital for examinations, and school children living in areas without access to public transportation are driven from home to school. The yearly revenue is around 120 million US dollars. To organize the transportation and plan the different tours effectively, FlexDanmark makes routing based on detailed speed maps built from GPS logs from more than 5,000 vehicles. Typically, 2 million GPS coordinates are delivered to FlexDanmark every night. FlexDanmark has a DW where the cleaned GPS data are integrated with other data such as weather data (driving speeds are related to the weather and are, e.g., lower when there is snow). The ETL procedure is implemented in Python. Among other things, the ETL procedure has to transform between different coordinate systems, do map matching to roads (GPS coordinates can be quite imprecise), do spatial matching to the closest weather station, do spatial matching to municipalities and zip code areas, and finally load the DW. The latter is done using **pygrametl**.

The trips handled by FlexDanmark are paid by or subsidized by public funds. To be able to analyze how money is spent, another DW at FlexDanmark holds data about payments for the trips, the taxi companies providing the vehicles, customers, etc. This DW integrates data from many different source systems and has some interesting challenges since payment details (i.e., facts in the DW) about already processed trips can be updated, but the history of these updates must be tracked in a similar way to how dimension changes are tracked for a type-2 SCD. Further, new sources and dimensions are sometimes added. The ETL procedure for the DW is also implemented in Python, but FlexDanmark has created a framework that using *templates can generate Python code* incl. **pygrametl** objects based on metadata parameters [2]. Thus, FlexDanmark can easily and efficiently generate ETL code that handles parallelism, versioning of facts, etc. when new sources and/or dimensions are added.

FlexDanmark's reasons for using code-based, programmatic ETL are manifold. FlexDanmark's DWs are rather advanced since they handle GPS data and versioned facts, respectively. To implement ETL flows for these things in traditional graphical tools was found to be hard. FlexDanmark did try to implement the map matching in a widely used commercial ETL tool but found it hard to accomplish this task. In contrast, it was found to be quite easy to do programmatically in Python where existing libraries easily could be used and also replaced with others when needed. Programmatic ETL does thus give FlexDanmark bigger flexibility. Yet another aspect is pricing since FlexDanmark is publicly funded. Here programmatic ETL building on free, open source software such as Python and **pygrametl** is desirable. It was also considered to use a free, open source graphical ETL tool, but after comparing a few programmatic solutions with their counterparts created using the graphical tool, it was found to be faster and more flexible to code the ETL flows.

In most cases where **pygrametl** is used, we are not aware for what since users are not obliged to register in any way. Some **pygrametl** users have, however, told us in private communication how they use **pygrametl**. We thus know that **pygrametl** is used in production systems from a wide variety of domains including health, advertising, real estate, public administration, and sales.

Based on the feedback we have received so far; we have been unable to extract guidelines or principles for how best to design programmatic ETL flows. The programming involved can vary from very little for a small proof of concept to a significant amount for a multi-source advanced DW. The principles to apply should thus be those already used in the organization. Reusing existing development principles should also reduce the time required to learn **pygrametl** as users then only have to learn a framework and not new development principles.

12   Experiences from Open-Sourcing pygrametl

When we published the first paper about **pygrametl**, we also made the source code available on our department's web page. From the logs, we could see that there were some downloads and we also received a few questions and comments.

Later, the source code was moved to Google Code, and the attention it received increased. When Google Code was closed, the code was moved to GitHub [39] where it got a lot more attention. The lesson we learned from this is that it is very important to publish source code at the places where people are used to looking for open source projects. Before we moved to GitHub, others had already created unofficial and unmaintained repositories with the `pygrametl` code on GitHub, just so it was available there. Similarly, we learned that it should be easy for users to install the framework. Thus, it needs to be available from the Python Package Index (PyPI) [40]. Again we experienced that unofficial and unmaintained copies were created before we published an official version. With `pygrametl` on PyPI it can easily be installed using the pip package manager by executing the following command on the command-line: `pip install pygrametl`.

As the number of changes we received from other users increased, it became harder to ensure that the existing code did not break without extending our testing procedures. To simplify this, we developed DTT. During development, it became clear it could be used to not just test `pygrametl` but also ETL flows.

Another lesson we learned, although not very surprising, is that good documentation is needed. By making a Beginner's Guide and examples available online [42], we have reduced the number of (repeated) questions to answer via e-mail and made it much easier to get started with `pygrametl`. It is also important to clearly describe what the tool is intended to do. For example, we have received multiple questions about how to do general data movement from one platform to another, despite `pygrametl` being an ETL framework for *dimensional* DWs.

We have also received some excellent contributions from users. They have, e.g., found minor mistakes in corner cases of the framework, removed performance bottlenecks, helped generalize features, and in general improved the functionality of `pygrametl`. An interesting example is `useorderby`. When performing a lookup `SlowlyChangingDimension` used to only retrieve the newest version of a row by first sorting them using `ORDER BY`. However, for some RDBMSs, a user found that transferring all versions of a row and selecting the newest version in the Python process provided significantly better performance. So, the parameter `useorderby` was added to `SlowlyChangingDimension` so users can choose which behavior they want. Similarly, a user found that `BatchFactTable` performed poorly with some RDBMSs due to its use of `executemany`. We found that some PEP 249 connectors implement `executemany` as a loop around `execute` or raises an error. So we added support for loading batches using one SQL statement run by `execute` instead of multiple SQL statements run by `executemany`.

Over time it has also become clear that some of the functionality provided by `pygrametl` is not being used. For examples, `Step`s seems to not be a useful feature for our users. While we have received comments, questions, and bug reports about most of the other functionality provided by `pygrametl`, we have received virtually nothing about `Step`s. It seems that users who choose to use programmatic ETL prefer not to think in the terms required by the graphical ETL tools. Thus, ideas from `Step`s have been reused in other parts of `pygrametl`, e.g., `MappingStep` was re-implemented as the `MappingSource` data source.

pygrametl is published under a 2-Clause BSD license. We chose this license as it is very permissive. The license allows proprietary use of the code and has no requirements about making derivative work publicly available. In principle, there is thus a risk that users could improve the pygrametl source code without sharing the improvements with us. However, we prefer to give users freedom in deciding how to use the pygrametl code and, as described above, we do get contributions from users despite them not being forced to by the license.

13   Related Work

13.1   Data Integration Tools

Many commercial ETL and data integration tools exist [4] and many methods for creating ETL flows have been proposed [1]. Among the vendors of the most popular products, we find big players like IBM, Informatica, Microsoft, Oracle, and SAP [20,21,30,32,46]. These vendors and many others provide powerful tools supporting integration between different kinds of sources and targets based on graphical design of the flows. Due to their wide field of functionality, the commercial tools often have steep learning curves and as previously mentioned, the user's productivity does not necessarily get high(er) from using a graphical tool. Many of the commercial tools also have high licensing costs.

Open source ETL tools are also available [55]. In some open source ETL tools, such as the popular PDI [34] and Talend [49], the user also specifies the ETL flow in a GUI. Scriptella [47] is an example of a tool where the ETL flow is specified in XML. This XML can, however, contain embedded code written in Java or a scripting language. pygrametl goes further than Scriptella and does not use XML around the code. Further, pygrametl offers DW-specialized functionality such as direct support for SCDs and snowflake schemas, to name a few.

The academic community has also been attracted to ETL, with multiple surveys published about the research [1,61] Most of the academic approaches, e.g., [48,60], use graphs or UML to model an ETL workflow. We challenge the idea that graphical programming of ETL is always easier than text-based programming. Grönniger et al. [16] have previously argued why text-based modeling is better than graphical modeling. Among other things, they point out that writing text is more efficient than drawing models, that it is easier to grasp details from text, and that the creative development can be hampered when definitions must be added to the graphical model. As graphical ETL tools often are model-driven such that the graphical model is turned into the executable code, these concerns are, in our opinion, also related to ETL development. Also, Petre [35] has previously argued against the widespread idea that graphical notation and programming always lead to more accessible and comprehensible results than what is achieved from text-based notation and programming. In her studies [35], she found that text overall was faster to use than graphics. Andersen et al. [2] also argue for using programmatic ETL and propose the framework SimpleETL which reduces the amount of boilerplate code required for pygrametl programs by generating code from a metadata specification.

13.2 Parallelism

As ETL tools often operate on very large amounts of data, parallelization is widely applied in ETL tools. Parallel execution can sometimes be achieved without the user doing anything to enable it. In PDI [34], for example, each *step* (shown as a box in the graphical representation of the ETL flow) executes in its own thread. It is also possible to define that several instances of a step should run in parallel and have the rows distributed among them in round robin fashion. In Microsoft's popular ETL tool SSIS [30] many threads are also used to execute a data flow. SSIS uses a more advanced policy than PDI and considers *execution trees* of transformations that can be processed by the same thread. An execution tree can be assigned one or more threads depending on its CPU utilization. Further, parameters can be used to limit the number of parallel threads. However, it is very different how well different designs for an ETL flow exploits parallelism. Therefore, how a tool applies parallelism must also be considered carefully when a graphical ETL tool is used.

ETLMR [25,26] modifies **pygrametl** to be used with MapReduce [6] on a cluster. With ETLMR it is thus easy to create scalable dimensional ETL solutions on MapReduce with few lines of code. CloudETL [27] is a Java-based framework for creating dimensional ETL flows that load data into DWs managed by Hive [59] using MapReduce. The user specifies the ETL flow using high-level constructs while CloudETL takes care of the parallelization. CloudETL offers support for efficient individual lookups, inserts, and updates of SCDs and thus shares some ideas with ETLMR and **pygrametl**.

In contrast to the graphical ETL tools [30,34], the user has complete control over the parallelization in **pygrametl** and can decide which parts should execute in parallel. The support for **TransformingSource** and **ProcessSource** makes it possible to group certain transformations together and run them in a separate thread or process. Also, the support for **Decoupled** objects (**DecoupledDimension** and **DecoupledFactTable**) makes it easy to process (some or all) dimensions and fact tables in parallel. The parallelization constructs provided by **pygrametl** allow the ETL flow to run on a single server with multiple cores. This does not scale as much as the cluster-based solutions [25–27] but does also have less overhead.

13.3 Testing

While many methods have been proposed for creating ETL flows and DWs in general, research about ensuring their correctness is much more limited [5]. As existing literature already has been surveyed by ElGamal et al. [10], Chandra and Gupta [5], and Homayouni et al. [19], we only summarize selected publications on testing strategies and tools for testing ETL flows.

Golfarelli and Rizzi [13] provide a comprehensive discussion of all aspects of DW testing with ETL testing described as the most complex and critical testing phase. They propose using not only real correct data for ETL test but also data simulating errors. In their following work, they propose how their approach can be used with an iterative DW design process, and they further validate their approach through a case study [14,15]. ElGamal et al. [11] propose an architecture-agnostic testing strategy that, as a result, can be used with existing DWs. A testing manual accompanies the paper with a detailed description of each test to guide users of the strategy [9]. However, the paper states that an evaluation discovered the need to point to tools that could be used to automate the tests. ETLDiff [54] is an approach for regression testing of an entire ETL flow. The tool explores the DW schema and executes a query that joins a fact table to its dimension tables. The first time this is done, the result is stored, and the results of subsequent executions are then compared to this expected result and any differences are pointed out. In the comparison, the actual values of surrogate keys are ignored while the tool still considers if facts are referencing the right dimension members. Guduric [17] describes that it is common for SSIS users to do testing by running their ETL flow on a sample database and then manually sample the outcome. To make this more effective and reliable, he proposes the tool SSISTester that allows SSIS packages to be tested using an interface similar to that used by the Visual Studio testing framework. The tool requires tests to be written in C#. Like with traditional unit testing, it is the responsibility of the tester to write code to set up the precondition, compare the achieved state with the desired outcome, and clean up. Marin [28] proposes a method for testing OLAP cubes using the source OLTP database as the truth. The approach is implemented in Microsoft Dynamics AX. To test a cube, MDX queries are executed on it with equivalent T-SQL queries executed on the OLTP source database. The MDX queries are created based on a coverage model so redundant queries are not included in the test set and the T-SQL queries are automatically generated from the MDX queries. While this approach is data-agnostic, due to the limitations of their query translation method, it is mostly suitable for cases where little to no transformation is performed on the source data when loaded. A tool developed at Cambia Health Solutions [22] executes SQL queries against a test database and validates the output against an expected result. It was specifically designed for staff with a strong SQL background but who lacked knowledge of general-purpose programming languages like Java and Python. Bijoux [31,51] is a tool for generating test data for ETL flows. The input to Bijoux is an ETL flow and the output is data sets generated by considering the different paths and constraints in the ETL flow. Homayouni et al. [18] propose testing the entire ETL flow by comparing properties (e.g., number of rows) of the data in the sources and the DW when loaded. Tests can automatically be generated to check these properties if mappings from the sources and the DW are available in a structured manner. For example, the paper demonstrates how the mappings can be extracted from definitions of SQL views.

Compared to DTT, multiple papers focus on methodology and do not present any concrete tools despite commonly stating the benefit of automation and testing early in the DW design process [9,11,13–15]. The proposed ETL testing tools either only test the finished DW and not the ETL flow during development [18,22,28,54], require that the test environment is manually prepared [17,22,54], require that the user knows how to program [17], or only support asserting equality [22,28,54] Last, the focus of Bijoux [31,51] is on evaluating quality characteristics (performance, completeness, etc.) and not on improving productivity and correctness like DTT. From this it is clear that DTT fulfills a niche not covered by the other tools by making it simple to test an ETL flow by *drawing* preconditions and postconditions as easy-to-read DTs.

14   Conclusion and Future Work

We have presented an up-to-date overview of *pygrametl*, a framework for programmatic ETL. We challenge the conviction that ETL flows should always be developed using a graphical ETL tool. We instead propose to let *ETL developers* (which are typically specialists) create ETL flows *by writing code*. To make this easy, **pygrametl** provides commonly used functionality, such as reading from data sources and filling dimensions and fact tables. In particular, we emphasize how easy it is to fill snowflaked and slowly changing dimensions. A single method call will do and **pygrametl** takes care of all needed lookups and insertions. Flow support allows users to implement their ETL flows using connected steps. **pygrametl** also simplifies testing ETL flows through *Drawn Table Testing* which makes it simple for users to specify preconditions and postconditions for an ETL flow using string-based *Drawn Tables*. Last, **pygrametl** provides functions for common transformations and simple abstractions that make it easy for users to parallelize their ETL flows.

Our evaluation and case study show that creating ETL flows with **pygrametl** provides high programmer productivity and that the created ETL flows have good run-time performance. **pygrametl**'s flexible support for fact and dimension tables makes it easy to fill the DW. Thus the user can concentrate on the transformations needed for the data where they benefit from the power and expressiveness of a real programming language to achieve high productivity.

pygrametl is available as open source and is used in proofs of concepts as well as production systems from a variety of different domains. By making the framework open source, we have learned the importance of publishing code at well-known places such as GitHub and the joy of users contributing improvements in the form of code, documentation, and ideas for how to improve **pygrametl**.

As future work, we are considering introducing a new API with fewer classes, but the same or more functionality. The current class hierarchy to some degree reflects that new functionality has been added along the way when someone needed it. Also, the way to load rows (plain SQL INSERTs, batched INSERTs, or by bulk loading) is currently defined by the individual classes. A more general approach could be by composition of loader classes into the classes that handle dimensions and fact tables. It would also be interesting to investigate if specialized code can be generated using a set of templates from which the user can select the features they require, such as bulk loading. This could potentially provide a big performance advantage if, e.g., branches could be eliminated. We are still gaining experiences with DTT, but already see several directions for future work. For the variables, it would be useful if expressions could be used such that users, e.g., could specify an expected value as $1 + 1 or define a variable using the state of another $2 = $1 / 86400. Another interesting direction is to determine if other kinds of asserts could be added to enable easy specification of a wider range of tests. It would also be relevant to add better support for other kinds of tests to the framework (e.g., stress testing and performance testing) to create a single complete test automation tool for DW projects. It would also be interesting to determine if specifying and modifying DTs can be simplified through better editor support and database integration. Last, a strength of **pygrametl** is the easy integration with other Python projects. So better integration with relevant projects such as Pandas [33] and/or PyArrow [38] would also be beneficial.

Acknowledgments. This research was, in part, supported by the DiCyPS center funded by Innovation Fund Denmark [7], the GOFLEX project funded by European Union grant number 731232 [50], and the SEMIOTIC project funded by Danish Council for Independent Research grant number 8022–00284B. We also thank all who helped improve **pygrametl**, particularly code and documentation contributors as well as users who provided feedback.

References

1. Ali, S.M.F., Wrembel, R.: From conceptual design to performance optimization of ETL workflows: current state of research and open problems. VLDB J. (VLDBJ) **26**(6), 777–801 (2017). https://doi.org/10.1007/s00778-017-0477-2
2. Andersen, O., Thomsen, C., Torp, K.: SimpleETL: ETL processing by simple specifications. In: 20th International Workshop on Design, Optimization, Languages and Analytical Processing of Big Data (DOLAP). CEUR-WS.org (2018)
3. Beck, K.: Test Driven Development: By Example, pp. 194–195. Addison-Wesley Professional, Boston (2002)
4. Beyer, M.A., Thoo, E., Selvage, M.Y., Zaidi, E.: Gartner magic quadrant for data integration tools (2020)
5. Chandra, P., Gupta, M.K.: Comprehensive survey on data warehousing research. Int. J. Inf. Technol. (IJIT) **10**(2), 217–224 (2018). https://doi.org/10.1007/s41870-017-0067-y
6. Dean, J., Ghemawat, S.: MapReduce: simplified data processing on large clusters. In: 6th Operating Systems Design and Implementation (OSDI), pp. 137–150. USENIX (2004)
7. DiCyPS - Center for Data-Intensive Cyber-Physical Systems. https://www.dicyps.dk/dicyps-in-english/. Accessed 10 Feb 2021
8. Django. https://djangoproject.com/. Accessed 10 Feb 2021
9. ElGamal, N.: Data warehouse test routine descriptions. Technical report, Cairo University (2016). https://doi.org/10.13140/RG.2.1.3755.5282
10. ElGamal, N., El Bastawissy, A., Galal-Edeen, G.: Towards a data warehouse testing framework. In: 2011 Ninth International Conference on ICT and Knowledge Engineering (ICT&KE), pp. 65–71. IEEE (2012). https://doi.org/10.1109/ICTKE.2012.6152416

11. ElGamal, N., El-Bastawissy, A., Galal-Edeen, G.H.: An architecture-oriented data warehouse testing approach. In: 21st International Conference on Management of Data (COMAD), pp. 24–34. CSI (2016)
12. GitHub Flavored Markdown Spec - Version 0.29-gfm, 06 April 2019. https://github.github.com/gfm/#tables-extension-. Accessed 10 Feb 2021
13. Golfarelli, M., Rizzi, S.: A comprehensive approach to data warehouse testing. In: 12th International Workshop on Data Warehousing and OLAP (DOLAP), pp. 17–24. ACM (2009). https://doi.org/10.1145/1651291.1651295
14. Golfarelli, M., Rizzi, S.: Data warehouse testing. Int. J. Data Warehous. Min. (IJDWM) **7**(2), 26–43 (2011). https://doi.org/10.4018/jdwm.2011040102
15. Golfarelli, M., Rizzi, S.: Data warehouse testing: a prototype-based methodology. Inf. Softw. Technol. (IST) **53**(11), 1183–1198 (2011). https://doi.org/10.1016/j.infsof.2011.04.002
16. Grönniger, H., Krahn, H., Rumpe, B., Schindler, M., Völkel, S.S.: Text-based modeling. In: 4th International Workshop on Language Engineering (ATEM) (2007)
17. Guduric, P.: SQL server - unit and integration testing of SSIS packages. MSDN Mag.: Microsoft J. Dev. **28**(8), 48–56 (2013). http://download.microsoft.com/download/a/3/1/a315bac2-8093-45fd-8d04-1a9f899aca53/mdn_0813dg.pdf
18. Homayouni, H., Ghosh, S., Ray, I.: An approach for testing the extract-transform-load process in data warehouse systems. In: 22nd International Database Engineering & Applications Symposium (IDEAS), pp. 236–245. ACM (2018). https://doi.org/10.1145/3216122.3216149
19. Homayouni, H., Ghosh, S., Ray, I.: Data warehouse testing. Adv. Comput. **112**, 223–273 (2019). https://doi.org/10.1016/bs.adcom.2017.12.005
20. IBM InfoSphere DataStage. https://www.ibm.com/ms-en/marketplace/datastage. Accessed 10 Feb 2021
21. Informatica. https://informatica.com. Accessed 10 Feb 2021
22. Iyer, S.: Enabling ETL test automation in solution delivery teams. In: Excerpt from PNSQC 2014 Proceedings, pp. 1–10. PNSQC.org (2014)
23. Kimball, R., Ross, M.: The Data Warehouse Toolkit, 2nd edn. Wiley, New York (2002)
24. Kimball, R., Ross, M., Thornthwaite, W., Mundy, J., Becker, B.: The Data Warehouse Lifecycle Toolkit, 2nd edn. Wiley, Indianapolis (2008)
25. Liu, X., Thomsen, C., Pedersen, T.B.: ETLMR: a highly scalable dimensional ETL framework based on MapReduce. In: Cuzzocrea, A., Dayal, U. (eds.) DaWaK 2011. LNCS, vol. 6862, pp. 96–111. Springer, Heidelberg (2011). https://doi.org/10.1007/978-3-642-23544-3_8
26. Liu, X., Thomsen, C., Pedersen, T.B.: ETLMR: a highly scalable dimensional ETL framework based on MapReduce. In: Hameurlain, A., Küng, J., Wagner, R., Cuzzocrea, A., Dayal, U. (eds.) Transactions on Large-Scale Data- and Knowledge-Centered Systems VIII. LNCS, vol. 7790, pp. 1–31. Springer, Heidelberg (2013). https://doi.org/10.1007/978-3-642-37574-3_1
27. Liu, X., Thomsen, C., Pedersen, T.B.: CloudETL: scalable dimensional ETL for hive. In: 18th International Database Engineering & Applications Symposium (IDEAS), pp. 195–206. ACM (2014). https://doi.org/10.1145/2628194.2628249
28. Marin, M.: A data-agnostic approach to automatic testing of multi-dimensional databases. In: 7th International Conference on Software Testing, Verification and Validation (ICST), pp. 133–142. IEEE (2014). https://doi.org/10.1109/ICST.2014.26
29. Martin, R.C.: Clean Code: A Handbook of Agile Software Craftsmanship, pp. 132–133. Pearson Education, London (2009)

30. Microsoft SQL Server Integration Services. https://docs.microsoft.com/en-us/sql/integration-services/sql-server-integration-services. Accessed 10 Feb 2021
31. Nakuçi, E., Theodorou, V., Jovanovic, P., Abelló, A.: Bijoux: data generator for evaluating ETL process quality. In: 17th International Workshop on Data Warehousing and OLAP (DOLAP), pp. 23–32. ACM (2014). https://doi.org/10.1145/2666158.2666183
32. Oracle Data Integrator. https://www.oracle.com/technetwork/middleware/data-integrator/overview/index.html. Accessed 20 Feb 2021
33. Pandas. https://pandas.pydata.org/. Accessed 10 Feb 2021
34. Pentaho Data Integration - Kettle. https://github.com/pentaho/pentaho-kettle. Accessed 10 Feb 2021
35. Petre, M.: Why looking isn't always seeing: readership skills and graphical programming. Commun. ACM (CACM) **38**(6), 33–44 (1995). https://doi.org/10.1145/203241.203251
36. PostgreSQL. https://postgresql.org. Accessed 10 Feb 2021
37. psycopg. https://www.psycopg.org/. Accessed 10 Feb 2021
38. PyArrow. https://pypi.org/project/pyarrow/. Accessed 10 Feb 2021
39. pygrametl - GitHub. https://github.com/chrthomsen/pygrametl. Accessed 10 Feb 2021
40. pygrametl - PyPI. https://pypi.org/project/pygrametl/. Accessed 10 Feb 2021
41. pygrametl.org - Bulk Loading. http://pygrametl.org/doc/examples/bulkloading.html. Accessed 10 Feb 2021
42. pygrametl.org - Documentation. http://pygrametl.org/doc/index.html. Accessed 10 Feb 2021
43. pygrametl.org - ETL Flow and Data generator. http://pygrametl.org/assets/pygrametlexa.zip. Accessed 10 Feb 2021
44. Python. https://python.org. Accessed 10 Feb 2021
45. Ruby on Rails. https://rubyonrails.org/. Accessed 10 Feb 2021
46. SAP Data Services. https://www.sap.com/products/data-services.html. Accessed 10 Feb 2021
47. Scriptella. https://scriptella.org. Accessed 10 Feb 2021
48. Simitsis, A., Vassiliadis, P., Terrovitis, M., Skiadopoulos, S.: Graph-based modeling of ETL activities with multi-level transformations and updates. In: Tjoa, A.M., Trujillo, J. (eds.) DaWaK 2005. LNCS, vol. 3589, pp. 43–52. Springer, Heidelberg (2005). https://doi.org/10.1007/11546849_5
49. Talend Open Studio for Data Integration. https://www.talend.com/products/data-integration/data-integration-open-studio/. Accessed 10 Feb 2021
50. The GoFlex Project. https://goflex-project.eu/. Accessed 10 Feb 2021
51. Theodorou, V., Jovanovic, P., Abelló, A., Nakuçi, E.: Data generator for evaluating ETL process quality. Inf. Syst. (IS) **63**, 80–100 (2017). https://doi.org/10.1016/j.is.2016.04.005
52. Thomsen, C., Andersen, O., Jensen, S.K., Pedersen, T.B.: Programmatic ETL. In: Zimányi, E. (ed.) eBISS 2017. LNBIP, vol. 324, pp. 21–50. Springer, Cham (2018). https://doi.org/10.1007/978-3-319-96655-7_2
53. Thomsen, C., Pedersen, T.B.: Building a web warehouse for accessibility data. In: 9th International Workshop on Data Warehousing and OLAP (DOLAP), pp. 43–50. ACM (2006). https://doi.org/10.1145/1183512.1183522
54. Thomsen, C., Pedersen, T.B.: ETLDiff: a semi-automatic framework for regression test of ETL software. In: Tjoa, A.M., Trujillo, J. (eds.) DaWaK 2006. LNCS, vol. 4081, pp. 1–12. Springer, Heidelberg (2006). https://doi.org/10.1007/11823728_1

55. Thomsen, C., Pedersen, T.B.: A survey of open source tools for business intelligence. Int. J. Data Warehous. Min. (IJDWM) **5**(3), 56–75 (2009). https://doi.org/10.4018/jdwm.2009070103

56. Thomsen, C., Pedersen, T.B.: pygrametl: a powerful programming framework for extract-transform-load programmers. In: 12th International Workshop on Data Warehousing and OLAP (DOLAP), pp. 49–56. ACM (2009). https://doi.org/10.1145/1651291.1651301

57. Thomsen, C., Pedersen, T.B.: pygrametl: a powerful programming framework for extract-transform-load programmers. Technical report, Aalborg University (2009). http://dbtr.cs.aau.dk/DBPublications/DBTR-25.pdf

58. Thomsen, C., Pedersen, T.B.: Easy and effective parallel programmable ETL. In: 14th International Workshop on Data Warehousing and OLAP (DOLAP), pp. 37–44. ACM (2011). https://doi.org/10.1145/2064676.2064684

59. Thusoo, A., et al.: Hive - a petabyte scale data warehouse using hadoop. In: 26th International Conference on Data Engineering (ICDE), pp. 996–1005. IEEE (2010). https://doi.org/10.1109/ICDE.2010.5447738

60. Trujillo, J., Luján-Mora, S.: A UML based approach for modeling ETL processes in data warehouses. In: Song, I.-Y., Liddle, S.W., Ling, T.-W., Scheuermann, P. (eds.) ER 2003. LNCS, vol. 2813, pp. 307–320. Springer, Heidelberg (2003). https://doi.org/10.1007/978-3-540-39648-2_25

61. Vassiliadis, P.: A survey of extract-transform-load technology. Int. J. Data Warehous. Min. (IJDWM) **5**(3), 1–27 (2009). https://doi.org/10.4018/jdwm.2009070101

A Data Warehouse of Wi-Fi Sessions for Contact Tracing and Outbreak Investigation

Guilherme Augusto Zagatti[1]([✉]) [iD], See-Kiong Ng[1,2] [iD],
and Stéphane Bressan[1,2] [iD]

[1] Institute of Data Science, National University of Singapore, Singapore, Singapore
[2] School of Computing, National University of Singapore, Singapore, Singapore
gzagatti@u.nus.edu, {seekiong,steph}@nus.edu.sg

Abstract. The COVID-19 pandemic has spurred the development of a large number of automated and semi-automated contact tracing frameworks. Many of these are reactive and require active client participation, such as installing a specific contact tracing app on the clients' smartphones, and they are often unable to scale in time to reach the requisite critical mass adoption. To be better prepared for the emergence and re-emergence of coronavirus epidemics, we seek to leverage on the availability of common existing digital infrastructure such as the increasingly ubiquitous Wi-Fi networks that can be readily activated to assist in large-scale contact tracing. We present and discuss the design, implementation, and deployment of a data warehouse of Wi-Fi sessions for contact tracing and disease outbreak investigation. We discuss the conceptual design of the data warehouse and present the logical model that implements the conceptual model. We describe the data staging procedures and discuss the analysis of the Wi-Fi session data for mobility-based contact tracing and disease outbreak investigation. Finally, we present the case where the data warehouse of Wi-Fi sessions is experimentally deployed at full scale on a large local university campus in Singapore.

Keywords: Data warehouse · COVID-19 · Contact tracing ·
Epidemiology

1 Introduction

The global spread of COVID-19 has spurred the development of a large number of automated and semi-automated (henceforth, digital) contact tracing frameworks that leverage digital telecommunication infrastructure [6,17]. These frameworks promise to increase the efficiency of traditional contact tracing strategies by increasing the speed at which potential infection targets are identified and isolated, thus breaking the chain of transmission. Such efficiency gains arise from

© Springer-Verlag GmbH Germany, part of Springer Nature 2021
A. Hameurlain and A Min Tjoa (Eds.): TLDKS XLVIII, LNCS 12670, pp. 85–104, 2021.
https://doi.org/10.1007/978-3-662-63519-3_4

the speed and scale of proximity estimation using the large-scale digital traces of human mobility readily available from electronic mobile devices and wireless infrastructures.

Most of these frameworks are based on the assumption that the likelihood of being infected by SARS-CoV 2 is a decreasing function of the distance from the disease vector and an increasing function of time given a certain distance. Indeed, empirical evidence [7] have indicated that contact and droplet transmissions which require close proximity (less than 2 m) and usually aggravated by duration are the main transmission channels. Other channels such as airborne transmission might play a limited role, while environmental and behavioural factors (e.g. mask-wearing, hand hygiene) are also important factors that determine transmission likelihood.

The widespread use of mobile devices and wireless services leads to large amounts of digital traces that can be mined for proximity estimation. However, even in the current COVID-19 pandemic, thus far none of the digital contact tracing tools has become the contact tracing tool *de jour* that can replace manual contact tracing. One of the major drawbacks of these tools is that they are a reactive remedy that requires both substantial intensive and extensive participation rates of usually a new contact tracing app or device. In terms of intensive participation, users are usually required to be in constant possession of their devices and to keep them connected to the target network continuously or at least frequently. In terms of extensive participation, a majority of the population must have access to the technology in order to reach the requisite critical mass for the contact tracing to work. In fact, low adoption rates not only distort contact tracing efforts but can also contribute to the spread of the virus in neglected sub-populations [1].

Digital contact tracing tools are split into centralized and distributed frameworks. Centralized frameworks are server- or network-based solutions that passively collects data from connected devices [18], such as Wi-Fi-based contact tracing which leverages on the existing enterprise Wi-Fi network systems' network monitoring and logging capabilities which constantly collect data on devices' associations to access points (APs) within the network to infer the co-location of clients through spatial and temporal proximity. It can provide comprehensive system-wide coverage that is useful for large-scale (e.g. population-wide) mobility outbreak investigations such as disease outbreak simulation, as well as facilitating manual human-in-the-loop contact tracing with co-location information based on proximity.

Distributed frameworks, on the other hand, are client-based approaches that provide increased privacy through decentralized proximity sensing—e.g. based on received signal strength (RSS) proximity detection using peer-to-peer Bluetooth Low Energy (BLE) signal exchange. In fact, BLE RSS-based proximity detection is fairly accurate [17] and currently underpins Google/Apple Exposure Notification (GAEN), thus far the most downloaded and most likely to remain as the dominant decentralized technology in the long-run. However, such client-based approaches require a critical mass of users to determine proximity effectively. They are often unable to scale in time to reach the requisite critical mass as users are reluctant to opt-in and install a specific contact tracing app on their smartphones or carry a special contact tracing device with them at all times.

As such, centralized solutions are attractive especially in times of emergency. As Wi-Fi contact tracing does not require any additional app or opt-ins, it is much easier to deploy at scale in a timely manner. The necessary data are already collected by the network for routine network monitoring such as syslogs, Simple Network Management Protocol (SNMP) reports or real-time tracking systems (RTLS) events. Although Wi-Fi contact tracing only works in areas with Wi-Fi coverage (usually indoor), it is still very useful for assisting in epidemic control given that enclosed indoor areas of high human traffic often have higher risks in spreading the disease. Furthermore, most of the common high-traffic public environments in modern cities such as offices, university campuses, shopping areas, and even public transport stations that are of a high risk of disease spreading are equipped with Wi-Fi infrastructures that can be rapidly deployed for contact tracing and scale to large numbers of users.

As the Wi-Fi data are collected by the infrastructure for network monitoring purposes, it is important to organize the data into a platform for analytical purposes that enables the relevant data and information to be easily extracted, visualized, analyzed and communicated to decision-makers and healthcare providers to make informed decisions on disease outbreaks in a timely manner. Indeed, Aruba [4] and Oracle [15] have developed in-house, proprietary contact tracing solutions that use Wi-Fi session logs. Their solution is mostly focused on human-in-the-loop contact tracing applications with shorter data retention and fewer dimensions. We propose our design and implementation of a data warehouse of Wi-Fi sessions not only for contact tracing but also for disease outbreak investigation, thus geared towards simulation and policy evaluation leveraging additional dimensions with prescriptive goals in mind.

This work proceeds as follow. First, in Sect. 2, we review related works with regards to data warehouse design and implementation. Next, in Sect. 3, we describe our solution in five stages: conceptual model, logical representation, physical implementation, data staging, and data analysis. Section 4 describes the implementation of our data warehouse using the Wi-Fi data of a large university campus in Singapore. Finally, we conclude in Sect. 5 with a summary outlook.

2 Related Works

Data warehouses are repositories architected to facilitate the organisation and analysis of operational (both historical and current) data to support decision making. Traditional conceptualizations of the warehouse, such as the one first introduced by Inmon [11], mostly followed top-down online transaction processing (OLTP) conceptual modelling with an emphasis on the normalization of integrated, detailed, summarized, historical and metadata.

More recently, Kimball [12] advocated a bottom-up approach. The proposed star schema comprises a fact table in the centre, and accompanying dimension tables radiating from the centre that provide context for the facts. The central fact table consists of measurable and quantifiable facts as *grains of analysis* that are the most fundamental elements of the data warehouse. The dimension tables contain information of descriptors that provide contexts for the facts. The inherently flattened structure of a star schema helps achieve the twin goals of understandability and performance. However, this simplicity comes at a cost of an inability to exploit additional knowledge about hierarchical relations between the dimensions. Without such contextual knowledge, it could be difficult to determine appropriate roll-up or drill-down paths.

Malinowski and Zimányi [13] acknowledged the importance of hierarchies in dimensions with a conceptual model for data warehouses called *MultiDim* that considered the existence of a large number of hierarchical structures. This is particularly important in the analysis of spatio-temporal dimensions which are highly hierarchical and for which *MultiDim* was effectively extended. Logical models then derived from the conceptual model described data warehouse tables and their relationship in the form of star or snowflake schemas.

The field of data warehouses had been developed mostly for business intelligence applications. With the rise of digitalization and the emergence of data-centric public health and disaster management, there is a new need to develop effective data warehousing solutions for these new application domains. One example is a data warehouse for malaria by [3]. The warehouse consisted of a collection of multiple facts table decomposed into three broad categories: historical, predictive and static. Historical facts include demographic and economic data, household surveys, interventions. Predictive facts contained the simulation outputs. The capability to manage large-scale predictive facts, such as the outputs of simulated disease outbreak for analysis (which is also targeted in our warehouse), is a key consideration for designing data warehousing solutions for public health and disaster management. Another example is [9] which uses electronic medical records (EMR) to develop a data warehouse for contact tracing and disease cluster identification in the community. The authors paired positive test results from on-site rapid tests and external laboratory results with general patient information. Information such as address, spoken language and employer were used to identify likely transmission chains and clusters in the community. In other words, there is much more demand for the data warehouse to support complex and ad hoc data analysis than traditional routine business analytic applications.

Moving beyond traditional business intelligence applications, Vaisman and Zimányi [19] considered a wide range of data warehouse systems that incorporated a multitude of different data types that were not used by typical business-oriented analysis of [12], such as geospatial, temporal, 3D, 4D (or mobility), text analytic, multimedia and graph data warehouses. As mentioned earlier, there is much more demand on the data warehouse's ability to accommodate complex data types and ad hoc data analytic queries for applications in fields such as medicine, social-media, biology, landscape survey and disaster management. For example, our current application requires a data warehouse solution effective for both mobility and network-centric data analysis.

With the advent of GPS technologies, data warehouse solutions for GPS-based mobility information such as vehicular trajectory warehouses have seen considerable development recently. [2] described a data warehouse for handling billions of GPS data to estimate real-time travel time for taxi drivers. They defined a GPS ping defined a fact grain associated with additional dimensions such as weather, calendar, vehicular and other extract-transform-load data. Alternatively, [14] considered a complete trajectory as the grain of analysis in their data warehouse, by recording trajectories using a moving object database called *HERMES*. Along the same lines, [20] and [5] recently introduced a *PostgreSQL* extension denoted *MobilityDB* with temporal types for representing moving objects in *PostgreSQL* which can be used to build trajectory-based fact tables. The use of *MobilityDB* for contact tracing had been reported in a blog post [8].

The proliferation of mobile phones has also generated large amounts of human mobility data based on mobile phone data. Flowkit [10,16] is one of the popular toolkits for analysing call detail records (CDR) to provide intelligence for disaster response and humanitarian needs with a large focus on the analysis of population mobility. CDR data are similar to the Wi-Fi session logs that we are considering in this work. CDR logs activities related to mobile phone usage such as calls, SMS and data. These activities are associated with a routing base station (analogous to wireless access points in the Wi-Fi networks in our case). Flowkit's CDR data warehouse captures the CDR activities of a mobile phone operator with its facts table. It also captures the majority of its dimensions directly into the facts table which limits its OLAP capabilities. However, the spatial dimension associated with a base station is a notable exception—it is captured in a snowflake structure to allow for a wide range of spatial aggregation. To improve performance, Flowkit is able to dynamically generate and store materialized views through a custom-built python library developed for interacting with the warehouse. In this work, we also explore the use of materialized views for improved query performance, a practice which is also recommended in [12] and [13].

3   Proposed Solution

We present our proposed solution for a Wi-Fi session data warehouse for contact tracing and disease outbreak investigation in four subsections. In the first subsection, we introduce the conceptual model to model the facts and relationships we want to represent in our spatio-temporal data warehouse without worrying about the implementation details. Next, we introduce the logical representation of our conceptual model in terms of an entity relational database. This second subsection presents the data warehouse in terms of facts and dimension tables following traditional star and snowflake schema representations. In the third subsection, we describe the physical implementation of our schema. Finally, in the fourth subsection, we discuss extract-transform-load (ETL) procedures for our data warehouse. We also discuss the analytical procedures to leverage the information in the data-warehouse towards contact tracing and disease outbreak investigation.

3.1   Conceptual Model

We develop a multidimensional conceptual model based on the *MultiDim* model [13] that enable us to focus on the relationship between facts and dimensions as well as on the hierarchical relationship of each dimension while abstracting away from specific implementation details. The conceptual model for our warehouse is presented as a diagram in Fig. 1. The graphical notation follows [13].

Wi-Fi session logs are generated during the normal operations of a Wi-Fi network which consists of a network of wireless access points and, optionally, wireless controllers. Any device within the radio signal range of a wireless access point can connect to it as long as it satisfies the required authentication requirements. For scalability as well as security reasons, large Wi-Fi networks are also mediated by wireless controllers which are responsible for routing the frames received by their wireless access point clients. The logging activity represents measurement events that take place in the physical world—e.g. the beep of the scanner [12]. It represents our *fact table grain*, measurable and quantifiable facts that represent the most fundamental element of the warehouse.

Wi-Fi networks typically generate session logs with the following entries: start and end time, access point id, user id, mac address, received signal strength and pull time. A Wi-Fi session tuple can be seen as an *n-ary* relationship between six different levels, namely: *user, mac address, status, protocol, ssid, access point* and *timestamp*.

The *user* level refers to the *userid* required for password authentication protocols (PAP) in large Wi-Fi networks. A *user* is associated with a *user class* such as student, staff, etc. in the university setting. The *mac address* uniquely identifies a device in the Wi-Fi network at a given point in time. Since mac addresses can be easily modified, it might not be possible to trivially track a single device through an extended period. For privacy reasons, *user* and *mac address* are hashed and we do not associate additional attributes with these levels. The *status* level indicates whether a session was completed or not by the time the logs were pulled from the system.

The fourth level, *protocol*, indicates the communication protocol used to establish the connection. The radio frequency used by the protocol is one of its associated attributes. Higher radio-frequencies usually correspond to a shorter wireless connection range. The *ssid* level refers to the service set ID (SSID) which identifies a particular network in natural language to its end users. Networks grant user access based on an authentication protocol, which is the attribute denoted *authentication type* associated with *ssid*. Multiple *user classes* are allowed to use multiple *ssid* networks but not necessarily all of them.

Access point is a *point* spatial data type[1]. It is associated with a name determined by (say) the IT department to identify a wireless access point. As the wireless access point does not determine and/or broadcast its own geographical coordinates, the IT department must follow strict installation procedures and adopt a consistent naming convention if it wishes to determine the precise location of a wireless access point by name. Each wireless access point is located

---

[1] All of the spatial data types are defined in more details in [13].

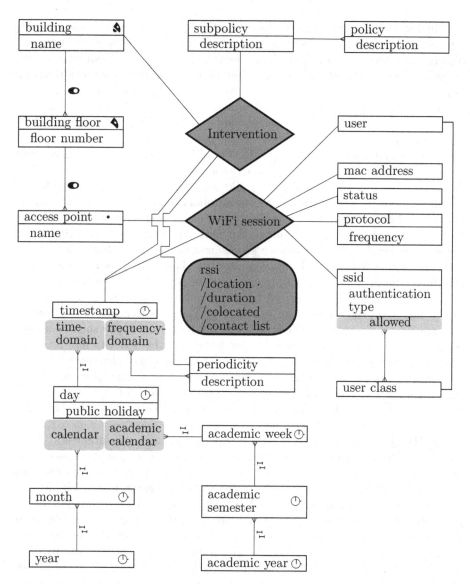

Fig. 1. Conceptual model of the Wi-Fi sessions data warehouse. Graphical notation follows [13].

inside a *building floor* which is a *surface* spatial data type that maps to building floors. A set of building floors is located inside a *building* which is a *surface set* spatial data type. The relationship connecting the different spatial levels is that of *covers/is covered by*.

Finally, the *timestamp* level is an *instant* temporal data type[2] that captures a precise point in time. Sessions can are determined by three different temporal dimensions: start, end, and pull time. Each Wi-Fi session spans an interval represented by its start and end time. Session information such as signal strength is polled at regular intervals denoted pull time. *Timestamp* is embedded in complex hierarchies which can be analysed following two paths: (1) the *frequency-domain* and (2) the *time-domain*. The *frequency-domain* corresponds to periodic analysis where the interest is to filter the data with time-intervals according to recurring cycles, such as daily interval between 10:00 and 14:00 (say), every Monday, every month of August, etc. More complex periodic intervals such as every other Monday from 15:00 to 17:00 should also be allowed, as events which affect the flow of people can also be scheduled in non-conventional cycles. To accommodate different types of cycles, the *periodicity* level has a single attribute called *description* that describes the cycle (e.g. Monday, August). The many-to-many relationship between *timestamp* and *periodicity* serves as a binary mask that allows us to filter the data with targeted periodic-intervals. The second path of analysis is the *time-domain*. This path is simpler and corresponds to coarser time-instants. A time data type is characterized by its granularity—in this path the higher in the hierarchy the coarser the granularity. The synchronization relationship corresponds to an overlap. When aggregating numerical types such as session duration, an allocation rule is required to apportion the quantity into a coarser scale. For instance, a duration that traverses multiple days. The *day* level which has an attribute public holiday is further split into two additional paths of analysis, *calendar* and *academic calendar* to cater specifically for our university use case. The former divides time according to the usual Gregorian calendar, while the later divides it according to business logic.

In *MultiDim*, facts are composed of dimensions and measurements. All of the session dimensions were described in the previous paragraphs. Session measurements (shown as a shaded round-cornered table in the figure) comprise both direct and indirect measurements. In terms of direct measurements, we have the received signal strength indicator (RSSI) which measures the strength of the connection in decibels (dB), serving as a proxy for the proximity of the device to the access point. Signal strength is measured at regular intervals—the pull time. A Wi-Fi session spanning a certain time interval may generate multiple logs with associated pull times and signal strengths. Along with direct measures, the diagram also depicts derived measures of different degrees of complexity, from session duration and device location to whether the user and device are co-located, and the contact list of users associated with the session. Note that other than the session duration and perhaps the device's location at a coarse level, the other measures would have to be computed from the Wi-Fi sessions using additional modelling frameworks. The computation involved could be challenging—for example, the duration measure must take into consideration that the users do not necessarily connect their device throughout their entire visit duration, the colocated measure must deal with the issue that the users' precise locations

---

[2] Again, all of the temporal data types are defined in more details in [13].

are not collected by the Wi-Fi network, while the contact list measure should account for the fact that the wireless access points do not necessarily cover the whole area of interest.

In addition to using the underlying mobility network to assist in contact tracing, the spatio-temporal dynamics of the population's mobility patterns can also be used to inform (or even predict) the effectiveness of epidemic controls, especially mobility-based interventions. For outbreak investigations, we model a second fact relationship denoted *intervention* to capture mobility-based intervention policies enacted to combat the spread of the disease. Our approach consists of defining an intervention with the following levels: *subpolicy, periodicity, building* and *timestamp*. *Subpolicy* refers to one of the sub-policies enacted by a parent policy. For instance, a zoning policy could divide the organisation into multiple zones. Each zone would consist of an intervention sub policy. The *periodicity* level determines the periodic intervals in which an intervention is active. For instance, a policy that prevents certain users from patronizing a cafeteria (say) could have its periodicity equal to *12:00 to 14:00 every working day*. An intervention that is always active would have its periodicity equal to *always*. *Building* determines to which locations the rule applies. In this warehouse, policies are specified at the coarsest possible level following implementation feasibility and business logic. Finally, the start and end time of the policy intervention is tracked by the *timestamp* level.

The proposed *n-ary* relationship provides a degree of abstraction to cater for different variations of mobility-based interventions. It also allows us to record hypothetical policy interventions for comparisons in investigating *what-if* scenarios and conducting simulation studies.

3.2 Logical Representation

For simplicity, we employ the star schema as the logical representation of the data warehouse with most of the hierarchical levels in the conceptual schema flattened into a single dimension table. The spatial hierarchy is split into two linked tables forming a snowflake structure for ease of management. Figure 2 depicts the logical representation in terms of an entity-relation diagram with two types of tables prefixed according to their definition, *facts* and *dimension*. In the tables, *key* refers to the table key attribute that must be unique. Table attributes with the suffix _key refers to foreign keys. Links between tables are denoted by arrows and referential integrity is expected. In other words, all arrows start with a foreign key in one table and end with a table key in another table.

Most of the dimension tables have a boolean attribute denoted *prepopulated*. This attribute indicates whether dimension records have been manually prepopulated or not. Most dimension records are unknown in advance and they must be derived from the fact grains—i.e. the raw data. Dimension tables are populated following a two-step process. First, we keep a copy of the dimension tables that have external attributes as text files. We manually add attributes from external sources—such as correspondence with information technology departments, OpenStreetMap, business calendars, etc.—to it. After raw data ingestion,

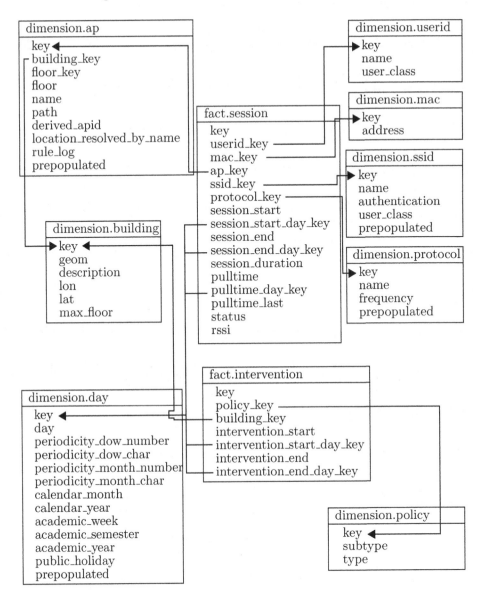

Fig. 2. Logical model of the Wi-Fi sessions data warehouse

whenever a new record that is not in the text file is identified in the dimension table residing in the data warehouse, those new records are manually added to the text file and populated with external sources. The dimension table in the warehouse is then updated to reflect the populated text file. We keep track of which dimension records have been pre-populated through the *prepopulated* boolean attribute which is only true if the dimension record resides in the text file. The pre-populated text files are stored for re-initializing the database whenever required.

A number of levels can be directly converted from the conceptual schema, namely: *user, mac address, ssid* and *protocol*. As mentioned in the previous subsection, user ids and mac addresses are hashed for privacy reasons and we are thus unable to link this information with administrative records. However, in our university campus use case, we can infer the user class from Wi-Fi session logs based on the class of the networks that they connect to. For each user, we identify all SSID networks they connected to, based on which we assign the most restrictive class to them. It is worth noticing that *user class* is repeated in both *dimension.userid* and *dimension.ssid* tables to keep the schema as simple as possible. Since there is a many-to-many relationship between *user class* and *ssid*, we use a comma-separated string in *dimension.ssid* to accommodate all the possible classes. Session status is stored in the facts table as an enumeration type rather than in a separate dimension table.

As mentioned earlier, the spatial hierarchy that maps wireless access point locations in the conceptual diagram has been structured as a snowflake in the logical diagram for ease of management. Both wireless access point locations and building-floor dimensions are collected in a single table, *dimension.ap*, while the building dimension belongs to a separate table. Wireless access points are labelled with a *name* and a *path*. It is often the case that the IT department may not have an authoritative list of wireless access points' actual geographical coordinates and relied on internal naming conventions to record the location of wireless access points. The flag *location_resolved_by_name* is used to indicate whether that is the case. We also include an attribute denoted *rule_log* which consists of a comma-separated string that indicates all the heuristics used to resolve the name of a wireless access point to geographical information. In our case, the wireless access point *name* can be split using regular expression rules into three parts: building, floor and access point ID. Based on the naming resolution, we can assign floor and building keys to each wireless access point. Whenever resolution fails, a missing value is assigned to either of these. Floor information is stored in two columns *floor* and *floor_key*. While it might seem redundant to record a floor key in the same table as the wireless access point location, this information becomes useful when accessing the warehouse from an API since *floor_key* uniquely identifies all building-floor combinations present in the data.

Since all building-floors have the same blueprint just shifted by a constant altitude, we only record spatial information in the *dimension.building* table which is linked to *dimension.ap*. The latter records the spatial data in the *geom* as a 2D-surface which usually requires relatively large disk space. The total number of floors is recorded in *max_floor* which allow the recovery of 3D-shapes. The coordinates of the centroid of the buildings are recorded in *lon* and *lat* which stands for longitude and latitude respectively.

We opt to snowflake this hierarchy for two main reasons. First, spatial operations of arbitrary complexity are made more efficient on the normalized table since they are repeated only once per building. The result of these operations can be easily merged with *dimension.ap* using the *building_key* attribute. This culminates into improved API access. For instance, our visualization application stores spatial data and aggregated facts separately. The data is then dynamically merged according to user interaction translating into better user experience. Second, the building dimension is also linked with *fact.intervention*. Having a single buildings table allows this information to be shared by both facts which reduce the risk of inconsistencies. The advantages and disadvantages of snowflaking are further discussed in [13].

The temporal data in the fact tables are recorded as both a timestamp and a day key which links to the *dimension.day* table. This table contains time- and frequency-domain attributes. As mentioned before, Wi-Fi sessions span a certain duration of time. The system polls the session at regular intervals to determine whether it is still ongoing or whether it was completed. At pull time, the received signal strength indicator is also recorded. Signal strength can be useful when estimating device location and distance between devices. For moderate high-frequency polling intervals as we have here (about every 5 min) the same session is recorded multiple times where only pull time and the signal strength indicator is updated. This not only adds considerable size to the facts table but also increases data ingestion time. To facilitate analysis at session-level we also add an attribute to the facts table denoted *pulltime_last* which indicates whether that was the last polled entry for a given session. This column is added during the consolidation phase and does add to the total data ingestion time.

As for interventions, we record each intervention event start and end time in *fact.intervention*. The table sees policies as a series of continuous interventions in time and space allowing for a great degree of flexibility in recording policies. A policy that zones the university in multiple sub-zones for a period of 2 months (say), would be recorded in this table as a series of rows. Each zone represents a sub-policy. There would be an entry for each building that the zone is applied to. The intervention start and end time would be represented by the first day the policy was in effect until the last. Alternatively, a policy that applies to a certain cafeteria only for working days lunch hours, would be represented in the table as a series of entries for each lunch hour interval while the policy is effective.

3.3 Physical Implementation

The data warehouse is implemented as an AgensGraph database to support both relational and network-centric analyses. This database is built on top of *PostgreSQL* and supports both relational and graph data models. Although our logical schema and most of our analytical operations are strictly based on relational models, the advantage of implementing the warehouse in AgensGraph is that it is possible to create data views using a graph data model. This is particularly relevant for creating tables of user proximity. In addition to that, spatial support is provided with the installation of PostGIS as an external module. The database is deployed with Docker containers to ensure it can be easily and consistently deployed.

All of the tables presented in the logical diagram are converted to database tables. We partition the *fact.session* table by session start date to improve query performance and create indices for session start and end. This procedure is recommended in [13]. We also add an indexed Boolean column *pulltime_last* to improve performance of session-level analysis—i.e. any analysis that does not use the received signal strength indicator or pull time. This column thus allows the quick selection of exactly one row per session from the facts table.

3.4   Data Staging

The Wi-Fi network produces session logs at regular intervals which includes both active sessions and those completed during the polling interval. In our use case, the logs are extracted as comma-delimited text files through a process managed by the IT department outside of our direct control. These files are loaded into the database using an extract-transform-load workflow developed in Airflow, a Python library to programmatically develop and deploy complex workflows. The process is broadly split into three parts, raw data pre-processing, ingestion and consolidation. Apart from the metadata stored by Airflow, we keep track of extract-transform-load events in a separate table in the data warehouse, *etl.etl*, which contains important metadata for managing the data staging procedure.

Since logs are produced at regular intervals, sessions that span multiple polling intervals might generate multiple log entries. We keep all the records since they contain the received signal strength reading at pull time. Incomplete sessions will have a missing value for the session end time. The session end time is only known after the session ends which means that all session logs before the last are likely to contain a missing value for the session end time. During the consolidation phase of the data staging procedure we update the session end time of each session with either its latest pull time—which reflects that the session is still ongoing, or in some cases that the session end time was never logged—or its latest session end time. During consolidation, we also determine which entry represents the last polled entry for each session, updating *pulltime_last* accordingly. Consolidation also ensures that data staging is idempotent meaning that it ensures the data warehouse does not carry duplicate entries even if the same log entry is ingested twice.

Wi-Fi session logs can contain noise or inconsistencies which are not always dealt with by the extract-transform-load process. About a quarter of the sessions have a start time later than the end time likely caused by logging inconsistencies (since the majority of which is within a few seconds of each other). During data staging, we fix this issue by replacing any pull-time or session end time earlier than the session start time with the session start time. In general, the extract-transform-load process only ensures that data formats are compatible with the database such that the data can be loaded into it. To avoid degrading performance and significantly altering the original data, instead of increasing the burden on the extract-transform-load process, we leave it as the job of the analysts to determine further data cleaning procedures appropriate for their analysis.

3.5   Data Analysis

Our proposed data warehouse should be able to answer queries related to contact tracing and outbreak investigation from *Can we find individuals who were in close vicinity to an infected individual for some time? Can we rank those individuals according to contact duration? Can we filter the contacts according to exposure distance?* to *How would the disease spread if a subset of individuals were initially infected? Which social distancing policies would be most effective to curb the spread of the disease?* Although none of these questions can be answered with complete certainty based on the limitations of the information in our Wi-Fi data warehouse, the warehouse should provide as much as evidence as possible in support or against the hypotheses.

The authors of both [13] and [12] have advocated derived facts and dimensions and materialized views to improve the performance of frequent queries. To accommodate additional dimensions and complementary facts required by frequent queries in the complex data analysis for contact tracing and outbreak investigation, our data warehouse stores the Wi-Fi session logs at the most granular level possible, and leaves any manipulation of the data to the data analysts. As discussed above, the data staging procedure does not eliminate all the inconsistencies present in the Wi-Fi session facts table but leaves it to the analysts to determine further appropriate data cleaning procedures for their analysis. Also, the data warehouse does not make any assumptions about the analysis of data, such as the identification of a person being stationary (i.e. whether the person has stayed in a location for a minimum period) and contact (i.e. whether two persons have come in close physical contact to each other) events, that are necessary for answering data analysis questions related to contact tracing and outbreak investigation. It is the analysts' task to determine working assumptions and heuristics.

Kimball [12] discusses complementary facts in the context of business processes. He advocates the concurrent use of transaction and snapshot facts. While transaction data is extremely detailed, its use is impractical when answering questions about the cumulative performance of the business at regular intervals for which snapshots—such as profitability tables—are much better placed. Kimball advocates a consensual approach that is valid for the whole business and evolves with time to compute snapshots. In the present case, transaction facts are represented by the pull time-level session data. Cumulative snapshots could include gathering and mobility facts. These snapshots are the output of heuristics and/or complex modelling frameworks. To accommodate different modelling approaches for computing agile snapshots (e.g. stationarity, co-location), we opt for the use of materialized views.

An example of a snapshot in the context of contact tracing is co-location. Co-location can be defined as any event in which two stationary *userids* shared a wireless access point for at least some time, say at least 10 min. For this analysis, we create a subset of stationary Wi-Fi sessions following [18]. The goal is to obtain the sessions that are most likely linked with stationary transitions of a single individual. First, we classify each *userid-mac* tuple into primary or non-primary. Each *userid* should have at most one primary tuple at any point in time. The primary tag identifies the device that is most likely in the possession of an individual as she/he moves around the organisation[3]. Our heuristics for classifying a device as primary for a given day is (1) at least 10% of all sessions with that device during the whole period were under 10 min and none of them was above 24 h—i.e. the device is likely a mobile[4] and (2) that was the mobile device that visited most access points on that given day.

The classified tuples represent an additional dimension which is created exclusively for analytical purposes. We save it as a materialized view, *dimension.userid_mac*. Second, we merge adjacent sessions that take place within the same wireless access point within 10 min of each other. Finally, we select only the merged sessions associated with primary tuples that last for at least 10 min. These sessions are likely to represent stationary events. This subset is saved as a materialized view for further analysis downstream, *views.stationary_session*. Alternative sub-setting procedures or even transformations of the raw data that yield more accurate stationary events could be considered in the future.

We can then create a materialized view listing all the contact events. This table can be regarded as a derived fact or snapshot—the *PostgreSQL* query creating this table is shown in Listing 1. During a contact tracing exercise, this table can be used to locate possible contacts of an infected user. These candidates can then be further manually verified by the organisation. The table can also be used to determine simulated infection events during a disease outbreak simulation exercise. Alternative definitions of co-location are possible and could be easily incorporated into the data warehouse as alternative views.

---

[3] As opposed to devices that might not be in the possession of an individual while connected to the network (e.g. a laptop computer in the library could be connected to the network while the individual is away for lunch).

[4] [18] mentions that mobile devices are likely to stay connected to the network while an individual is walking, but laptops and similar devices likely hibernate while the individual is on the move. Laptops are also likely to remain static in the workplace overnight, while mobile devices are almost always in the possession of an individual.

```
CREATE MATERIALIZED VIEW IF NOT EXISTS views.contact_list AS
SELECT *
FROM (
    SELECT
        a.userid_key AS userid_key,
        b.userid_key AS userid_key_other,
        a.ap_key,
        GREATEST(a.session_start, b.session_start) AS overlap_start,
        LEAST(a.session_end, b.session_end) AS overlap_end,
        LEAST(a.session_end, b.session_end) -
            GREATEST(a.session_start, b.session_start) AS overlap_duration
    FROM views.stationary_session a, views.stationary_session b
    WHERE
        a.ap_key = b.ap_key AND
        (a.session_start, a.session_end) OVERLAPS
            (b.session_start, b.session_end) AND
        a.userid_key <> b.userid_key
) f
WHERE f.overlap_duration > '10 minutes'
ORDER BY userid_key, userid_key_other, overlap_end;

CREATE UNIQUE INDEX IF NOT EXISTS
ix_contact_list_userid_key_userid_key_other_overlap_start
ON views.contact_list (userid_key, userid_key_other, overlap_start);
```

Listing 1: Creating a materialized view for contact events.

4   Case Study

The design, implementation, and deployment of a data warehouse of Wi-Fi sessions were motivated by the emergence of COVID-19 in Singapore. The first COVID-19 infection in Singapore was recorded on 18th January 2020. While none of the subsequent infections occurred at the university, an outbreak of the disease at the university campus has remained a possibility. With the progression of the disease in the country and the constant threat of re-occurrence, the government and the university have implemented measures to enforce social distancing and reduce the spread of the disease in the country.

It was thus important to put in place, as rapidly as possible, a data warehouse that could make use of data collected by the existing infrastructure to assist in manual contact tracing and outbreak investigations. The university shared Wi-Fi logs with selected researchers under strict security and privacy constraints for the development of solutions for the analysis of gathering and mobility data.

We implemented a data warehouse of Wi-Fi sessions using data from a large local university covering the period from 3rd December 2019 to 17th January 2021[5]. Pulled data was missing from 30th July 2020 to 26th October 2020 inclusive and 19th November 2020. The university hosts approximately 51,000 students and staff, and the sessions are spread over 227 different buildings. The

---

[5] Latest data at the time of writing of this document.

facts table contains a total of 400 million entries comprising 55 million sessions from about 87,000 different users with an average of 8 sessions per user per day.

The warehouse is hosted in a server running with Intel Xeon E5 v4 2.20 GHz with 40 CPU cores and 500 GB of total memory. The warehouse is deployed via Docker containers, only 20 CPU cores and 100 GB of memory are made available to it. Loading and consolidating the complete raw data took approximately 26 h, split into 18 and 8 h for each of these tasks respectively. In total, 322 files with median size of 208 MB–maximum size 830 MB–each representing a full day of data pull were ingested into the data warehouse. In terms of ingestion time, the median duration was 42 min (or 0.08 MB per second). During the ingestion process there were clear outliers for which the total loading time was above 4 h. Fact tables are consolidated per session start date since that is how they are partitioned. The median file will contain sessions that span about 24 days. Median consolidation time per table was 50 min–maximum 2 h. Our architecture is set-up to ingest files pulled on a daily basis.

We developed two visualisation and analytics applications as depicted in Fig. 3. The first application serves to visualize floor-level density throughout the day. The application can be used to identify crowded regions. It takes advantage of materialized views that pre-compute building-floor session counts at regular 15 min interval for the whole duration of the data. The materialized view uses *PostgreSQL* in-built function, *generate_series*, to expand Wi-Fi session intervals into multiple smaller, aligned intervals. Session counts are then grouped by

(a) Campus density visualization

(b) Building details

(c) Individual trajectory for contact tracing

(d) Contact tracing application

Fig. 3. Visualisation and Analytics

building-floor and interval. The second application consists of a contact-tracer which depicts all user ids that shared a wireless access point with a target user id. The application shows both the shared intervals and cumulative duration. It takes advantage of the materialized view to pre-compute contacts discussed in the previous section.

For outbreak investigation, we have also developed an agent-based disease simulator using the Julia programming language that connects directly to the data warehouse. The simulator uses as input the materialized contact list and the list of places visited per user to simulate the spread of disease. The simulator outputs contagion flows between buildings. Simulator parameters and output can be easily incorporated into the warehouse for further comparative analysis. We plan to incorporate intervention data into simulations to determine optimal intervention policies.

5   Conclusion

Emerging infectious diseases are a constant threat to public health. In particular, the emergence and re-emergence of coronavirus epidemics, as well as other outbreaks that are of pandemic scale, have led to a worldwide need to develop new methods and techniques for better epidemic preparedness and effective epidemic control.

With the widespread availability of digitized data and digital infrastructures for data collection, there is an opportunity to shift to digital real-time data collection and analysis for better disease outbreak preparedness and responses. In this work, we have looked into the organization and exploitation of large-scale data readily available from common existing digital infrastructure such as Wi-Fi access points to improve the situational awareness for mobility-based contact tracing and outbreak investigation. In addition to providing useful timely information to assist manual contact tracing, the mobility patterns in the Wi-Fi data can also provide a fine-grained understanding of the dynamics of infectious disease spread through human communities to facilitate pre-planning and the development of effective mitigation strategies.

In this paper, we have presented the design, implementation, and deployment of a data warehouse of Wi-Fi sessions for contact tracing and disease outbreak investigation. We discussed the conceptual design of the data warehouse and presented the logical model for the conceptual model. We described the data staging procedures and discussed the analysis of the Wi-Fi session data for mobility-based contact tracing and disease outbreak investigation. We followed the best-practices advocated in [12,13] and [19], focusing on designing our data warehouse to cater to the rapid evolution of business requirements in pandemic control and the complexity of the associated data analysis tasks. While we have focused on Wi-Fi sessions data and pandemic-related data mining applications in this work, the design considerations are broadly applicable to other mobility mining data sources involving check-ins, such as cellular phones or geotagged social media traces.

As of January 2021, the project is live. Further information can be found in <http://ids.nus.edu.sg/cofi.html>. The data warehouse schema, deployment and visualization code, and example analytical queries are available in the Github repository <https://github.com/NUS-IDS/cofi>.

References

1. Alkhatib, A.: We need to talk about digital contact tracing. Interactions **27**(4), 84–89 (2020). https://doi.org/10.1145/3404205
2. Andersen, O., Krogh, B.B., Thomsen, C., Torp, K.: An advanced data warehouse for integrating large sets of GPS data. In: Proceedings of the 17th International Workshop on Data Warehousing and OLAP - DOLAP 2014, Shanghai, China. ACM Press (2014). https://doi.org/10.1145/2666158.2666172
3. Arifin, S.M.N., Madey, G.R., Vyushkov, A., Raybaud, B., Burkot, T.R., Collins, F.H.: An online analytical processing multi-dimensional data warehouse for malaria data. Database (2017). https://doi.org/10.1093/database/bax073
4. Aruba: Contact Tracing (2020). https://www.arubanetworks.com/solutions/contact-tracing/
5. Bakli, M., Sakr, M., Zimányi, E.: Distributed Spatiotemporal Trajectory Query Processing in SQL (2020)
6. Braithwaite, I., Callender, T., Bullock, M., Aldridge, R.W.: Automated and partly automated contact tracing: a systematic review to inform the control of COVID-19. Lancet Digit. Health **2**(11) (2020). https://doi.org/10.1016/S2589-7500(20)30184-9
7. CDC: Scientific Brief: SARS-CoV-2 and Potential Airborne Transmission (2020). https://www.cdc.gov/coronavirus/2019-ncov/more/scientific-brief-sars-cov-2.html
8. Cybertec: Intersecting Tracks of individuals – MobilityDB (2020)
9. DeWitt, M.E.: Automatic contact tracing for outbreak detection using hospital electronic medical record data. MedRxiv (2020). https://doi.org/10.1101/2020.09.08.20190876
10. Gray, J., et al.: Flowminder/FlowKit: 1.10.0. Zenodo (2020). https://doi.org/10.5281/zenodo.3873357
11. Inmon, W.H.: The data warehouse and data mining. Commun. ACM **39**(11), 49–51 (1996). https://doi.org/10.1145/240455.240470
12. Kimball, R.: The Data Warehouse Toolkit: The Definitive Guide to Dimensional Modeling, 3rd edn. Wiley, Indianapolis (2013)
13. Malinowski, E., Zimányi, E.: Advanced Data Warehouse Design: From Conventional to Spatial and Temporal Applications. DCSA, 1st edn. Springer, Berlin (2008). https://doi.org/10.1007/978-3-540-74405-4
14. Marketos, G., Frentzos, E., Ntoutsi, I., Pelekis, N., Raffaetà, A., Theodoridis, Y.: Building real-world trajectory warehouses. In: Proceedings of the Seventh ACM International Workshop on Data Engineering for Wireless and Mobile Access. MobiDE 2008, New York. Association for Computing Machinery (2008). https://doi.org/10.1145/1626536.1626539
15. Oracle: Contact Tracing APIs in Oracle Database. https://blogs.oracle.com/oraclespatial/contact-tracing-apis-in-oracle-database (2020)
16. Power, D., et al.: FlowKit: Unlocking the Power of Mobile Data for Humanitarian and Development Purposes. Technical Report (2019)

17. Shubina, V., Holcer, S., Gould, M., Lohan, E.S.: Survey of decentralized solutions with mobile devices for user location tracking, proximity detection, and contact tracing in the COVID-19 Era. Data **5**(4), 87 (2020). https://doi.org/10.3390/data5040087

18. Trivedi, A., Zakaria, C., Balan, R., Shenoy, P.: WiFiTrace: Network-based Contact Tracing for Infectious Diseases Using Passive WiFi Sensing. arXiv:2005.12045 (2020)

19. Vaisman, A., Zimányi, E.: Data Warehouse Systems. DSA, Springer, Heidelberg (2014). https://doi.org/10.1007/978-3-642-54655-6

20. Vaisman, A., Zimányi, E.: Mobility data warehouses. ISPRS Int. J. Geo-Inf. **8**(4), 170 (2019). https://doi.org/10.3390/ijgi8040170

Convergence Proof for Actor-Critic Methods Applied to PPO and RUDDER

Markus Holzleitner[1(✉)], Lukas Gruber[1], José Arjona-Medina[1],
Johannes Brandstetter[1], and Sepp Hochreiter[1,2]

[1] ELLIS Unit Linz and LIT AI Lab, Institute for Machine Learning,
Johannes Kepler University Linz, Linz, Austria
[2] Institute of Advanced Research in Artificial Intelligence (IARAI), Vienna, Austria

Abstract. We prove under commonly used assumptions the convergence of actor-critic reinforcement learning algorithms, which simultaneously learn a policy function, the actor, and a value function, the critic. Both functions can be deep neural networks of arbitrary complexity. Our framework allows showing convergence of the well known Proximal Policy Optimization (PPO) and of the recently introduced RUDDER. For the convergence proof we employ recently introduced techniques from the two time-scale stochastic approximation theory.

Previous convergence proofs assume linear function approximation, cannot treat episodic examples, or do not consider that policies become greedy. The latter is relevant since optimal policies are typically deterministic. Our results are valid for actor-critic methods that use episodic samples and that have a policy that becomes more greedy during learning.

1 Introduction

In reinforcement learning, popular methods like Proximal Policy Optimization (PPO) [41] lack convergence proofs. Convergence proofs for these methods are challenging, since they use deep neural networks, episodes as samples, policies that become greedy, and previous policies for trust region methods. For Q-learning, convergence to an optimal policy has been proven in [5,47] as well as for TD(λ) in [11]. Convergence of SARSA to an optimal policy has been established for policies that become greedy, like "greedy in the limit with infinite exploration" (GLIE) or "restricted rank-based randomized" (RRR) [42]. Policy gradient methods converge to a local optimum, since the "policy gradient theorem" [43, Chapter 13.2] shows that they form a stochastic gradient of the objective. Stochastic gradients converge according to the stochastic approximation theory to an optimum [6–8,24,25,37,45]. Temporal difference (TD) convergences to a local optimum with smooth function approximation like by neural networks [28]. Also Deep Q-Networks (DQNs) [31,32] use a single neural network, therefore be shown to converge, as done in [12]. However it is assumed that every training set of reward-state transitions is drawn iid and that a global minimum of the Q-function on the training set is provided.

© Springer-Verlag GmbH Germany, part of Springer Nature 2021
A. Hameurlain and A Min Tjoa (Eds.): TLDKS XLVIII, LNCS 12670, pp. 105–130, 2021.
https://doi.org/10.1007/978-3-662-63519-3_5

We prove the convergence of general actor-critic reinforcement learning algorithms [43, Chapter 13.5]. Recently, actor-critic methods have had a considerable success, e.g. at defeating humans in the game Dota 2 [34] and in mastering the game of Starcraft II [46]. Actor-critic algorithms simultaneously learn a policy function, the actor, and a critic function that estimates values, action-values, advantages, or redistributed rewards. The critic is responsible for credit assignment, that is, which action or state-action pair was responsible for receiving a reward. Using this credit assignment, a policy function is updated to increase the return. Actor-critic algorithms are typically policy gradient methods, but can also be reward redistribution methods like RUDDER [3] or "backpropagation through a model" [4, 33, 38, 39]. Actor-critic algorithms have been only proven to converge for simple settings like for the neural networks that are linear [21, 22, 27, 48, 49]. In contrast to these convergence proofs, in our setting both functions can be deep neural networks of arbitrary complexity, though they should not share weights.

The main contribution of this paper is to provide a convergence proof for general actor-critic reinforcement learning algorithms. We apply this convergence proof to two concrete actor-critic methods. First, we establish convergence of a practical variant of Proximal Policy Optimization (PPO) [41]. PPO is an actor-critic on-policy gradient method with trust region penalties to ensure a small policy gap [40]. Secondly, we prove convergence of the recently introduced RUDDER [3]. RUDDER targets the problem of sparse and delayed rewards by reward redistribution which directly and efficiently assigns reward to relevant state-action pairs. Thus, RUDDER dramatically speeds up learning for sparse and delayed rewards. In RUDDER, the critic is the reward redistributing network, which is typically an LSTM.

The main proof techniques are recent developments from the two time-scale stochastic approximation theory [7]. The recent addition to the theory is the introduction of controlled Markov processes [16], which can treat policies that become more greedy and trust region methods that use previous policies. The two time-scale stochastic approximation framework has been applied previously to show convergence of actor-critic algorithms [21, 22] and, more recently, of Linear Quadratic Regulator (LQR) problems [48] and off-policy TD learning [49]. However, only tabular cases or linear function approximations have been considered. In a recent work, convergence was shown for variants of PPO and Trust Region Policy Optimization (TRPO) equipped with neural networks [27]. However, again the neural networks were only linear, the policy was energy-based, and the Kullback-Leibler term of the trust-region method was modified.

We aim at generalizing these proofs to learning settings which use deep neural networks, use episodes, use policies that become greedy, and use trust region methods. Therefore, the idea of stationary distributions on state-action pairs does not apply [21, 22] and we have to enrich the framework by a controlled Markov process which describes how the policy becomes more greedy and how to use previous policies. While we are developing a framework to ensure convergence, it does not imply convergence to an optimal policy. Such proofs are in general difficult for methods that use deep neural networks, since locally stable attractors may not correspond to optimal policies [15,26,29]. However, convergence to a locally optimal policy can be proven for linear approximation to Q-values [23,44]. Our main contributions to the convergence proof are, that we:

- use a Markov control in the two time-scale stochastic approximation framework,
- use episodes as samples instead of transitions,
- allow policies to become greedy,
- allow objectives that use previous policies (trust region methods).

In the next section, the main theorem is provided, which shows local convergence of actor-critic methods. Next, we formulate the results for PPO and RUDDER as corollaries. The third section gives a roadmap for the corresponding proofs, thereby introducing the precise framework and the results from stochastic approximation theory [7,16]. Finally, we discuss the technical assumptions and details for the proofs.

2   The Main Results

2.1   Abstract Setting and Main Theorem

Preliminaries. We consider a finite MDP defined by the 4-tuple $\mathcal{P} = (\mathcal{S}, \mathcal{A}, \mathcal{R}, p)$ (we assume a discount factor $\gamma = 1$) where the state space $\mathcal{S}$ and the action space $\mathcal{A}$ consist of finitely many states s and actions a and $\mathcal{R}$ the set of rewards r which are bounded. Let us denote by $|\mathcal{A}|$ and $|\mathcal{S}|$ the corresponding cardinalities and $K_R > 0$ an upper bound on the absolute values of the rewards. For a given time step t, the random variables for state, action, and reward are S_t, A_t and $R_{t+1} = R(S_t, A_t)$, respectively. Furthermore, $\mathcal{P}$ has transition-reward distributions $p(S_{t+1} = s', R_{t+1} = r \mid S_t = s, A_t = a)$. By π we denote an associated Markov policy. The (undiscounted) return of a sequence of length T at time t is $G_t = \sum_{k=0}^{T-t} R_{t+k+1}$. As usual, the action-value function for a given policy π is $q^\pi(s, a) = \mathrm{E}_\pi[G_t \mid S_t = s, A_t = a]$. The goal is to find the optimal policy $\pi^* = \operatorname{argmax}_\pi \mathrm{E}_\pi[G_0]$. We assume that the states s are time-aware (time t can be extracted from each state) in order to guarantee stationary optimal policies.

The abstract actor-critic setting is assumed to have two loss functions: L_h for the policy and L_g for the critic. Additionally we have the following building blocks:

- We consider two classes of parameters, denoted by $\boldsymbol{\omega} \in \mathbb{R}^m$ and $\boldsymbol{\theta} \in \mathbb{R}^k$. Moreover, $\boldsymbol{z}$ denotes an additional controlled Markov process with values in a compact metric space that may allow e.g. to force the policy to get more greedy and for treating trust region methods which rely on previous policies (it may be used for other purposes as well, e.g. Markovian sampling). $\boldsymbol{z}$ will be defined in a similar abstract way as done in [16] to make the setting as general as possible. We defer the technical details to Sect. 3.1.

- The first loss $L_h(\boldsymbol{\theta}, \boldsymbol{\omega}, \boldsymbol{z})$ is minimized with respect to $\boldsymbol{\theta}$ in order to find an optimal policy. This is achieved by updating a sufficiently smooth policy $\pi(\boldsymbol{\theta}, \boldsymbol{z})$, that can be controlled by $\boldsymbol{z}$. We will discuss in Sect. 3.2, how π can be constructed in specific situations. Next we consider two optional possibilities, how $L_h(\boldsymbol{\theta}, \boldsymbol{\omega}, \boldsymbol{z})$ may be defined: it may equal the expectation (i) $E_{\tau \sim \pi(\boldsymbol{\theta}, \boldsymbol{z})} [\phi(\tau, \boldsymbol{\theta}, \boldsymbol{\omega}, \boldsymbol{z})]$ or (ii) $E_{\tau \sim \breve{\pi}} [\phi(\pi(.; \boldsymbol{\theta}, \boldsymbol{z}), \tau, \boldsymbol{\theta}, \boldsymbol{\omega}, \boldsymbol{z})]$ where the expectations are taken over whole episodes $\tau = (s_0, a_0, \ldots, s_T, a_T)$ (sequences) that are generated via (i) $\pi(\boldsymbol{\theta}, \boldsymbol{z})$ or (ii) a behavioral policy $\breve{\pi}$, respectively. It will be clear from the context, which of these two possibilities we are using. The function ϕ can be interpreted as a per-sample loss for a sufficiently smooth neural network, that tries to find the optimal policy, evaluated only on a single trajectory τ. The detailed smoothness assumptions on L_h that need to be imposed are discussed in Sect. 3.2. The gradient of $L_h(\boldsymbol{\theta}, \boldsymbol{\omega}, \boldsymbol{z})$ will be denoted by $h(\boldsymbol{\theta}, \boldsymbol{\omega}, \boldsymbol{z})$.
- The second loss is given by $L_g(\boldsymbol{\theta}, \boldsymbol{\omega}, \boldsymbol{z}) = E_{\tau \sim \pi(\boldsymbol{\theta}, \boldsymbol{z})} [\Phi(g(\tau; \boldsymbol{\omega}, \boldsymbol{z}), \tau, \boldsymbol{\theta}, \boldsymbol{\omega}, \boldsymbol{z})]$ and is minimized with respect to $\boldsymbol{\omega}$ in order to find an optimal critic function $g(\tau; \boldsymbol{\omega}, \boldsymbol{z})$. The functions g and Φ should again be sufficiently smooth, such that $L_g(\boldsymbol{\theta}, \boldsymbol{\omega}, \boldsymbol{z})$ satisfies (L1)–(L3) from Sect. 3.2. Φ can be seen as the per-sample loss for the critic g. The gradient of L_g will be denoted by f.
- Since the expectations cannot be computed analytically, we do not have the exact gradients $h(\boldsymbol{\theta}, \boldsymbol{\omega}, \boldsymbol{z})$ and $f(\boldsymbol{\theta}, \boldsymbol{\omega}, \boldsymbol{z})$. Therefore, the expectations are approximated by sampling sequences τ and computing the average gradient on the sampled sequences. In our case, the stochastic approximations $\hat{h}$ and $\hat{f}$ of the gradients h and f respectively, are created by randomly inserting only one sample trajectory τ, i.e. we are dealing with online stochastic gradients. A formal description of the sampling process can be found in Sect. 3.2. Our losses are then minimized using online stochastic gradient descent (SGD) with learning rates $a(n)$ and $b(n)$, where the integer $n \geqslant 0$ denotes the timestep of our iteration.

For a given n, let us now state the discussed building blocks in a more compact and formal way:

$$
\begin{aligned}
L_h(\boldsymbol{\theta}_n, \boldsymbol{\omega}_n, \boldsymbol{z}_n) =& E_{\tau \sim \pi(\boldsymbol{\theta}_n, \boldsymbol{z}_n)} [\phi(\tau, \boldsymbol{\theta}_n, \boldsymbol{\omega}_n, \boldsymbol{z}_n)], \\
h(\boldsymbol{\theta}_n, \boldsymbol{\omega}_n, \boldsymbol{z}_n) =& E_{\tau \sim \pi(\boldsymbol{\theta}_n, \boldsymbol{z}_n)} [\nabla_{\theta_n} \log \pi(\boldsymbol{\theta}_n, \boldsymbol{z}_n) \, \phi(\tau, \boldsymbol{\theta}_n, \boldsymbol{\omega}_n, \boldsymbol{z}_n) \\
& + \nabla_{\theta_n} \phi(\tau, \boldsymbol{\theta}_n, \boldsymbol{\omega}_n, \boldsymbol{z}_n)],
\end{aligned}
\tag{1}
$$

where the first possibility for the policy loss L_h and its gradient h is listed. h is computed by the Policy Gradient Theorem, which can be found e.g. in [43, Chapter 13.2]. Next we discuss the expressions for the second possibility for L_h (when sampling via a behavioral policy $\breve{\pi}$):

$$L_h(\boldsymbol{\theta}_n, \boldsymbol{\omega}_n, \boldsymbol{z}_n) = \mathrm{E}_{\tau \sim \tilde{\pi}} \left[\phi(\pi(.; \boldsymbol{\theta}_n, \boldsymbol{z}_n), \tau, \boldsymbol{\theta}_n, \boldsymbol{\omega}_n, \boldsymbol{z}_n) \right],$$
$$h(\boldsymbol{\theta}_n, \boldsymbol{\omega}_n, \boldsymbol{z}_n) = \mathrm{E}_{\tau \sim \tilde{\pi}} \left[\nabla_{\boldsymbol{\theta}_n} \phi(\pi(.; \boldsymbol{\theta}_n, \boldsymbol{z}_n), \tau, \boldsymbol{\theta}_n, \boldsymbol{\omega}_n, \boldsymbol{z}_n) \right]. \tag{2}$$

The expressions for our second loss L_g and its gradient f are as follows:

$$L_g(\boldsymbol{\theta}_n, \boldsymbol{\omega}_n, \boldsymbol{z}_n) = \mathrm{E}_{\tau \sim \pi(\boldsymbol{\theta}_n, \boldsymbol{z}_n)} \left[\Phi(g(\tau; \boldsymbol{\omega}_n, \boldsymbol{z}_n), \tau, \boldsymbol{\theta}_n, \boldsymbol{\omega}_n, \boldsymbol{z}_n) \right],$$
$$f(\boldsymbol{\theta}_n, \boldsymbol{\omega}_n, \boldsymbol{z}_n) = \mathrm{E}_{\tau \sim \pi(\boldsymbol{\theta}_n, \boldsymbol{z}_n)} \left[\nabla_{\boldsymbol{\omega}_n} \Phi(g(\tau; \boldsymbol{\omega}_n, \boldsymbol{z}_n), \tau, \boldsymbol{\theta}_n, \boldsymbol{\omega}_n, \boldsymbol{z}_n) \right], \tag{3}$$

and finally, the iterative algorithm that optimizes the losses by online SGD, is given by:

$$\boldsymbol{\theta}_{n+1} = \boldsymbol{\theta}_n - a(n)\, \hat{h}(\boldsymbol{\theta}_n, \boldsymbol{\omega}_n, \boldsymbol{z}_n),$$
$$\boldsymbol{\omega}_{n+1} = \boldsymbol{\omega}_n - b(n)\, \hat{f}(\boldsymbol{\theta}_n, \boldsymbol{\omega}_n, \boldsymbol{z}_n). \tag{4}$$

Main Theorem. Our main result will guarantee local convergence for (4). To this end we fix a starting point $(\boldsymbol{\theta}_0, \boldsymbol{\omega}_0)$ and determine an associated neighborhood $V_0 \times U_0$ which can be constructed by the loss assumptions (L1)–(L3) given in Sect. 3.2. The iterates (4) will always stay in $V_0 \times U_0$ by these assumptions. Furthermore, let us denote the loss functions that result after considering the "limit" of the control sequence $\boldsymbol{z}_n \to \boldsymbol{z}$ by $L_h(\boldsymbol{\theta}, \boldsymbol{\omega})$ (and similarly $L_g(\boldsymbol{\theta}, \boldsymbol{\omega})$). Again we refer to Sect. 3.1 for a precise account on this informal description. Moreover, we denote a local minimum of $L_g(\boldsymbol{\theta}, \cdot)$ by $\boldsymbol{\lambda}(\boldsymbol{\theta})$, whereas $\boldsymbol{\theta}^*(\boldsymbol{\theta}_0, \boldsymbol{\omega}_0))$ should indicate a local minimum of $L_h(\cdot, \boldsymbol{\lambda}(\cdot))$ in $V_0 \times U_0$. Also here we refer to Sect. 3.2 for a precise discussion. We can now state our main theorem:

Theorem 1. *Fix a starting point $(\boldsymbol{\theta}_0, \boldsymbol{\omega}_0)$. Determine the associated neighborhood $V_0 \times U_0$ as in Sect. 3.2. Assume learning rates like (A4) for the time-scales $a(n)$ and $b(n)$ mentioned in Sect. 3.1. Also take the loss assumptions in Sect. 3.2 for granted.*

Then Eq. (4) converges to a local minimum $(\boldsymbol{\theta}^*(\boldsymbol{\theta}_0, \boldsymbol{\omega}_0), \boldsymbol{\lambda}(\boldsymbol{\theta}^*(\boldsymbol{\theta}_0, \boldsymbol{\omega}_0)))$ of the associated losses (i) Eq. (1) or (ii) Eq. (2) and Eq. (3):

$$(\boldsymbol{\theta}_n, \boldsymbol{\omega}_n) \to (\boldsymbol{\theta}^*(\boldsymbol{\theta}_0, \boldsymbol{\omega}_0), \boldsymbol{\lambda}(\boldsymbol{\theta}^*(\boldsymbol{\theta}_0, \boldsymbol{\omega}_0))) \ a.s. \ as \ n \to \infty.$$

2.2   Convergence Proof for PPO

The main theorem is applied to prove convergence of PPO. Our PPO variant uses deep neural networks, softmax outputs for the policy network, regularization, trust region, or exploration terms. Regularization can be entropy, weight decay, or a trust region penalty like the Kullback-Leibler divergence. All functions are assumed to be sufficiently smooth, i.e. at least three times continuously differentiable and bounded wrt. the parameters. The losses should satisfy (L1)–(L3) from Sect. 3.2. The PPO algorithm aims at minimizing the following losses:

$$L_h(\boldsymbol{\theta}_n, \boldsymbol{\omega}_n, \boldsymbol{z}_n) = \mathrm{E}_{\tau \sim \pi(\boldsymbol{\theta}_n, \boldsymbol{z}_n)} \left[- G_0 + (z_2)_n \, \rho(\tau, \boldsymbol{\theta}_n, \boldsymbol{z}_n)\right], \tag{5}$$

$$L_g^{\mathrm{TD}}(\boldsymbol{\theta}_n, \boldsymbol{\omega}_n, \boldsymbol{z}_n) = \mathrm{E}_{\tau \sim \pi(\boldsymbol{\theta}_n, \boldsymbol{z}_n)} \left[\frac{1}{2} \sum_{t=0}^{T} \left(\delta^{\mathrm{TD}}(t)\right)^2\right], \tag{6}$$

$$L_g^{\mathrm{MC}}(\boldsymbol{\theta}_n, \boldsymbol{\omega}_n, \boldsymbol{z}_n) = \mathrm{E}_{\tau \sim \pi(\boldsymbol{\theta}_n, \boldsymbol{z}_n)} \left[\frac{1}{2} \sum_{t=0}^{T} \left(G_t - \hat{q}^\pi(s_t, a_t; \boldsymbol{\omega}_n)\right)^2\right], \tag{7}$$

$$\boldsymbol{\theta}_{n+1} = \boldsymbol{\theta}_n - a(n) \, \hat{h}(\boldsymbol{\theta}_n, \boldsymbol{\omega}_n, \boldsymbol{z}_n),$$
$$\boldsymbol{\omega}_{n+1} = \boldsymbol{\omega}_n - b(n) \, \hat{f}(\boldsymbol{\theta}_n, \boldsymbol{\omega}_n, \boldsymbol{z}_n). \tag{8}$$

Let us now briefly describe the terms in Eq. (5)–(8):

- $\hat{q}^\pi(s_t, a_t; \boldsymbol{\omega})$ is a function that approximates the Q-value $q^\pi(s_t, a_t)$.
- $\delta^{\mathrm{TD}}(t) = R(s_t, a_t) + \hat{q}^\pi(s_{t+1}, a_{t+1}; \boldsymbol{\omega}_{n-1}) - \hat{q}^\pi(s_t, a_t; \boldsymbol{\omega}_n)$ is the temporal difference error.
- The exact gradients $h(\boldsymbol{\theta}_n, \boldsymbol{\omega}_n, \boldsymbol{z}_n)$ (from the Policy Gradient Theorem assuming causality and subtracting a baseline [43, Chapter 13.2]), $f^{\mathrm{TD}}(\boldsymbol{\theta}_n, \boldsymbol{\omega}_n, \boldsymbol{z}_n)$ and $f^{\mathrm{MC}}(\boldsymbol{\theta}_n, \boldsymbol{\omega}_n, \boldsymbol{z}_n)$ of the respective losses can be found in Sects. A.1 and A.3 in the appendix.
- $\boldsymbol{z}_n = ((z_1)_n, (z_2)_n, (z_1)_{n-1}, (z_2)_{n-1}, \boldsymbol{\theta}_{n-1}, \boldsymbol{\omega}_{n-1})$ denotes an additional controlled Markov process with values in compact sets. The controlled Markov process is essential to define the trust region term of PPO which uses previous values of $\boldsymbol{\theta}$ and z_1. Here, $z_1 \in [1, \beta]$ increases from 1 to $\beta > 1$ and $z_2 \in [0, (z_2)_0]$ decreases from $(z_2)_0 > 1$ to 0. z_1 controls the amount of greediness and z_2 the regularization. Details can be found in Sect. 3.2.
- $\pi(\boldsymbol{\theta}_n, \boldsymbol{z}_n)$ is a softmax policy that depends on $(z_1)_n$ to make it more greedy. We will introduce it precisely in Sect. 3.2, especially Eq. (14) there. π is learned using $\hat{q}$ and updated in every time-step.
- $\rho(\tau, \boldsymbol{\theta}_n, \boldsymbol{z}_n)$ includes the trust region term of PPO and may also include regularization terms like weight decay or entropy regularization. For example, $\rho(\tau, \boldsymbol{\theta}_n, \boldsymbol{z}_n) = \mathrm{KL}_\epsilon(\pi(\boldsymbol{\theta}_{n-1}, (z_1)_{n-1}), \pi(\boldsymbol{\theta}_n, (z_1)_n))$, where $\mathrm{KL}_\epsilon(\boldsymbol{p}, \boldsymbol{q}) = \mathrm{KL}(\tilde{\boldsymbol{p}}, \tilde{\boldsymbol{q}})$ with $\tilde{p}_i = (p_i + \epsilon)/(1 + k\epsilon)$.

The next corollary states that the above described PPO algorithms (TD and MC versions) converge.

Corollary 1 (Convergence PPO). *Fix a starting point $(\boldsymbol{\theta}_0, \boldsymbol{\omega}_0)$. Determine the associated neighborhood $V_0 \times U_0$ as in Sect. 3.2. Assume learning rates like (A4) for the time-scales $a(n)$ and $b(n)$ mentioned in Sect. 3.1. Also take the loss assumptions in Sect. 3.2 for granted.*

Using the same notation as in Theorem 1, the PPO algorithm Eq. (8) converges to a local minimum $(\boldsymbol{\theta}^*(\boldsymbol{\theta}_0, \boldsymbol{\omega}_0), \boldsymbol{\lambda}(\boldsymbol{\theta}^*(\boldsymbol{\theta}_0, \boldsymbol{\omega}_0)))$ of the associated losses Eq. (5) and either Eq. (6) or Eq. (7):

$$(\boldsymbol{\theta}_n, \boldsymbol{\omega}_n) \to (\boldsymbol{\theta}^*(\boldsymbol{\theta}_0, \boldsymbol{\omega}_0), \boldsymbol{\lambda}(\boldsymbol{\theta}^*(\boldsymbol{\theta}_0, \boldsymbol{\omega}_0))) \text{ a.s. as } n \to \infty.$$

Proof. We apply Theorem 1 since all its assumption are fulfilled. □

2.3   Convergence Proof for RUDDER

The main theorem is applied to prove convergence of RUDDER, which excels for tasks with sparse and delayed rewards [2]. For a recent application, see [35]. Again, we assume enough smoothness for all functions, i.e. they are at least three times continuously differentiable wrt. the parameters and bounded. The losses should satisfy (L1)–(L3) from Sect. 3.2. We formulate the RUDDER algorithm as a minimization problem of square losses $L_h(\boldsymbol{\theta}_n, \boldsymbol{\omega}_n, \boldsymbol{z}_n)$ and $L_g(\boldsymbol{\theta}_n, \boldsymbol{\omega}_n, \boldsymbol{z}_n)$:

$$
L_h = E_{\tau \sim \check{\pi}} \left[\frac{1}{2} \sum_{t=0}^{T} \left(R_{t+1}(\tau; \boldsymbol{\omega}_n) - \hat{q}(s_t, a_t; \boldsymbol{\theta}_n) \right)^2 + (z_2)_n \, \rho_\theta(\tau, \boldsymbol{\theta}_n, \boldsymbol{z}_n) \right],
$$

(9)

$$
L_g = E_{\tau \sim \pi(\theta_n, z_n)} \left[\frac{1}{2} \left(\sum_{t=0}^{T} \tilde{R}_{t+1} - g(\tau; \boldsymbol{\omega}_n) \right)^2 + (z_2)_n \, \rho_\omega(\tau, \boldsymbol{\theta}_n, \boldsymbol{z}_n) \right],
$$
(10)

$$
\boldsymbol{\theta}_{n+1} = \boldsymbol{\theta}_n - a(n) \, \hat{h}(\boldsymbol{\theta}_n, \boldsymbol{\omega}_n, \boldsymbol{z}_n),
$$
$$
\boldsymbol{\omega}_{n+1} = \boldsymbol{\omega}_n - b(n) \, \hat{f}(\boldsymbol{\theta}_n, \boldsymbol{\omega}_n, \boldsymbol{z}_n).
$$
(11)

Let us now briefly describe the terms in Eq. (9)–(11):

- $\hat{q}(s, a; \boldsymbol{\theta}_n)$ is a function parametrized by $\boldsymbol{\theta}_n$ that approximates the Q-value $q(s, a)$. Note that the policy loss L_h implicitly depends on the policy π via $\hat{q}$.
- The expressions for $h(\boldsymbol{\theta}_n, \boldsymbol{\omega}_n, \boldsymbol{z}_n)$ and $f(\boldsymbol{\theta}_n, \boldsymbol{\omega}_n, \boldsymbol{z}_n)$ can be found in Sect. A.2 in the appendix.
- $\tilde{R}$ is the original MDP reward.
- $R(\tau; \boldsymbol{\omega}_n)$ is the redistributed reward based on the return decomposition of g with parameter vector $\boldsymbol{\omega}_n$. For a state-action sequence τ the realization of its redistributed reward R is computed from $g(\tau; \boldsymbol{\omega}_n)$ and the realization of return variable $\sum_{t=0}^{T} \tilde{R}_{t+1}$. In practice, g can be an LSTM-network, or, e.g. in [35], g is obtained by a profile model.
- $\rho_\theta(\tau, \boldsymbol{\theta}_n, \boldsymbol{z}_n)$ is a regularization term for the learning of the Q-value approximation $\hat{q}$.
- $\rho_\omega(\tau, \boldsymbol{\theta}_n, \boldsymbol{z}_n)$ is a regularization term for the learning of the reward redistribution function g.
- $\check{\pi}$ is a behavioral policy that does not depend on the parameters.
- $\boldsymbol{z}_n = ((z_1)_n, (z_2)_n, (z_1)_{n-1}, (z_2)_{n-1}, \boldsymbol{\theta}_{n-1}, \boldsymbol{\omega}_{n-1})$ denotes an additional Markov process, where we use the same construction as in the PPO setting. Details can again be found in Sect. 3.2.
- $\pi(\boldsymbol{\theta}_n, \boldsymbol{z}_n)$ is a softmax policy applied to $(z_1)_n \, \hat{q}$ (see Eq. (14) for a precise introduction). It depends on $(z_1)_n > 1$ which makes it more greedy and $\boldsymbol{\theta}_n$ is updated in every time-step.

The next corollary states that the RUDDER algorithm converges.

Corollary 2 (Convergence RUDDER). *Fix a starting point (θ_0, ω_0). Determine the associated neighborhood $V_0 \times U_0$ as in Sect. 3.2. Assume learning rates like (A4) for the time-scales $a(n)$ and $b(n)$ mentioned in Sect. 3.1. Also take the loss assumptions in Sect. 3.2 for granted. Using the same notation as in Theorem 1, the RUDDER algorithm Eq. (11) converges to a local minimum $(\theta^*(\theta_0, \omega_0), \lambda(\theta^*(\theta_0, \omega_0)))$ of the associated losses Eq. (9) and Eq. (10):*

$$(\theta_n, \omega_n) \;\to\; (\theta^*(\theta_0, \omega_0), \lambda(\theta^*(\theta_0, \omega_0))) \; a.s. \; as \; n \;\to\; \infty.$$

Proof. We apply Theorem 1 since all its assumptions are fulfilled. □

3   Assumptions and Proof of Theorem 1

This section aims at presenting the theoretical framework from [16] and [7] that we want to apply to prove Theorem 1. We formulate the convergence result Theorem 2 and the assumptions (A1)–(A7) that we need to ensure in order to get there. Then we discuss how it can be applied to our setting.

3.1   The Stochastic Approximation Theory: Borkar and Karmakar and Bhatnagar

For this section we use the formulations in [14,16]. Stochastic approximation algorithms are iterative procedures to find stationary points (minimum, maximum, saddle point) of functions when only noisy observations are provided. We use two time-scale stochastic approximation algorithms, i.e. two coupled iterations moving at different speeds. Convergence of these interwoven iterates can be ensured by assuming that one step size is considerably smaller than the other. The slower iterate is assumed to be slow enough to allow the fast iterate to converge while simultaneously being perturbed by the slower. The perturbations of the slower should be small enough to ensure convergence of the faster. The iterates map at time step $n \geqslant 0$ the fast variable $\omega_n \in \mathbb{R}^k$ and the slow variable $\theta_n \in \mathbb{R}^m$ to their new values:

$$\theta_{n+1} = \theta_n - a(n)\,(h(\theta_n, \omega_n, z_n) + (m_1)_n), \tag{12}$$

$$\omega_{n+1} = \omega_n - b(n)\,(f(\theta_n, \omega_n, z_n) + (m_2)_n), \tag{13}$$

where:

- $h(.) \in \mathbb{R}^m$ and $f(.) \in \mathbb{R}^k$ are mappings for Eq. (12) and Eq. (13), respectively.
- $a(n)$ and $b(n)$ are step sizes for Eq. (12) and Eq. (13), respectively.
- $(m_1)_n$ and $(m_2)_n$ are martingale difference sequences for Eq. (12) and Eq. (13), respectively.
- z_n denotes the common Markov control process for Eq. (12) and Eq. (13).

We assume that all the random variables are defined on a common probability space $(\Omega, \mathfrak{A}, P)$ with associated sigma algebra $\mathfrak{A}$ and probability measure P. Let us continue with an informal summary of the assumptions needed to ensure convergence of (12)–(13). More precise technical details can be found in Sect. A.4 in the appendix and in [16].

(A1) *Assumptions on the controlled Markov processes*: z_n takes values in a compact metric space S. It is controlled by the iterate sequences θ_n and ω_n and additionally by a random process a_n taking values in a compact metric space W. The dynamics wrt. n are specified by a transition kernel. Be aware that this control setting can in general be different than the already introduced MDP setting.

(A2) *Assumptions on the update functions*: f, and h are jointly continuous as well as Lipschitz in their first two arguments, and uniformly w.r.t. the third.

(A3) *Assumptions on the additive noise*: For $i = 1, 2$ the $(m_i)_n$ are martingale difference sequences with bounded second moments.

(A4) *Assumptions on the learning rates*: Informally, the sums of the positive $a(n)$ and $b(n)$ diverge, while their squared sums converge. $a(n)$ goes to zero faster than $b(n)$.

(A5) *Assumptions on the transition kernels*: The transition kernels of z_n are continuous wrt. the topology of weak convergence of probability measures.

(A6) *Assumptions on the associated ODEs*: We consider occupation measures which intuitively give for the controlled Markov process the probability or density to observe a particular state-action pair from $S \times W$ for given θ and ω and a given control. A precise definition of these occupation measures can be found e.g. on page 68 of [7] or page 5 in [16]. We need the following assumptions:

- We assume that there exists only one such ergodic occupation measure for z_n on $S \times W$, denoted by $\Gamma_{\theta,\omega}$. A main reason for assuming uniqueness is that it enables us to deal with ODEs instead of differential inclusions. Moreover, set $\tilde{f}(\theta, \omega) = \int f(\theta, \omega, z)\, \Gamma_{\theta,\omega}(\mathrm{d}z, W)$.
- For $\theta \in \mathbb{R}^m$, the ODE $\dot{\omega}(t) = \tilde{f}(\theta, \omega(t))$ has a unique asymptotically stable equilibrium $\lambda(\theta)$ with attractor set B_θ such that $\lambda : \mathbb{R}^m \to \mathbb{R}^k$ is a Lipschitz map with global Lipschitz constant.
- The Lyapunov function $V(\theta, .)$ associated to $\lambda(\theta)$ is continuously differentiable.
- Next define $\tilde{h}(\theta) = \int h(\theta, \lambda(\theta), z)\, \Gamma_{\theta,\lambda(\theta)}(\mathrm{d}z, W)$. The ODE $\dot{\theta}(t) = \tilde{h}(\theta(t))$ has a global attractor set A.
- For all θ, with probability 1, ω_n for $n \geqslant 1$ belongs to a compact subset Q_θ of B_θ "eventually".

This assumption is an adapted version of (A6)' of [16] to avoid too many technicalities (e.g. [16] uses a different control for each iterate).

(A7) *Assumption of bounded iterates*: The iterates θ_n and ω_n are uniformly bounded almost surely.

Convergence for Eq. (12)–(13) is given by Theorem 1 in [16]:

Theorem 2 (Karmakar & Bhatnagar). *Under the assumptions (A1)–(A7), the iterates Eq. (12) and Eq. (13) converge:*

$$(\theta_n, \omega_n) \to \cup_{\theta^* \in A}(\theta^*, \lambda(\theta^*)) \quad a.s. \quad as\ n \to \infty.$$

3.2   Application to Proof of Main Result

Next we describe how Theorem 2 yields Theorem 1 by discussing the validity of (A1)–(A7). We additionally mention details about their concrete realization in the context of PPO and RUDDER. We conclude by a discussion on how we can allow our policies to become sufficiently greedy over time.

Ad (A1): Controlled Markov Process for the Abstract Setting: For Eq. (1)–(3) we assume to have a controlled process that fulfills the previously discussed requirements for (A1).

Ad (A1): Controlled Markov Process for PPO and RUDDER: In our applications to RUDDER and PPO, however, the Markov control will have a much simpler form: z_n mainly consists of real sequences which obey the Markov property. Also we do not have any additional control in these situations. More concretely: $z_n = ((z_1)_n, (z_2)_n, (z_1)_{n-1}, (z_2)_{n-1}, \theta_{n-1}, \omega_{n-1})$ with $(z_1)_n \in [1, \beta]$ for some $\beta > 1$, and $(z_2)_n \in [0, (z_2)_0]$ for some $(z_2)_0 > 1$. $(z_1)_n$ can be defined by $(z_1)_0 = 1$ and $(z_1)_{n+1} = (1 - \frac{1}{\beta})(z_1)_n + 1$. It consists of the partial sums of a geometric series converging to $\beta > 1$. For $(z_2)_n$ we can use any sequence satisfying the Markov Property and converging to zero, e.g. $(z_2)_0 = C$ and $(z_2)_{n+1} = \alpha(z_2)_n$ with $\alpha < 1$ or $(z_2)_{n+1} = \frac{(z_2)_n}{(z_2)_n + \alpha}$ with $1 < \alpha$. z_n then is a time-homogeneous Markov process with unique invariant measure, cf. Sect. A.6 in the appendix.

Let us now describe the meaning of this process for RUDDER and PPO: The component $(z_1)_n$ is used as a slope parameter for the softmax policy and goes to a large value β to make the policy greedy. The softmax policy is introduced in the following rather abstract way: For a sufficiently smooth function (deep neural network) $\psi(s; \theta) = (\psi^1(s; \theta), \dots, \psi^{|\mathcal{A}|}(s; \theta))$, a softmax policy $\pi(\theta, z_1)$ is defined as

$$\pi(a^i \mid s; \theta, z_1) = \frac{\exp(z_1 \, \psi^i(s; \theta))}{\sum_j \exp(z_1 \, \psi^j(s; \theta))}. \tag{14}$$

For RUDDER and PPO we use $\psi(s; \theta) = \hat{q}(s; \theta_n)$ with $\hat{q}^i(s; \theta_n)$ approximating $q^\pi(s, a^i)$. The component $(z_2)_n$ is used to weight an additional term in the objective and goes to zero over time. We require $(z_1)_{n-1}$ and θ_{n-1} for the trust-region term ρ, for which we have to reconstruct the old policy. Further details, especially concerning β, can be found in Sect. 3.2 and Sect. A.7 in the appendix.

Ad (A3): Martingale Difference Property and the Probabilistic Setting: Here we describe the sampling process more formally:

- The baseline probability space is given by $\Omega = [0, 1]$, $P = \mu$ and $\mathfrak{A} = \mathfrak{B}([0, 1])$, with μ denoting the Lebesgue measure and $\mathfrak{B}([0, 1])$ the Borel σ-algebra on $[0, 1]$.

- Next we introduce the set of all trajectories obtained by following π as $\tilde{\Omega}_\pi = \{\tau = (s, a)_{0:T} | \tau$ is chosen wrt. $\pi, S_0 = s_0, A_0 = a_0\}$. Its power set serves as related σ-algebra $\tilde{\mathfrak{A}}_\pi$.
- We endow $\tilde{\mathfrak{A}}_\pi$ with a probability measure: $\tilde{P}_\pi(\tau) = \prod_{t=1}^T p(s_t \mid s_{t-1}, a_{t-1}) \pi(a_t \mid s_t)$, which computes the probability of choosing a sequence τ with starting point (s_0, a_0). $\tilde{\mathfrak{A}}_\pi$ can be ordered according to the magnitude of the values of its events on P_π. We denote this ordering by $\leq$.
- We define $S_\pi : \Omega \to \tilde{\Omega}_\pi$ as $S_\pi : x \mapsto \mathrm{argmax}_{\tau \in \tilde{\Omega}_\pi} \left\{ \sum_{\eta \leq \tau} \tilde{P}_\pi(\eta) \leq x \right\}$. This map is well defined and measurable and it describes how to get one sample from a multinomial distribution with probabilities $\tilde{P}_\pi(\tau)$, where $\tau \in \tilde{\Omega}_\pi$.
- Now we are in the position to describe the sampling process. As mentioned already in the beginning, we use an online update, i.e. we introduce functions $\hat{h}$ and $\hat{f}$, where $\hat{h}$ approximates h by using one sample trajectory instead of the expectation, the same goes for $\hat{f}$. More formally, for f we define $\hat{f}(\boldsymbol{\theta}_n, \boldsymbol{\omega}_n, \boldsymbol{z}_n)$: $[0, 1] \to \mathbb{R}^k$ as $x \mapsto S_{\pi(\boldsymbol{\theta}_n, \boldsymbol{z}_n)}(x) = \tau \mapsto \nabla_{\boldsymbol{\omega}_n} \Phi(g(\tau; \boldsymbol{\omega}_n, \boldsymbol{z}_n), \tau, \boldsymbol{\theta}_n, \boldsymbol{\omega}_n, \boldsymbol{z}_n)$.
- Finally we can define the martingale errors as

$$(\boldsymbol{m}_1)_{n+1} = \hat{h}(\boldsymbol{\theta}_n, \boldsymbol{\omega}_n, \boldsymbol{z}_n) - h(\boldsymbol{\theta}_n, \boldsymbol{\omega}_n, \boldsymbol{z}_n)$$

and

$$(\boldsymbol{m}_2)_{n+1} = \hat{f}(\boldsymbol{\theta}_n, \boldsymbol{\omega}_n, \boldsymbol{z}_n) - f(\boldsymbol{\theta}_n, \boldsymbol{\omega}_n, \boldsymbol{z}_n).$$

Further details (regarding the sampling process and the bounds for the second moments) can be found in Sects. A.5 and A.6 in the appendix.

Ad (A2) and (A6): Smoothness of h and f and Stability of ODEs via Assumptions on Losses. We make the following assumptions on the loss functions of Eq. (1) (or Eq. (2)) and Eq. (3):

(L1) π, g, Φ and ϕ all have compact support and are at least three times continuously differentiable wrt. their parameters $\boldsymbol{\theta}$ and $\boldsymbol{\omega}$.

(L2) For each fixed $\boldsymbol{\theta}$ all critical points of $L_g(\boldsymbol{\theta}, \boldsymbol{\omega})$ are isolated local minima and there are only finitely many. The local minima $\{\lambda_i(\boldsymbol{\theta})\}_{i=1}^{k(\boldsymbol{\theta})}$ of $L_g(\boldsymbol{\theta}, .)$ can be expressed locally as at least twice continuously differentiable functions with associated domains of definitions $\{V_{\lambda_i(\boldsymbol{\theta})}\}_{i=1}^{k(\boldsymbol{\theta})}$.

(L3) Locally in $V_{\lambda_i(\boldsymbol{\theta})}$, $L_h(\boldsymbol{\theta}, \lambda_i(\boldsymbol{\theta}))$ has only one local minimum.

Some remarks concerning these assumptions are in order:

- *Comment on (L1):* The parameter space of networks can be assumed to be bounded in practice.
- *Comment on (L2):* For each starting point $(\boldsymbol{\theta}_0, \boldsymbol{\omega}_0)$ we can find a neighborhood $U_{\boldsymbol{\theta}_0}(\boldsymbol{\omega}_0)$ that connects $\boldsymbol{\omega}_0$ with a local minimum $\lambda_i(\boldsymbol{\theta}_0)$ of $L_g(\boldsymbol{\theta}_0, \cdot)$, so that $U_{\boldsymbol{\theta}_0}(\boldsymbol{\omega}_0)$ contains no further critical points, e.g. a small neighborhood around the steepest descent path on the loss surface of $L_g(\boldsymbol{\theta}_0, \cdot)$ starting at $\boldsymbol{\omega}_0$. Next we apply the implicit function theorem (IFT) to find a neighborhood V_0 around $\boldsymbol{\theta}_0$, such that $\lambda_i(\boldsymbol{\theta})$ is twice continuously differentiable there. The

IFT can be applied to $f(\boldsymbol{\theta}, \cdot) = \nabla_\omega L_g(\boldsymbol{\theta}, \cdot) = 0$, since the associated Hessian is positive definite and thus invertible. It can even be shown that it is twice continuously differentiable, using analytic versions of the IFT.

- *Comment on (L3):* In a similar vein, for each $\boldsymbol{\theta} \in V_0$ we can construct neighborhoods $U_\theta(\omega_0)$ around ω_0 with $\lambda_i(\boldsymbol{\theta})$ as unique associated local minimum (we may have to shrink V_0). Define $\cup_{\theta \in V_0}(\{\boldsymbol{\theta}\} \times U_\theta(\omega_0)) = V_0 \times U_0$.

- *Comment on compatibility with global setting:* By using a suitable regularization (e.g. weight decay) for the networks, we can assume that the algorithm Eq. (12) and Eq. (13) always stays in $V_0 \times U_0$. This heuristically justifies that for $(\boldsymbol{\theta}_0, \omega_0)$ we localize to $V_0 \times U_0$.

- *Comment on drawbacks of assumptions:* A completely rigorous justification of this argument would require a more thorough analysis of SGD, which would of course be a very interesting future research direction. For SGD with one time scale, a result in this direction can be found in [30]. It would be interesting to extend it to two timescales.

- *Comment on requirements for critical points:* It is also a widely accepted (but yet unproven) conjecture that the probability of ending in a poor local minimum is very small for sufficiently large networks, see e.g. [10, 17–20]. Thus, we can ensure that Eq. (12) and Eq. (13) really converges to a useful quantity (a high quality local minimum), if our networks are large enough.

Using these smoothness assumptions, it is not hard to ensure the required properties in (A2) and (A6) by relating the analysis of the loss surfaces of L_g and L_h to a stability analysis of the corresponding gradient systems. Further technical details can be found in Sect. A.6 in the appendix.

Ad (A5) and (A7): Transition Kernel and Bounded Iterates: The transition kernel is continuous (c.f. Sect. A.6 in the appendix). Boundedness of $\boldsymbol{\theta}_n$ and ω_n is achieved by weight decay terms in practice.

Proof of Theorem 1

Proof. In the previous paragraphs we discussed how the assumptions of Theorem 2 can be fulfilled.   □

Finite Greediness Is Sufficient to Converge to the Optimal Policy. Regularization terms are weighted by $(z_2)_n$ which converges to zero, therefore the optimal policies are the same as without the regularization. There exists an optimal policy π^* that is deterministic according to Proposition 4.4.3 in [36]. We want to ensure via a parameter $(z_1)_n$ that the policy becomes more greedy during learning. If the policy is not greedy enough, estimates of the action-value or the advantage function may misguide the algorithm and the optimal policy is not found. For example, huge negative rewards if not executing the optimal actions may avoid convergence to the optimal policy if the policy is not greedy enough. $(z_1)_n$ directly enters the policy according to Eq. (14). We show that we can estimate how large $(z_1)_n$ must become in order to ensure that Q-value and policy gradient methods converge to an optimal policy, if it is the local minimum of the loss function (we cannot ensure this). For policy gradients, the optimal actions receive always the largest gradient and the policy converges to the optimal policy. The required greediness will be measured by the parameter $\beta > 1$. *In practical applications we know that β exists but do not know its value, since it depends on characteristics of the task and the optimal Q-values.* For a more formal treatment c.f. Sect. A.7 in the appendix, especially Lemma 2.

Conclusions and Outlook. We showed local convergence of an abstract actor-critic setting and applied it to a version of PPO and RUDDER under practical assumptions. We intend to apply our results to similar practically relevant settings, e.g. the PPO algorithm discussed in [41]. A further future direction is to guarantee convergence to an optimal policy. It would also be interesting to relax some of the required assumptions on the loss functions (e.g. by extending the techniques in [30] to two timescales) or elaborate on convergence rates.

Acknowledgments. The ELLIS Unit Linz, the LIT AI Lab, the Institute for Machine Learning, are supported by the Federal State Upper Austria. IARAI is supported by Here Technologies. We thank the projects AI-MOTION (LIT-2018-6-YOU-212), DeepToxGen (LIT-2017-3-YOU-003), AI-SNN (LIT-2018-6-YOU-214), DeepFlood (LIT-2019-8-YOU-213), Medical Cognitive Computing Center (MC3), PRIMAL (FFG873979), S3AI (FFG-872172), DL for granular flow (FFG-871302), ELISE (H2020-ICT-2019-3 ID: 951847), AIDD (MSCA-ITN-2020 ID: 956832). We thank Janssen Pharmaceutica, UCB Biopharma SRL, Merck Healthcare KGaA, Audi.JKU Deep Learning Center, TGW LOGISTICS GROUP GMBH, Silicon Austria Labs (SAL), FILL Gesellschaft mbH, Anyline GmbH, Google Brain, ZF Friedrichshafen AG, Robert Bosch GmbH, Software Competence Center Hagenberg GmbH, TÜV Austria, and the NVIDIA Corporation.

A   Appendix

This appendix is meant to provide the reader with details and more precise descriptions of several parts of the main text, including e.g. exact formulations of the algorithms and more technical proof steps. Sections A.1 and A.2 provide the full formulation of the PPO and RUDDER algorithm, respectively, for which we ensure convergence. Section A.3 describes how the causality assumption leads to the formulas for PPO. In Sect. A.4 we discuss the precise formulations of the assumptions from [16]. Section A.5 gives further details about the probabilistic setup that we use to formalize the sampling process while Sect. A.6 gives formal details on how to ensure the assumptions from [16] to obtain our main convergence result Theorem 1. The last Sect. A.7 discusses arguments how to deduce the optimal policy from the approximate ones.

A.1   Further Details on PPO

Here we describe the minimization problem for the PPO setup in a more detailed way by including the exact expression for the gradients of the respective loss functions:

$$L_h(\boldsymbol{\theta}_n, \boldsymbol{\omega}_n, \boldsymbol{z}_n) = \mathrm{E}_{\tau \sim \pi(\boldsymbol{\theta}_n, \boldsymbol{z}_n)} \left[- G_0 + (z_2)_n \, \rho(\tau, \boldsymbol{\theta}_n, \boldsymbol{z}_n) \right], \tag{15}$$

$$h(\boldsymbol{\theta}_n, \boldsymbol{\omega}_n, \boldsymbol{z}_n) =$$

$$\mathrm{E}_{\tau \sim \pi(\boldsymbol{\theta}_n, \boldsymbol{z}_n)} \left[- \sum_{t=0}^{T} \nabla_{\boldsymbol{\theta}} \log \pi(a_t \mid s_t; \boldsymbol{\theta}_n, \boldsymbol{z}_n) \, (\hat{q}^{\pi}(s_t, a_t; \boldsymbol{\omega}_n) - \hat{v}^{\pi}(s_t; \boldsymbol{\omega}_n)) \right.$$

$$\left. + (z_2)_n \sum_{t=0}^{T} \nabla_{\boldsymbol{\theta}_n} \log \pi(a_t \mid s_t; \boldsymbol{\theta}_n, \boldsymbol{z}_n) \, \rho(\tau, \boldsymbol{\theta}_n, \boldsymbol{z}_n) + (z_2)_n \nabla_{\boldsymbol{\theta}_n} \rho(\tau, \boldsymbol{\theta}_n, \boldsymbol{z}_n) \right], \tag{16}$$

$$L_g^{\mathrm{TD}}(\boldsymbol{\theta}_n, \boldsymbol{\omega}_n, \boldsymbol{z}_n) = \mathrm{E}_{\tau \sim \pi(\boldsymbol{\theta}_n, \boldsymbol{z}_n)} \left[\frac{1}{2} \sum_{t=0}^{T} \left(\delta^{\mathrm{TD}}(t) \right)^2 \right], \tag{17}$$

$$f^{\mathrm{TD}}(\boldsymbol{\theta}_n, \boldsymbol{\omega}_n, \boldsymbol{z}_n) = \mathrm{E}_{\tau \sim \pi(\boldsymbol{\theta}_n, \boldsymbol{z}_n)} \left[- \sum_{t=0}^{T} \delta^{\mathrm{TD}}(t) \, \nabla_{\boldsymbol{\omega}_n} \hat{q}^{\pi}(s_t, a_t; \boldsymbol{\omega}_n) \right], \tag{18}$$

$$L_g^{\mathrm{MC}}(\boldsymbol{\theta}_n, \boldsymbol{\omega}_n, \boldsymbol{z}_n) = \mathrm{E}_{\tau \sim \pi(\boldsymbol{\theta}_n, \boldsymbol{z}_n)} \left[\frac{1}{2} \sum_{t=0}^{T} \left(G_t - \hat{q}^{\pi}(s_t, a_t; \boldsymbol{\omega}_n) \right)^2 \right], \tag{19}$$

$$f^{\mathrm{MC}}(\boldsymbol{\theta}_n, \boldsymbol{\omega}_n, \boldsymbol{z}_n) =$$

$$\mathrm{E}_{\tau \sim \pi(\boldsymbol{\theta}_n, \boldsymbol{z}_n)} \left[- \sum_{t=0}^{T} \left(G_t - \hat{q}^{\pi}(s_t, a_t; \boldsymbol{\omega}_n) \right) \nabla_{\boldsymbol{\omega}_n} \hat{q}^{\pi}(s_t, a_t; \boldsymbol{\omega}_n) \right], \tag{20}$$

$$\boldsymbol{\theta}_{n+1} = \boldsymbol{\theta}_n - a(n) \, \hat{h}(\boldsymbol{\theta}_n, \boldsymbol{\omega}_n, \boldsymbol{z}_n), \boldsymbol{\omega}_{n+1} = \boldsymbol{\omega}_n - b(n) \, \hat{f}(\boldsymbol{\theta}_n, \boldsymbol{\omega}_n, \boldsymbol{z}_n). \tag{21}$$

A.2   Further details on RUDDER

In a similar vein we present the minimization problem of RUDDER in more detail:

$$L_h(\boldsymbol{\theta}_n, \boldsymbol{\omega}_n, \boldsymbol{z}_n) =$$

$$\mathrm{E}_{\tau \sim \check{\pi}} \left[\frac{1}{2} \sum_{t=0}^{T} \left(R_{t+1}(\tau; \boldsymbol{\omega}_n) - \hat{q}(s_t, a_t; \boldsymbol{\theta}_n) \right)^2 + (z_2)_n \, \rho_{\boldsymbol{\theta}}(\tau, \boldsymbol{\theta}_n, \boldsymbol{z}_n) \right] \tag{22}$$

$$h(\boldsymbol{\theta}_n, \boldsymbol{\omega}_n, \boldsymbol{z}_n) =$$

$$\mathrm{E}_{\tau \sim \check{\pi}} \left[- \sum_{t=0}^{T} \left(R_{t+1}(\tau; \boldsymbol{\omega}_n) - \hat{q}(s_t, a_t; \boldsymbol{\theta}_n) \right) \nabla_{\boldsymbol{\theta}} \hat{q}(s_t, a_t; \boldsymbol{\theta}_n) + (z_2)_n \nabla_{\boldsymbol{\theta}} \rho_{\boldsymbol{\theta}}(\tau, \boldsymbol{\theta}_n, \boldsymbol{z}_n) \right] \tag{23}$$

$$L_g(\boldsymbol{\theta}_n, \boldsymbol{\omega}_n, \boldsymbol{z}_n) =$$

$$\mathrm{E}_{\tau \sim \pi(\boldsymbol{\theta}_n, \boldsymbol{z}_n)} \left[\frac{1}{2} \left(\sum_{t=0}^{T} \tilde{R}_{t+1} - g(\tau; \boldsymbol{\omega}_n) \right)^2 + (z_2)_n \, \rho_{\boldsymbol{\omega}}(\tau, \boldsymbol{\theta}_n, \boldsymbol{z}_n) \right] \tag{24}$$

$$f(\boldsymbol{\theta}_n, \boldsymbol{\omega}_n, \boldsymbol{z}_n) = \mathrm{E}_{\tau \sim \pi(\boldsymbol{\theta}_n, \boldsymbol{z}_n)} \left[- \left(\sum_{t=0}^{T} \tilde{R}_{t+1} - g(\tau; \boldsymbol{\omega}_n) \right) \nabla_{\boldsymbol{\omega}} g(\tau; \boldsymbol{\omega}_n) \right.$$

$$\left. + (z_2)_n \, \nabla_{\boldsymbol{\omega}} \rho_{\boldsymbol{\omega}}(\tau, \boldsymbol{\theta}_n, \boldsymbol{z}_n) \right], \tag{25}$$

$$\boldsymbol{\theta}_{n+1} = \boldsymbol{\theta}_n - a(n) \, \hat{h}(\boldsymbol{\theta}_n, \boldsymbol{\omega}_n, \boldsymbol{z}_n), \boldsymbol{\omega}_{n+1} = \boldsymbol{\omega}_n - b(n) \, \hat{f}(\boldsymbol{\theta}_n, \boldsymbol{\omega}_n, \boldsymbol{z}_n). \tag{26}$$

A.3   Causality and Reward-To-Go

This section is meant to provide the reader with more details concerning the causality assumption that leads to the formula for h in Eq. (15) for PPO. We can derive a formulation of the policy gradient with reward-to-go. For ease of notation, instead of using $\tilde{P}_\pi(\tau)$ as in previous sections, we here denote the probability of state-action sequence $\tau = \tau_{0,T} = (s_0, a_0, s_1, a_1, \ldots, s_T, a_T)$ with policy π as

$$p(\tau) = p(s_0)\, \pi(a_0 \mid s_0) \prod_{t=1}^{T} p(s_t \mid s_{t-1}, a_{t-1})\, \pi(a_t \mid s_t)$$

$$= p(s_0) \prod_{t=1}^{T} p(s_t \mid s_{t-1}, a_{t-1}) \prod_{t=0}^{T} \pi(a_t \mid s_t). \tag{27}$$

The probability of state-action sequence $\tau_{0,t} = (s_0, s_0, s_1, a_1, \ldots, s_t, a_t)$ with policy π is

$$p(\tau_{0,t}) = p(s_0)\, \pi(a_0 \mid s_0) \prod_{k=1}^{t} p(s_k \mid s_{k-1}, a_{k-1})\, \pi(a_k \mid s_k)$$

$$= p(s_0) \prod_{k=1}^{t} p(s_k \mid s_{k-1}, a_{k-1}) \prod_{k=0}^{t} \pi(a_k \mid s_k). \tag{28}$$

The probability of state-action sequence $\tau_{t+1,T} = (s_{t+1}, a_{t+1}, \ldots, s_T, a_T)$ with policy π given (s_t, a_t) is

$$p(\tau_{t+1,T} \mid s_t, a_t) = \prod_{k=t+1}^{T} p(s_k \mid s_{k-1}, a_{k-1})\, \pi(a_k \mid s_k)$$

$$= \prod_{k=t+1}^{T} p(s_k \mid s_{k-1}, a_{k-1}) \prod_{k=t+1}^{T} \pi(a_k \mid s_k). \tag{29}$$

The expectation of $\sum_{t=0}^{T} R_{t+1}$ is

$$\mathrm{E}_\pi \left[\sum_{t=0}^{T} R_{t+1} \right] = \sum_{t=0}^{T} \mathrm{E}_\pi \left[R_{t+1} \right]. \tag{30}$$

With $R_{t+1} \sim p(r_{t+1} \mid s_t, a_t)$, the random variable R_{t+1} depends only on (s_t, a_t). We define the expected reward $\mathrm{E}_{r_{t+1}}[R_{t+1} \mid s_t, a_t]$ as a function $r(s_t, a_t)$ of (s_t, a_t):

$$r(s_t, a_t) := \mathrm{E}_{r_{t+1}}\left[R_{t+1} \mid s_t, a_t \right] = \sum_{r_{t+1}} p(r_{t+1} \mid s_t, a_t)\, r_{t+1}. \tag{31}$$

Causality. We assume that the reward $R_{t+1} = R(s_t, a_t) \sim p(r_{t+1} \mid s_t, a_t)$ only depends on the past but not on the future. The state-action pair (s_t, a_t) is determined by the past and not by the future. Relevant is only how likely we observe (s_t, a_t) and not what we do afterwards.

Causality is derived from the Markov property of the MDP and means:

$$\mathrm{E}_{\tau \sim \pi} [R_{t+1}] = \mathrm{E}_{\tau_{0,t} \sim \pi} [R_{t+1}]. \tag{32}$$

That is

$$
\begin{aligned}
\mathrm{E}_{\tau \sim \pi} [R_{t+1}] &= \sum_{s_1} \sum_{a_1} \sum_{s_2} \sum_{a_2} \cdots \sum_{s_T} \sum_{a_T} p(\tau)\, r(s_t, a_t) \\
&= \sum_{s_1} \sum_{a_1} \sum_{s_2} \sum_{a_2} \cdots \sum_{s_T} \sum_{a_T} \prod_{l=1}^{T} p(s_l \mid s_{l-1}, a_{l-1}) \prod_{l=1}^{T} \pi(a_l \mid s_l)\, r(s_t, a_t) \\
&= \sum_{s_1} \sum_{a_1} \sum_{s_2} \sum_{a_2} \cdots \sum_{s_t} \sum_{a_t} \prod_{l=1}^{t} p(s_l \mid s_{l-1}, a_{l-1}) \prod_{l=1}^{t} \pi(a_l \mid s_l)\, r(s_t, a_t) \\
&\quad \sum_{s_{t+1}} \sum_{a_{t+1}} \sum_{s_{t+2}} \sum_{a_{t+2}} \cdots \sum_{s_T} \sum_{a_T} \prod_{l=t+1}^{T} p(s_l \mid s_{l-1}, a_{l-1}) \prod_{l=t+1}^{T} \pi(a_l \mid s_l) \\
&= \sum_{s_1} \sum_{a_1} \sum_{s_2} \sum_{a_2} \cdots \sum_{s_t} \sum_{a_t} \prod_{l=1}^{t} p(s_l \mid s_{l-1}, a_{l-1}) \prod_{l=1}^{t} \pi(a_l \mid s_l)\, r(s_t, a_t) \\
&= \mathrm{E}_{\tau_{0,t} \sim \pi} [R_{t+1}]. \tag{33}
\end{aligned}
$$

Policy Gradient Theorem. We now assume that the policy π is parametrized by $\boldsymbol{\theta}$, that is, $\pi(a_t \mid s_t) = \pi(a_t \mid s_t; \boldsymbol{\theta})$. We need the gradient with respect to $\boldsymbol{\theta}$ of $\prod_{t=a}^{b} \pi(a_t \mid s_t)$:

$$
\begin{aligned}
\nabla_\theta \prod_{t=a}^{b} \pi(a_t \mid s_t; \boldsymbol{\theta}) &= \sum_{s=a}^{b} \prod_{t=a, t \neq s}^{b} \pi(a_t \mid s_t; \boldsymbol{\theta})\, \nabla_\theta \pi(a_s \mid s_s; \boldsymbol{\theta}) \\
&= \prod_{t=a}^{b} \pi(a_t \mid s_t; \boldsymbol{\theta}) \sum_{s=a}^{b} \frac{\nabla_\theta \pi(a_s \mid s_s; \boldsymbol{\theta})}{\pi(a_s \mid s_s; \boldsymbol{\theta})} \\
&= \prod_{t=a}^{b} \pi(a_t \mid s_t; \boldsymbol{\theta}) \sum_{s=a}^{b} \nabla_\theta \log \pi(a_s \mid s_s; \boldsymbol{\theta}). \tag{34}
\end{aligned}
$$

It follows that

$$\nabla_\theta \mathrm{E}_\pi [R_{t+1}] = \mathrm{E}_\pi \left[\sum_{s=1}^{t} \nabla_\theta \log \pi(a_s \mid s_s; \boldsymbol{\theta})\, R_{t+1} \right]. \tag{35}$$

We only have to consider the **reward to go**. Since a_0 does not depend on π, we have $\nabla_\theta E_\pi [R_1] = 0$. Therefore

$$\nabla_\theta E_\pi \left[\sum_{t=0}^{T} R_{t+1} \right] = \sum_{t=0}^{T} \nabla_\theta E_\pi [R_{t+1}]$$

$$= E_\pi \left[\sum_{t=1}^{T} \sum_{k=1}^{t} \nabla_\theta \log \pi(a_k \mid s_k; \boldsymbol{\theta}) \, R_{t+1} \right]$$

$$= E_\pi \left[\sum_{k=1}^{T} \sum_{t=k}^{T} \nabla_\theta \log \pi(a_k \mid s_k; \boldsymbol{\theta}) \, R_{t+1} \right]$$

$$= E_\pi \left[\sum_{k=1}^{T} \nabla_\theta \log \pi(a_k \mid s_k; \boldsymbol{\theta}) \sum_{t=k}^{T} R_{t+1} \right]$$

$$= E_\pi \left[\sum_{k=1}^{T} \nabla_\theta \log \pi(a_k \mid s_k; \boldsymbol{\theta}) \, G_k \right]. \tag{36}$$

We can express this by Q-values.

$$E_\pi \left[\sum_{k=1}^{T} \nabla_\theta \log \pi(a_k \mid s_k; \boldsymbol{\theta}) \, G_k \right]$$

$$= \sum_{k=1}^{T} E_\pi [\nabla_\theta \log \pi(a_k \mid s_k; \boldsymbol{\theta}) \, G_k]$$

$$= \sum_{k=1}^{T} E_{\tau_{0,k} \sim \pi} [\nabla_\theta \log \pi(a_k \mid s_k; \boldsymbol{\theta}) \, E_{\tau_{k+1,T} \sim \pi} [G_k \mid s_k, a_k]]$$

$$= \sum_{k=1}^{T} E_{\tau_{0,k} \sim \pi} [\nabla_\theta \log \pi(a_k \mid s_k; \boldsymbol{\theta}) \, q^\pi(s_k, a_k)]$$

$$= E_{\tau \sim \pi} \left[\sum_{k=1}^{T} \nabla_\theta \log \pi(a_k \mid s_k; \boldsymbol{\theta}) \, q^\pi(s_k, a_k) \right]. \tag{37}$$

We have finally:

$$\nabla_\theta E_\pi \left[\sum_{t=0}^{T} R_{t+1} \right] = E_{\tau \sim \pi} \left[\sum_{k=1}^{T} \nabla_\theta \log \pi(a_k \mid s_k; \boldsymbol{\theta}) \, q^\pi(s_k, a_k) \right]. \tag{38}$$

A.4   Precise statement of Assumptions

Here we provide a precise formulation of the assumptions from [16]. The formulation we use here is mostly taken from [14]:

(A1) *Assumptions on the controlled Markov processes:* The controlled Markov process z takes values in a compact metric space S. It is controlled by the iterate sequences $\boldsymbol{\theta}_n\}$ and $\boldsymbol{\omega}_n$ and furthermore $\boldsymbol{z}_n$ by a random process $\boldsymbol{a}_n$ taking values in a compact metric space W. For B Borel in S the $\boldsymbol{z}_n$ dynamics for $n \geqslant 0$ is determined by a transition kernel $\tilde{p}$:

$$\mathrm{P}(\boldsymbol{z}_{n+1} \in B | \boldsymbol{z}_l, \boldsymbol{a}_l, \boldsymbol{\theta}_l, \boldsymbol{\omega}_l, l \leqslant n) = \int_B \tilde{p}(\mathrm{d}\boldsymbol{z} | \boldsymbol{z}_n, \boldsymbol{a}_n, \boldsymbol{\theta}_n, \boldsymbol{\omega}_n). \qquad (39)$$

(A2) *Assumptions on the update functions:* $h : \mathbb{R}^{m+k} \times S^{(1)} \to \mathbb{R}^m$ is jointly continuous as well as Lipschitz in its first two arguments, and uniformly w.r.t. the third. This means that for all $\boldsymbol{z} \in S$:

$$\|h(\boldsymbol{\theta}, \boldsymbol{\omega}, \boldsymbol{z}) - h(\boldsymbol{\theta}', \boldsymbol{w}', \boldsymbol{z})\| \leqslant L^{(1)} \left(\|\boldsymbol{\theta} - \boldsymbol{\theta}'\| + \|\boldsymbol{\omega} - \boldsymbol{\omega}'\|\right). \qquad (40)$$

Similarly for f, where the Lipschitz constant is $L^{(2)}$.

(A3) *Assumptions on the additive noise:* For $i = 1, 2$, $\{(\boldsymbol{m}_i)_n\}$ are martingale difference sequences with bounded second moments. More precisely, $(\boldsymbol{m}_i)_n$ are martingale difference sequences w.r.t. increasing σ-fields

$$\mathfrak{F}_n = \sigma(\boldsymbol{\theta}_l, \boldsymbol{\omega}_l, (\boldsymbol{m}_1)_l, (\boldsymbol{m}_2)_l, \boldsymbol{z}_l, l \leqslant n), \qquad (41)$$

satisfying $\mathrm{E}\left[\|(\boldsymbol{m}_i)_n\|^2 \mid \mathfrak{F}_n\right] \leqslant B_i$ for $n \geqslant 0$ and given constants B_i.

(A4) *Assumptions on the learning rates:*

$$\sum_n a(n) = \infty, \quad \sum_n a^2(n) < \infty, \qquad (42)$$

$$\sum_n b(n) = \infty, \quad \sum_n b^2(n) < \infty, \qquad (43)$$

and $a(n) = \mathrm{o}(b(n))$. Furthermore, $a(n), b(n), n \geqslant 0$ are non-increasing.

(A5) *Assumptions on the transition kernels:* The state-action map

$$S \times W \times \mathbb{R}^{m+k} \ni (\boldsymbol{z}, \boldsymbol{a}, \boldsymbol{\theta}, \boldsymbol{\omega}) \mapsto \tilde{p}(\mathrm{d}\boldsymbol{y} \mid \boldsymbol{z}, \boldsymbol{a}, \boldsymbol{\theta}, \boldsymbol{\omega}) \qquad (44)$$

is continuous (the topology on the spaces of probability measures is induced by weak convergence).

(A6) *Assumptions on the associated ODEs:* We consider occupation measures which intuitively give for the controlled Markov process the probability or density to observe a particular state-action pair from $S \times W$ for given $\boldsymbol{\theta}$ and $\boldsymbol{\omega}$ and a given control. A precise definition of these occupation measures can be found e.g. on page 68 of [7] or page 5 in [16]. We have following assumptions:

- We assume that there exists only one such ergodic occupation measure for $\boldsymbol{z}_n$ on $S \times W$, denoted by $\Gamma_{\boldsymbol{\theta}, \boldsymbol{\omega}}$. A main reason for assuming uniqueness is that it enables us to deal with ODEs instead of differential inclusions. Moreover, set

$$\tilde{f}(\boldsymbol{\theta}, \boldsymbol{\omega}) = \int f(\boldsymbol{\theta}, \boldsymbol{\omega}, \boldsymbol{z}) \, \Gamma_{\boldsymbol{\theta}, \boldsymbol{\omega}}(\mathrm{d}\boldsymbol{z}, W). \qquad (45)$$

- We assume that for $\boldsymbol{\theta} \in \mathbb{R}^m$, the ODE $\dot{\boldsymbol{\omega}}(t) = \tilde{f}(\boldsymbol{\theta}, \boldsymbol{\omega}(t))$ has a unique asymptotically stable equilibrium $\boldsymbol{\lambda}(\boldsymbol{\theta})$ with attractor set B_θ such that $\boldsymbol{\lambda} : \mathbb{R}^m \to \mathbb{R}^k$ is a Lipschitz map with global Lipschitz constant.
- The Lyapunov function $V(\boldsymbol{\theta}, .)$ associated to $\boldsymbol{\lambda}(\boldsymbol{\theta})$ is continuously differentiable.
- Next define

$$\tilde{h}(\boldsymbol{\theta}) = \int h(\boldsymbol{\theta}, \boldsymbol{\lambda}(\boldsymbol{\theta}), \boldsymbol{z}) \, \Gamma_{\boldsymbol{\theta}, \boldsymbol{\lambda}(\boldsymbol{\theta})}(\mathrm{d}\boldsymbol{z}, W). \tag{46}$$

We assume that the ODE $\dot{\boldsymbol{\theta}}(t) = \tilde{h}(\boldsymbol{\theta}(t))$ has a global attractor set A.
- For all $\boldsymbol{\theta}$, with probability 1, $\boldsymbol{\omega}_n$ for $n \geqslant 1$ belongs to a compact subset Q_θ of B_θ "eventually".

This assumption is an adapted version of (A6)' of [16], to avoid too many technicalities (e.g. in [16] two controls are used, which we avoid here to not overload notation).

(A7) *Assumption of bounded iterates:* $\sup_n \|\boldsymbol{\theta}_n\| < \infty$ and $\sup_n \|\boldsymbol{\omega}_n\| < \infty$ a.s.

A.5   Further Details concerning the Sampling Process

Let us formulate the construction of the sampling process in more detail: We introduced the function S_π in the main paper as follows:

$$S_\pi : \Omega \to \tilde{\Omega}_\pi, \quad x \mapsto \underset{\tau \in \tilde{\Omega}_\pi}{\mathrm{argmax}} \left\{ \sum_{\eta \leq \tau} \tilde{P}_\pi(\eta) \leq x \right\}. \tag{47}$$

Now S_π basically divides the interval $[0, 1]$ into finitely many disjoint subintervals, such that the i-th subinterval I_i maps to the i-th element $\tau_i \in \tilde{\Omega}_\pi$, and additionally the length of I_i is given by $\tilde{P}_\pi(\tau_i)$. S_π is measurable, because the pre-image of any element of the sigma-algebra $\mathfrak{A}_\pi$ wrt. S_π is just a finite union of subintervals of $[0, 1]$, which is clearly contained in the Borel-algebra. Basically S_π just describes how to get one sample from a multinomial distribution with (finitely many) probabilities $\tilde{P}_\pi(\tau)$, where $\tau \in \tilde{\Omega}_\pi$. Compare with inverse transform sampling, e.g. Theorem 2.1.10. in [9] and applications thereof. For the reader's convenience let us briefly recall this important concept here in a formal way:

Lemma 1 (Inverse transform sampling). *Let X have continuous cumulative distribution $F_X(x)$ and define the random variable Y as $Y = F_X(X)$. Then Y is uniformly distributed on $(0, 1)$.*

A.6   Further Details for Proof of Theorem 1

Here we provide further technical details needed to ensure the assumptions stated before to prove our main theorem Theorem 1.

Ad (A1): Assumptions on the Controlled Markov Processes: Let us start by discussing more details for controlled processes that appear in the PPO and RUDDER setting. Let us focus on the process related to $(z_1)_n$: Let $\beta > 1$ and let the real sequence z_n be defined by $(z_1)_1 = 1$ and $(z_1)_{n+1} = (1 - \frac{1}{\beta})(z_1)_n + 1$. The z_n's are nothing more but the partial sums of a geometric series converging to β.

The sequence $(z_1)_n$ can also be interpreted as a time-homogeneous Markov process $(\boldsymbol{z}_1)_n$ with transition probabilities given by

$$P(z, y) = \delta_{(1 - \frac{1}{\beta})z+1}, \tag{48}$$

where δ denotes the Dirac measure, and with the compact interval $[1, \beta]$ as its range. We use the standard notation for discrete time Markov processes, described in detail e.g. in [13]. Its unique invariant measure is clearly δ_β. So integrating wrt. this invariant measure will in our case just correspond to taking the limit $(z_1)_n \to \beta$.

Ad (A2): h and f are Lipschitz: By the mean value theorem it is enough to show that the derivatives wrt. $\boldsymbol{\theta}$ and $\boldsymbol{\omega}$ are bounded uniformly wrt. $\boldsymbol{z}$. We only show details for f, since for h similar considerations apply. By the explicit formula for L_g, we see that $f(\boldsymbol{\theta}, \boldsymbol{\omega}, \boldsymbol{z})$ can be written as:

$$\sum_{\substack{s_1, \dots, s_T \\ a_1, \dots, a_T}} \prod_{t=1}^{T} p(s_t \mid s_{t-1}, a_{t-1}) \pi(a_t \mid s_t, \boldsymbol{\theta}, \boldsymbol{z}) \nabla_\omega \Phi(g(\tau; \boldsymbol{\omega}, \boldsymbol{z}), \tau, \boldsymbol{\theta}, \boldsymbol{\omega}, \boldsymbol{z}). \tag{49}$$

The claim can now be readily deduced from the assumptions (L1)–(L3).

Ad (A3): Martingale Difference Property and Estimates: From the results in the main paper on the probabilistic setting, $(\boldsymbol{m}_1)_{n+1}$ and $(\boldsymbol{m}_2)_{n+1}$ can easily be seen to be martingale difference sequences with respect to their filtrations $\mathfrak{F}_n$. Indeed, the sigma algebras created by $\boldsymbol{\omega}_n$ and $\boldsymbol{\theta}_n$ already describe $\tilde{\mathfrak{A}}_{\pi_{\theta_n}}$, and thus:

$$\mathrm{E}[(\boldsymbol{m}_i)_{n+1}|\mathfrak{F}_n] = \mathrm{E}[\hat{f}(\boldsymbol{\theta}_n, \boldsymbol{\omega}_n, \boldsymbol{z}_n)|\mathfrak{F}_n] - \mathrm{E}[f(\boldsymbol{\theta}_n, \boldsymbol{\omega}_n, \boldsymbol{z}_n)] = 0. \tag{50}$$

It remains to show that

$$\mathrm{E}[\|(\boldsymbol{m}_i)_{n+1}\|^2|\mathfrak{F}_n] \leq B_i \text{ for } i = 1, 2. \tag{51}$$

This, however, is also clear, since all the involved expressions are bounded uniformly again by the assumptions (L1)–(L3) on the losses (e.g. one can observe this by writing down the involved expressions explicitly as indicated in the previous point (A2)).

Ad (A4): Assumptions on the Learning Rates: These standard assumptions are taken for granted.

Ad (A5):Transition Kernels: The continuity of the transition kernels is clear from Eq. (48) (continuity is wrt. to the weak topology in the space of probability measures. So in our case, this again boils down to using continuity of the test functions).

Ad (A6): Stability Properties of the ODEs:
- By the explanations for (A1) we mentioned that integrating wrt. the ergodic occupation measure in our case corresponds to taking the limit $z_n \to z$ (since our Markov processes can be interpreted as sequences). Thus $\tilde{f}(\boldsymbol{\theta}, \boldsymbol{\omega}) = f(\boldsymbol{\theta}, \boldsymbol{\omega}, z)$. In the sequel we will also use the following abbreviations: $f(\boldsymbol{\theta}, \boldsymbol{\omega}) = f(\boldsymbol{\theta}, \boldsymbol{\omega}, z)$, $h(\boldsymbol{\theta}, \boldsymbol{\omega}) = h(\boldsymbol{\theta}, \boldsymbol{\omega}, z)$, etc. Now consider the ODE

$$\dot{\boldsymbol{\omega}}(t) = f(\boldsymbol{\theta}, \boldsymbol{\omega}(t)), \tag{52}$$

where $\boldsymbol{\theta}$ is fixed. Equation (52) can be seen as a gradient system for the function L_g. By standard results on gradient systems (cf. e.g. Sect. 4 in [1] for a nice summary), which guarantee equivalence between strict local minima of the loss function and asymptotically stable points of the associated gradient system, we can use the assumptions (L1)–(L3) and the remarks thereafter from the main paper to ensure that there exists a unique asymptotically stable equilibrium $\boldsymbol{\lambda}(\boldsymbol{\theta})$ of Eq. (52).
- The fact that $\boldsymbol{\lambda}(\boldsymbol{\theta})$ is smooth enough can be deduced by the Implicit Function Theorem as discussed in the main paper.
- For Eq. (52) $L_g(\boldsymbol{\theta}, \boldsymbol{\omega}) - L_g(\boldsymbol{\theta}, \boldsymbol{\lambda}(\boldsymbol{\theta}))$ can be taken as associated Lyapunov function $V_{\boldsymbol{\theta}}(\boldsymbol{\omega})$, and thus $V_{\boldsymbol{\theta}}(\boldsymbol{\omega})$ clearly is differentiable wrt. $\boldsymbol{\omega}$ for any $\boldsymbol{\theta}$.
- The slow ODE $\dot{\boldsymbol{\theta}}(t) = h(\boldsymbol{\theta}(t), \boldsymbol{\lambda}(\boldsymbol{\theta}(t)))$ also has a unique asymptotically stable fixed point, which again is guaranteed by our assumptions and the standard results on gradient systems.

Ad (A7): Assumption of Bounded Iterates: This follows from the assumptions on the loss functions.

A.7   Finite Greediness is Sufficient to Converge to the Optimal Policy

Here we provide details on how the optimal policy can be deduced using only a finite parameter $\beta > 1$. The Q-values for policy π are:

$$q^{\pi}(s_t, a_t) = \mathrm{E}_{\pi} \left[\sum_{\tau=t}^{T} R_{\tau+1} \mid s_t, a_t \right]$$

$$= \sum_{\substack{s_t, \dots, s_T \\ a_t, \dots, a_T}} \prod_{\tau=t}^{T-1} p(s_{\tau+1} \mid s_\tau, a_\tau) \prod_{\tau=t}^{T} \pi(a_\tau \mid s_\tau) \sum_{\tau=t}^{T} R_{\tau+1}. \tag{53}$$

The optimal policy π^* is known to be deterministic $\left(\prod_{t=1}^{T} \pi^*(a_t \mid s_t) \in \{0,1\} \right)$. Let us assume that the optimal policy is also unique. Then we are going to show the following result:

Lemma 2. *For* $i_{\max} = \arg\max_i q^{\pi^*}(s, a^i)$ *and* $v^{\pi^*}(s) = \max_i q^{\pi^*}(s, a^i)$. *We define*

$$0 < \epsilon < \min_{s, i \neq i_{\max}} (v^{\pi^*}(s) - q^{\pi^*}(s, a^i)), \tag{54}$$

We assume a function $\psi(s, a^i)$ *that defines the actual policy* π *via*

$$\pi(a^i \mid s; \beta) = \frac{\exp(\beta \, \psi(s, a^i))}{\sum_j \exp(\beta \, \psi(s, a^j))}. \tag{55}$$

We assume that the function ψ *already identified the optimal actions, which will occur during learning at some time point when the policy is getting more greedy:*

$$0 < \delta < \min_{s, i \neq i_{\max}} (\psi(s, a^{i_{\max}}) - \psi(s, a^i)). \tag{56}$$

Hence,

$$\lim_{\beta \to \infty} \pi(a^i \mid s; \beta) = \pi^*(a^i \mid s). \tag{57}$$

We assume that

$$\beta >$$
$$\max \left(\frac{\log(|\mathcal{A}| - 1)}{\delta}, -\log \left(\frac{\epsilon}{2T \, (|\mathcal{A}| - 1) \, |\mathcal{S}|^T \, |\mathcal{A}|^T \, (T+1) \, K_R} \right) / \delta \right). \tag{58}$$

Then we can make the statement for all s:

$$\forall_{j, j \neq i} : \quad q^{\pi}(s, a^i) > q^{\pi}(s, a^j) \;\Rightarrow\; i = i_{\max}, \tag{59}$$

therefore the Q-values $q^{\pi}(s, a^i)$ *determine the optimal policy as the action with the largest Q-value can be chosen.*

More importantly, β *is large enough to allow Q-value based methods and policy gradients converge to the optimal policy if it is the local minimum of the loss functions. For Q-value based methods the optimal action can be determined if the optimal policy is the minimum of the loss functions. For policy gradients the optimal action receives always the largest gradient and the policy converges to the optimal policy.*

Proof. We already discussed that the optimal policy π^* is known to be deterministic $\left(\prod_{t=1}^{T} \pi^*(a_t \mid s_t) \in \{0,1\}\right)$. Let us assume that the optimal policy is also unique. Since

$$\pi(a^i \mid s; \beta) = \frac{\exp(\beta \ (\psi(s, a^i) - \psi(s, a^{i_{\max}})))}{\sum_j \exp(\beta \ \psi(s, a^j) - \psi(s, a^{i_{\max}}))}, \tag{60}$$

we have

$$\begin{aligned}
\pi(a^{i_{\max}} \mid s; \beta) &= \frac{1}{1 + \sum_{j, j \neq i_{\max}} \exp(\beta \ \psi(s, a^j) - \psi(s, a^{i_{\max}}))} \\
&> \frac{1}{1 + (|\mathcal{A}| - 1) \ \exp(-\beta \ \delta)} \\
&= 1 - \frac{(|\mathcal{A}| - 1) \ \exp(-\beta \ \delta)}{1 + (|\mathcal{A}| - 1) \ \exp(-\beta \ \delta)} \\
&> 1 - (|\mathcal{A}| - 1) \ \exp(-\beta \ \delta)
\end{aligned} \tag{61}$$

and for $i \neq i_{\max}$

$$\begin{aligned}
\pi(a^i \mid s; \beta) &= \frac{\exp(\beta \ (\psi(s, a^i) - \psi(s, a^{i_{\max}})))}{1 + \sum_{j, j \neq i_{\max}} \exp(\beta \ \psi(s, a^j) - \psi(s, a^{i_{\max}}))} \\
&< \exp(-\beta \ \delta).
\end{aligned} \tag{62}$$

For $\prod_{t=1}^{T} \pi^*(a_t \mid s_t) = 1$, we have

$$\begin{aligned}
\prod_{t=1}^{T} \pi(a_t \mid s_t) &> (1 - (|\mathcal{A}| - 1) \ \exp(-\beta \ \delta))^T \\
&> 1 - T \ (|\mathcal{A}| - 1) \ \exp(-\beta \ \delta),
\end{aligned} \tag{63}$$

where in the last step we used that $(|\mathcal{A}| - 1) \exp(-\beta\delta) < 1$ by definition of β in (58) so that an application of Bernoulli's inequality is justified. For $\prod_{t=1}^{T} \pi^*(a_t \mid s_t) = 0$, we have

$$\prod_{t=1}^{T} \pi(a_t \mid s_t) < \exp(-\beta \ \delta). \tag{64}$$

Therefore

$$\left| \prod_{t=1}^{T} \pi^*(a_t \mid s_t) - \prod_{t=1}^{T} \pi(a_t \mid s_t) \right| < T \ (|\mathcal{A}| - 1) \ \exp(-\beta \ \delta). \tag{65}$$

Using Eq. (65) and the definition of β in Eq. (58) we get:

$$\left| q^{\pi^*}(s, a^i) - q^\pi(s, a^i) \right|$$

$$= \left| \sum_{\substack{s_1,..,s_T \\ a_1,...,a_T}} \prod_{t=1}^T p(s_t \mid s_{t-1}, a_{t-1}) \left(\prod_{t=1}^T \pi^*(a_t \mid s_t) - \prod_{t=1}^T \pi(a_t \mid s_t) \right) \sum_{t=0}^T R_{t+1} \right|$$

$$< \sum_{\substack{s_1,..,s_T \\ a_1,...,a_T}} \prod_{t=1}^T p(s_t \mid s_{t-1}, a_{t-1}) \left| \prod_{t=1}^T \pi^*(a_t \mid s_t) - \prod_{t=1}^T \pi(a_t \mid s_t) \right| (T+1) \, K_R$$

$$< \sum_{\substack{s_1,..,s_T \\ a_1,...,a_T}} \left| \prod_{t=1}^T \pi^*(a_t \mid s_t) - \prod_{t=1}^T \pi(a_t \mid s_t) \right| (T+1) \, K_R$$

$$< |\mathcal{S}|^T \, |\mathcal{A}|^T \, \frac{\epsilon}{2|\mathcal{S}|^T \, |\mathcal{A}|^T \, (T+1) \, K_R} \, (T+1) \, K_R \;=\; \epsilon/2. \tag{66}$$

Now from the condition that $q^\pi(s, a^i) > q^\pi(s, a^j)$ for all $j \neq i$ we can conclude that

$$q^{\pi^*}(s, a^j) - q^{\pi^*}(s, a^i)$$
$$< (q^\pi(s, a^j) + \epsilon/2) - (q^\pi(s, a^i) - \epsilon/2) < \epsilon \tag{67}$$

for all $j \neq i$. Thus for $j \neq i$ it follows that $j \neq i_{\max}$ and consequently $i = i_{\max}$.   □

References

1. Absil, P.A., Kurdyka, K.: On the stable equilibrium points of gradient systems. Syst. Control Lett. **55**(7), 573–577 (2006)
2. Arjona-Medina, J.A., Gillhofer, M., Widrich, M., Unterthiner, T., Brandstetter, J., Hochreiter, S.: RUDDER: Return decomposition for delayed rewards (2018). ArXiv https://arxiv.org/abs/1806.07857
3. Arjona-Medina, J.A., Gillhofer, M., Widrich, M., Unterthiner, T., Brandstetter, J., Hochreiter, S.: RUDDER: return decomposition for delayed rewards. In: Advances in Neural Information Processing Systems, vol. 33 (2019). ArXiv https://arxiv.org/abs/1806.07857
4. Bakker, B.: Reinforcement learning by backpropagation through an LSTM model/critic. In: IEEE International Symposium on Approximate Dynamic Programming and Reinforcement Learning, pp. 127–134 (2007). https://doi.org/10.1109/ADPRL.2007.368179
5. Bertsekas, D.P., Tsitsiklis, J.N.: Neuro-Dynamic Programming. Athena Scientific, Belmont (1996)
6. Bhatnagar, S., Prasad, H.L., Prashanth, L.A.: Stochastic Recursive Algorithms for Optimization. Lecture Notes in Control and Information Sciences, 1st edn., p. 302. Springer, London (2013). https://doi.org/10.1007/978-1-4471-4285-0
7. Stochastic Approximation. TRM, vol. 48. Hindustan Book Agency, Gurgaon (2008). https://doi.org/10.1007/978-93-86279-38-5

8. Borkar, V.S., Meyn, S.P.: The O.D.E. method for convergence of stochastic approximation and reinforcement learning. SIAM J. Control Optim. **38**(2), 447–469 (2000). https://doi.org/10.1137/S0363012997331639

9. Casella, G., Berger, R.L.: Statistical Inference. Wadsworth and Brooks/Cole, Stanley (2002)

10. Choromanska, A., Henaff, M., Mathieu, M., Arous, G.B., LeCun, Y.: The loss surfaces of multilayer networks. In: Proceedings of the Eighteenth International Conference on Artificial Intelligence and Statistics, pp. 192–204 (2015)

11. Dayan, P.: The convergence of TD(λ) for general λ. Mach. Learn. **8**, 341 (1992)

12. Fan, J., Wang, Z., Xie, Y., Yang, Z.: A theoretical analysis of deep q-learning. CoRR abs/1901.00137 (2020)

13. Hairer, M.: Ergodic properties of Markov processes. In: Lecture Notes (2018)

14. Heusel, M., Ramsauer, H., Unterthiner, T., Nessler, B., Klambauer, G., Hochreiter, S.: GANs trained by a two time-scale update rule converge to a Nash equilibrium. In: Guyon, I., et al. (eds.) Advances in Neural Information Processing Systems, vol. 30. pp. 6626–6637. Curran Associates, Inc. (2017). Preprint arXiv:1706.08500

15. Jin, C., Netrapalli, P., Jordan, M.I.: Minmax optimization: Stable limit points of gradient descent ascent are locally optimal. arXiv:1902.00618 (2019)

16. Karmakar, P., Bhatnagar, S.: Two time-scale stochastic approximation with controlled Markov noise and off-policy temporal-difference learning. Math. Oper. Res. (2017). https://doi.org/10.1287/moor.2017.0855

17. Kawaguchi, K.: Deep learning without poor local minima. In: Lee, D.D., Sugiyama, M., Luxburg, U.V., Guyon, I., Garnett, R. (eds.) Advances in Neural Information Processing Systems, vol. 29. pp. 586–594 (2016)

18. Kawaguchi, K., Bengio, Y.: Depth with nonlinearity creates no bad local minima in ResNets. Neural Netw. **118**, 167–174 (2019)

19. Kawaguchi, K., Huang, J., Kaelbling, L.P.: Effect of depth and width on local minima in deep learning. Neural Comput. **31**(6), 1462–1498 (2019)

20. Kawaguchi, K., Kaelbling, L.P., Bengio, Y.: Generalization in deep learning. arXiv:1710.05468 (2017)

21. Konda, V.R., Borkar, V.S.: Actor-critic-type learning algorithms for Markov decision processes. SIAM J. Control Optim. **38**(1), 94–123 (1999). https://doi.org/10.1137/S036301299731669X

22. Konda, V.R., Tsitsiklis, J.N.: Actor-critic algorithms. In: Advances in Neural Information Processing Systems, pp. 1008–1014 (2000)

23. Konda, V.R., Tsitsiklis, J.N.: On actor-critic algorithms. SIAM J. Control Optim. **42**(4), 1143–1166 (2003). https://doi.org/10.1137/S0363012901385691

24. Kushner, H.J., Clark, D.S.: Stochastic Approximation Methods for Constrained and Unconstrained Systems. Applied Mathematical Sciences. Springer, New York (1978). https://doi.org/10.1007/978-1-4684-9352-8

25. Kushner, H.J., Yin, G.G.: Stochastic Approximation and Recursive Algorithms and Applications. Stochastic Modelling and Applied Probability. Springer, New York (2003). https://doi.org/10.1007/b97441

26. Lin, T., Jin, C., Jordan, M.I.: On gradient descent ascent for nonconvex-concave minimax problems. arXiv:1906.00331 (2019)

27. Liu, B., Cai, Q., Yang, Z., Wang, Z.: Neural proximal/trust region policy optimization attains globally optimal policy. In: Advances in Neural Information Processing Systems, vol. 33. arXiv:1906.10306 (2019)

28. Maei, H.R., Szepesvári, C., Bhatnagar, S., Precup, D., Silver, D., Sutton, R.S.: Convergent temporal-difference learning with arbitrary smooth function approximation. In: Bengio, Y., Schuurmans, D., Lafferty, J.D., Williams, C.K.I., Culotta, A. (eds.) Advances in Neural Information Processing Systems, vol. 22. pp. 1204–1212. Curran Associates, Inc. (2009)

29. Mazumdar, E.V., Jordan, M.I., Sastry, S.S.: On finding local Nash equilibria (and only local Nash equilibria) in zero-sum games. arXiv:1901.00838 (2019)

30. Metrikopoulos, P., Hallak, N., Kavis, A., Cevher, V.: On the almost sure convergence of stochastic gradient descent in non-convex problems. In: Advances in Neural Information Processing Systems, vol. 34 (2020). arXiv:2006.11144

31. Mnih, V., et al.: Playing atari with deep reinforcement learning. arXiv:1312.5602 (2013)

32. Mnih, V., et al.: Human-level control through deep reinforcement learning. Nature **518**(7540), 529–533 (2015). https://doi.org/10.1038/nature14236

33. Munro, P.W.: A dual back-propagation scheme for scalar reinforcement learning. In: Proceedings of the Ninth Annual Conference of the Cognitive Science Society, Seattle, WA, pp. 165–176 (1987)

34. Open, A.I., et al.: Dota 2 with large scale deep reinforcement learning. arXiv:1912.06680 (2019)

35. Patil, V.P., et al.: Align-RUDDER: learning from few demonstrations by reward redistribution. arXiv:2009.14108 (2020)

36. Puterman, M.L.: Markov Decision Processes, 2nd edn. Wiley, Hoboken (2005)

37. Robbins, H., Monro, S.: A stochastic approximation method. Ann. Math. Stat. **22**(3), 400–407 (1951). https://doi.org/10.1214/aoms/1177729586

38. Robinson, A.J.: Dynamic error propagation networks. Ph.D. thesis, Trinity Hall and Cambridge University Engineering Department (1989)

39. Robinson, T., Fallside, F.: Dynamic reinforcement driven error propagation networks with application to game playing. In: Proceedings of the 11th Conference of the Cognitive Science Society, Ann Arbor, pp. 836–843 (1989)

40. Schulman, J., Levine, S., Moritz, P., Jordan, M.I., Abbeel, P.: Trust region policy optimization. arXiv:1502.05477 (2015). 31st International Conference on Machine Learning (ICML), Proceedings of Machine Learning Research, vol. 37

41. Schulman, J., Wolski, F., Dhariwal, P., Radford, A., Klimov, O.: Proximal policy optimization algorithms. arXiv:1707.06347 (2018)

42. Singh, S., Jaakkola, T., Littman, M., Szepesvári, C.: Convergence results for single-step on-policy reinforcement-learning algorithms. Mach. Learn. **38**, 287–308 (2000). https://doi.org/10.1023/A:1007678930559

43. Sutton, R.S., Barto, A.G.: Reinforcement Learning: An Introduction, 2nd edn. MIT Press, Cambridge (2018)

44. Sutton, R.S., McAllester, D., Singh, S., Mansour, Y.: Policy gradient methods for reinforcement learning with function approximation. In: Advances in Neural Information Processing Systems, pp. 1057–1063 (2000)

45. Tsitsiklis, J.N.: Asynchronous stochastic approximation and q-learning. Mach. Learn. **16**(3), 185–202 (1994). https://doi.org/10.1023/A:1022689125041

46. Vinyals, O., et al.: Grandmaster level in StarCraft II using multi-agent reinforcement learning. Nature **575**(7782), 350–354 (2019). https://doi.org/10.1038/s41586-019-1724-z

47. Watkins, C.J.C.H., Dayan, P.: Q-learning. Mach. Learn. **8**, 279–292 (1992)

48. Xu, T., Zou, S., Liang, Y.: Two time-scale off-policy TD learning: non-asymptotic analysis over Markovian samples. Adv. Neural Inf. Process. Syst. **32**, 10633–10643 (2019)

49. Yang, Z., Chen, Y., Hong, M., Wang, Z.: Provably global convergence of actor-critic: a case for linear quadratic regulator with ergodic cost. Adv. Neural Inf. Process. Syst. **32**, 8351–8363 (2019)

Revival of MAS Technologies in Industry

Petr Kadera[✉], Václav Jirkovský, and Vladimír Mařík

Czech Institute of Informatics, Robotics, and Cybernetics, Czech Technical
University in Prague, Jugoslávských Partyzánů 3, 160 00 Prague, Czech Republic
{petr.kadera,vaclav.jirkovsky,vladimir.marik}@cvut.cz

Abstract. Multi-Agent Systems (MAS) were proposed in the mid-1980s
to provide a means for control of complex distributed systems. Although
the topic received significant attention from the research community,
which resulted in many methodologies and theoretical concepts, industrial practitioners' adoption remained low. A wave of innovations referred
to as Industry 4.0 brought new technologies focused on easier integration of heterogeneous systems. Semantic technologies were recognized as
a suitable tool for the axiomatic information modelling of production
systems, and the OPC-UA communication standard brought a means
of secure communication and principles of object-oriented information
modelling to the layer of process control. In this paper, a new MAS
Platform - Cluster 4.0 Integration Platform is introduced. It utilizes (1)
semantics to explicitly describe products, production, and resources for
their easier integration and exploitation and (2) OPC-UA to connect
software agents to physical machines.

Keywords: Multi-agent systems · Ontology · Object-oriented
modelling · System integration

1 Expectations

The concept of Multi-Agent Systems (MAS) was proposed in the mid-1980s. It
was highly appreciated by both the scientific and the industrial communities
immediately as it has promised an interesting way how to manage the control of
complex manufacturing systems and solutions. Within the following two decades,
basic theoretical foundations of MAS were built, and active developments in the
field of technology and tools for its support began. In 1996, FIPA (Foundation for
Intelligent Physical Agents) was established. Its main objective was the scientific
substantiation of standards in the field of agents and MAS. Later, in 2005,

This work was supported by institutional resources for research by the
Czech Technical University in Prague, the EU Structural funds and the Ministry of Education of the Czech Republic within the project 'Cluster 4.0'
(reg. No. CZ.02.1.01/0.0/0.0/16_026/0008432), and the RICAIP project that has
received funding from the European Union's Horizon 2020 research and innovation
programme under grant agreement No. 857306.

© Springer-Verlag GmbH Germany, part of Springer Nature 2021
A. Hameurlain and A Min Tjoa (Eds.): TLDKS XLVIII, LNCS 12670, pp. 131–144, 2021.
https://doi.org/10.1007/978-3-662-63519-3_6

FIPA became one of the standardization committees in IEEE. At that time, it was expected that MAS-technologies are ready to capture the leadership as a substantially new design paradigm for handling complex industrial distributed systems.

This concept appeared very attractive and natural for understanding and implementations because it suggested building systems and solving problems similarly as the natural complex systems carry out in reality, particularly through communication interactions and underlying self-organization.

2 Past of Using Agents in Industry

However, at the beginning of the 2000s, something in the development of MAS theory and technologies got wrong. Successful solutions in the field of intelligent applications that were implemented during this period by the world's leading IT companies, particularly Apple, Facebook, Google, SAP, were not related to MAS or MAS-technologies at all.

Muller [15], after a detailed analysis of the industrial MAS systems, indicated in 2014: "While there is ample evidence that Multi-Agent Systems and Technologies are vigorous as a research area, it is unclear what practical application impact this research area has accomplished to date."

While forecasting the MAS-application development, the very important roadmap [10] stated in 2005, that for MAS technology, it is unrealistic to reach the industrial maturity level for another 20 years.

The authors [1] also complain about the weaknesses of methodologies for designing MAS developed by that time. Indeed, by that time, several well-developed MAS methodologies were created and tested; for example, Gaia, MaSE, ADELFE, MESSAGE, Prometheus etc., although they were not supported by adequate tools. The intensity of research activities intended to design MAS methodologies and supporting software tools was quite high almost until 2010. However, unfortunately, currently only a small number of methodologies and tools remain to be the subjects of further developments.

Among leaders of industrial MAS deployment is Rockwell Automation, Inc., which made indispensable investments into the research and design activities in the MAS area [20] and spent nearly two decades to make pioneering research and development in the application of holonic and MAS in the industrial automation domain. They went through a long path from the first simple prototypes of holonic control systems (holoblocs) as an extension of the function blocks that were created more or less spontaneously and ad hoc, to the development of a comprehensive bundle of advanced methodologies, practices, and tools that cover all aspects of design, implementation, validation, and monitoring of agent-based real-time control systems.

Rockwell Automation started from the classical "old-fashioned" approaches to "novel" control paradigms. For the very first time Rockwell implemented Holonic Agent Architecture, Object-oriented design, Distributed Control Systems (DCS) with a clear differentiation between higher-level and lower-level agents, sniffers to observe and evaluate the communication traffic, Agent Applications, Simulation Support including one of the very first agent-based simulation tool for agent-based systems MAST, developed semantic technologies and ontology services provided by specialized agents, etc.

Practice has shown that many applications for which MAS-technology was considered as the most promising one [15], were successfully implemented later using other technologies. Among them, the most competitive ones were service-oriented technologies, grid computing, autonomous, ubiquitous and cloud computing, etc. The aforementioned technologies appeared much later but were able to quickly outperform the MAS-technologies, first of all, in engineering aspects.

In addition to discussed MAS achievements, it is important to mention recently developed new software engineering technologies which are related to MAS as supporting technologies or utilize the principles of MAS under new, up-to-date labels (SOA, Twins, IoT or Cyber-Physical Systems, etc.). These are bringing a strong revival of the MAS solutions in industry these days [7].

Cyber-Physical Systems (CPS) refer to a specific category of systems with integrated computational and physical capabilities. Interconnected CPS components collaborating in a peer-to-peer way facilitate to meet increasing requirements for flexibility and re-configurability. Such networks are named industrial cyber-physical systems (iCPS). But still, they use the basic principles of MAS, despite the fact that the authors do not like to mention this.

The next step of agent development was declared in relation to the service-oriented architectures (SOA) [14]. SOA as a style of software design, is not being considered as a product or a follower of MAS. But there are many parallels between the agents and web services: agents provide capabilities to other agents in the same way as services are provided in service-oriented systems, and also similar but less formalized messages are used to exchange data.

Holonic multi-agent system, introduced in the important paper [18], can be considered as an enhanced version of multi-agent systems with pre-defined classes of agents: orders, products, resources and staff (later advanced by task agent, the function of satisfaction and bonuses, etc.) which can recursively form holarchies as bottom-up structures (comparing with the top-down hierarchies). In the beginning, the holonic MAS solutions were mostly used for control of near-to-physical layer devices in manufacturing exploring the IEC 16499 standard, but later were applied in the complex managerial problems [16].

The new trend is the application of semantic technologies (ontologies) to enhance the capabilities of agents for representing and exchanging knowledge, and thus to increase the openness, intelligence and flexibility of MAS solutions [8]. The other quite important aspect of the viability of MAS is their capability to learn from own experience. Distributed Machine Learning principles could enhance the capabilities (and thus reputation) of MAS, but these are still underdeveloped, despite the fact intensive research is being carried out in this field. The technologies mentioned above, namely clear way of agentification of physical systems, exploration of semantic/ontological structures and machine learning significantly change engineering landscape of MAS solutions.

The clear vision for extended deployment of MAS in industrial solutions was provided by the German Industry 4.0 initiative presented at the Hannover Fair by Prof. Wolfgang Wahlster in 2013 [6]. This vision considers virtualization of physical entities (machines, transportation means, conveyors, robots, persons, semi-products and products) by digital twins, communication and negotiation concerning the manufacturing decisions in the virtual space. It expects a broad exploration of ontological knowledge structures and Machine Learning principles. The digital twins to which the information about both the global goals and the capabilities to negotiate were added, represent nothing else just agents. Agent technology seems to be ideal for fulfilling the visions of Industry 4.0.

The Industry 4.0 approach is strongly contributing to deployment of MAS technologies in industry mentioned above: (a) by clear definition of digital twins/agents respecting their autonomy, (b) the way of engineering thinking is being changed from centralized to distributed manner rapidly across the engineering community, (c) by supporting the enhanced cooperation between academia and industry by building large research centers with flexible experimental production facilities (testbeds), placed in academia, but open to industry. The testbeds force the developers to create generic software platforms enabling reuse of the control code as the production tasks vary quite frequently and it is impossible to develop the code for each use-case from the scratch.

Such a testbed, one of the largest in Europe, with 26 robots of different types, flexible transportation conveyor structure, with autonomous self-guided transportation vehicles has been built at the Czech Technical University with the EU Project RICAIP. Around this testbed, the European Center for Advance Industrial Production is being organized. The very first algorithms were oriented towards exploration of agents, building an ontology architecture to deploy semantic information and to system modeling and integration. Let us describe these efforts in more detail.

3   Cluster 4.0 Integration Platform

The Cluster 4.0 Integration Platform (C4IP) implements planning and orchestration services for industrial manufacturing and is based on the MAS paradigm. Particular agents represent specific hardware resources or product agents that communicate with each other to achieve a requested goal, i.e., producing a specific product in the cheapest way. The multi-agent approach brings to the manufacturing domain flexibility in the planning and orchestration of manufacturing operations. The overall production plan is divided into smaller tasks (operations of the recipe) which are planned separately, assuming resources available at the time of planning. This dynamic approach slices the global planning problem into local tasks solved by individual agents and thus provides more flexibility in comparison to the case when the complete plan is calculated at the beginning of production. The multi-agent approach facilitates the management of the resources and products dynamically at the runtime. New resources may be added/removed from the platform on-the-fly, and new products may be ordered during the run-time without changing the configuration of the platform or interrupting ongoing production.

The multi-agent platform implements FIPA specifications. These specifications define standards for agent communication to facilitate understanding of agents and interoperability of different multi-agent systems. FIPA specifications define elements of the message that determine the meaning of the message and how the message should be further processed. This includes, for example, the identification of an agent to whom the response should be sent. FIPA specifications also introduce the concept of so-called performative, which identifies the type of the message, whether it is a request message, response message, or a reject message.

The physical system and the products are described semantically in the ontology together with capabilities and properties of the manufacturing facility (e.g., operations provided by machines, the composition of a product including its production recipe). The recipe concept also included in the ontology specifies operations that must be performed during the production and their ordering. The agent-based distributed planning splits the recipe into a sequence of operations conducted by selected agents. Because various agents can offer various operations, the agent-specific implementation of an operation is described by one or more manufacturing activities. In other words, a set of manufacturing activities represents an internal recipe describing a specific agent conducts a specific operation. Each agent creates for every operation a dedicated Job that manages the correct execution of the general operation by the specific machine. The top-level job represents a single operation of the production recipe. Within the job execution, the agent invokes production operations on the connected physical machine or submits requests to other agents to satisfy prerequisites needed for the job (e.g., the robot may need to supply material and transport the product to its station before executing its own task). Receiving a request from an agent invokes a new job that can recursively submit requests to other agents.

The entire life cycle of production negotiation is based on the Plan-Commit-Execute protocol [5]. Execution of particular production recipe step is performed in three phases, Planning phase, Commit phase and Execute phase. The diagram of the negotiation flow is depicted in Fig. 1.

Within the Planning phase, the plan of tasks needed to perform the job is created. This phase is split into two steps. First, the request is sent to the directory service agent. The directory service agent performs semantic matchmaking and returns a list of agents capable of executing the job. The request from the product agent is then sent to the suitable agents. Upon request from the product agent, the machine agent checks its resources. If needed, the machine agent may submit requests to other agents to fulfill all requirements needed to perform the job. If the machine agent is capable of fulfilling all requirements for the job, it evaluates the overall price for the job and sends a message with the success result back to the product agent. Next, the product agent evaluates responses obtained from all machine agents and selects the best option.

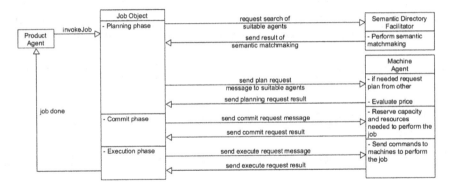

Fig. 1. Inter-agent negotiation life cycle.

During the commit phase, the product agent requests all agents involved in the selected plan sequence to reserve their resources needed to perform the job. These agents are thus reserved for the specific job and cannot accept other jobs in the given time slot.

Within the execute phase, the commitments from the previous phase are fulfilled. The hardware agents send commands to the machines and monitor the execution of the tasks. After successful execution of each operation, the product agent is notified and may start the subsequent operation of its production recipe.

3.1 Platform Overview

The agents may be divided into two fundamental groups: core agents and machines' agents. Production agents represent Orders and Products to be manufactured. They are related to specific product description in the ontology. The product agent sequentially negotiates execution of particular operations composing the product recipe. Core of the platform includes the service agents and the product agents. The hardware agents may be running as separate applications outside the platform core. The architecture is displayed in Fig. 2.

3.1.1 C4IP Core Platform Agents

The platform agents represent a backbone of the platform and provide services such as service discovery, monitoring, and communication with external product order service.

Directory service agent is the key element of the platform. The directory service agent provides three main capabilities as follows:

1. Directory service manages running services.
2. Directory service registers resource capabilities and additional information when started.
3. Directory service ensures matching of resources capable of performing specific production operation requested by the product.

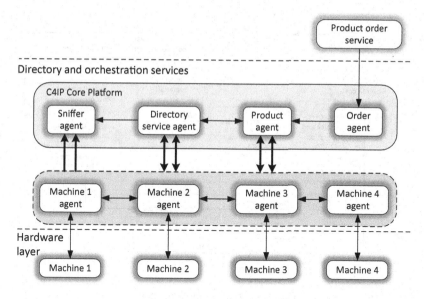

Fig. 2. C4IP platform architecture.

Logger agent collects, stores, and visualises log messages from all agents. It is a necessary supportive tool to develop and debug agent-based applications.

Order agent collects orders from external Product order service (e.g., an ERP system) and creates and initiates the corresponding Product agent.

Product agent is responsible for transformation of the product recipe into physical product. This agents guarantees the correct operation ordering with respect to the technological requirements.

3.1.2 Machines' Agents

Agents of this category represent application-specific production resources, typically production machines or logistics equipment. They offer their operations to other agents via the Directory Service Agent, ensure correct execution of requested operations, and provide an interface to physical machines.

KukaRobot agent – represents robots of the production line of two types: Kuka Agilus and Kuka iiwa. The manufacturing activity provided by these robots is Pick and Place. The KukaRobot agent provides two types of operations, namely AssembleJob and SupplyMaterialJob. Following diagram Fig. 3 shows workflow of the AssembleJob planning logic. The job is created upon request from the product agent. The job checks whether the requested material is available in the local warehouse and if not, the robot agent requests supply of the material from other agents. Then it is checked whether the (partly assembled) product is already present at one of the stations used by the robot. If not, the robot agent requests reservation of the station and requests transport of the product or empty shuttle to the reserved station. Finally, the robot's task, i.e.,

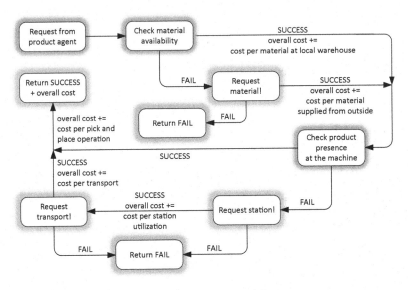

Fig. 3. Assemble job workflow.

the Pick and place activity itself, is added to the plan. The response with planning result and cost for the job is sent to the product agent.

Station agent – since some of the positioning units on the production line are shared between two robots, the system must ensure that given station is reserved for the job executed by specific robot. For this reason, Station agents are implemented within the platform. These are passive agents, they don't actively negotiate with other agents, but only commit to requesting plan if not already committed to another one. The station agents also provide on request information about possible commitment to other agents.

Shuttle agent – the shuttle agent represents particular Montrac shuttle on the production line. The manufacturing activity is transporting and the shuttle agent provides two operations, TransportJob and ClearStationJob. Workflow of the transport job is displayed in Fig. 4.

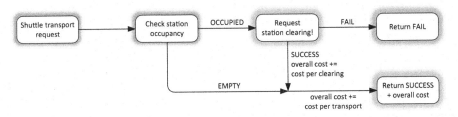

Fig. 4. Transport job workflow.

3.2   Connections of Agents to Machines via OPC UA

Agents for control of manufacturing systems are composed of high-level and low-level parts. The former is implemented using object-oriented programming approaches using C++ or Java and is responsible for finding the optimal cooperation schema among multiple agents. The latter ensures real-time control of connected machines and is based on the IEC 61131 or IEC 61499 standards for Programmable Logical Controllers (PLCs) programming. In the past, the interconnection of these two layers was implemented using a shared data tags in PLCs' memory. The creation of the correct structure of data tags was a tedious and error-prone task. This challenge was aimed by Agent Development Environment (ADE) [17], a specialized supportive tool for easy configuration of industrial MAS using automated generation of control code. However, generated code was difficult to be understood by engineers - this complicated debugging actions.

OPC Unified Architecture (OPC UA) standard [9] is a secure and vendor-independent mechanism for exchanging data in industrial automation as well as for information modelling. OPC UA standard overcomes the main disadvantage of its predecessor (OPC Data Access together with OPC Historical Data Access and OPC Alarm&Events)—COM[1] dependency of OPC. Therefore, the OPC UA was designed for the replacement of all existing COM-based specification to be platform-independent with extensible modelling capabilities.

OPC UA provides a means for data transport and modelling [11]. The data transport component optimizes binary TPC protocol for high-performance intranet communication and enables communication via Web Services. The data modelling component uses rules and building blocks to create and expose an information model—a formal definition of a data structure.

3.3   Semantic Description of the Production

At the beginning of the 21st century, semantic technologies came into the focus of MAS researchers. Thus, the MAS area shifted closer towards semantic interoperability and advanced methods for expressing and handling knowledge. One of the first examples was presented in [19], where is described developed ontology in the Web Ontology Language (OWL)[2] for product orders, production plans and description of the manufacturing system, including transportation aspects. Similarly to several other attempts, the ontology provides a proper conceptualization of a given domain and is closed to the required conceptualization for the C4IP platform. However, this ontology has several drawbacks for the purpose of C4IP platform—one of the obstacles is for example semantic heterogeneity. The given domain is described with different granularity and from a different point of view. Furthermore, the conceptualization of resources is insufficient for given needs.

---

[1] https://www.microsoft.com/com/default.mspx.
[2] OWL - https://www.w3.org/TR/owl-features/.

In general, the ontology's key role is to model a product, its structure, relations, and limitations among its parts described as axioms in description logics. Next, it should model relevant production operations together with detailed production steps of production machines to precisely define the overall production process if needed. Therefore, previously developed PPR ontology [4] was adopted. PPR ontology is derived from DIGICOR Core Ontology (DCO) [3] and Cyber-physical system Ontology for Component Integration (COCI) [2]. The ontology may be perceived from three different perspectives—the product-related: a description of the product architecture and features; the operation-related: a description of operations required for production and composition of a recipe; the workstation-related: a description of various resources, primarily machines and tools.

The product part describes a structure of the product and related material of its parts. Next, it has a relation to a given recipe together with a name and a description. The most important parts (i.e., the operation and workstation-related parts) are shown in Fig. 5.

The operation part shows the direct connection between operations and recipes and also manufacturing activities. Moreover, the important property is enabling to establish dependencies between operations with the help of the "preceding operation" property. On the other hand, the workstation part presents the relation between workstations and their composition from the given resources (e.g., machines or tools) and operations.

The PPR ontology conceptualization provides all of the required means (in the knowledge-based perspective) for the integration of low-level components with high-level parts of a control system. The interaction of users or surrounding systems with C4IP is with the help of unambiguous and shared concepts. With the description of a product and overall relevant recipe. This information is passed into MAS. The product agent with this information has all of the

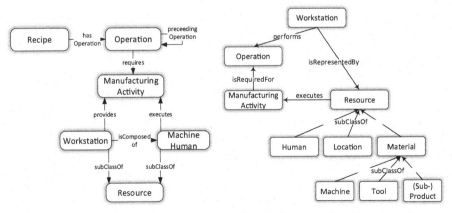

(a) Operation-related Ontology Part   (b) Workstation-related Ontology Part

Fig. 5. PPR Ontology

needed specifications to start the negotiation and then execute relevant operations specified by manufacturing activities. The operation of the PPR ontology is equivalent to operations of agents, and the mentioned manufacturing activities are related to the capabilities of particular machine agents.

Furthermore, the exploitation of PPR ontology has other advantages. For example, the separation of the knowledge-base from a control algorithm (typically hard-coded knowledge in the algorithm) enables easy deployments of the platform to other applications compared to legacy approaches.

4 Demonstration

In this section, the application of semantic technologies and OPC UA for the facilitation of MAS is described. The approach presented in this paper is applied to the truck assembling use-case, which was tested in the testbed for Industry 4.0 at CIIRC CTU. The truck consists of three main parts in several variants (and colours)—truck cabin, truck base, and truck bed in different variants, e.g., fence bed, dumper bed, tank.

PPR ontology described in Sect. 3.3 is exploited for the modelling of the product, i.e., the truck, together with its components, relations among them, and their properties. Next, the PPR ontology describes related operations and manufacturing activities (see Fig. 5) required for the truck assembling. Other important resources modelled in PPR ontology are the testbed equipment, e.g., Kuka robots (iiwa and Agilus) and a transportation system. Robotic operations are mainly AssembleJob and SupplyMaterialJob. Both of them are represented by the pick and place manufacturing activity. The transportation system ensures the transport operations.

As mentioned above, pieces of information about products and operations are not explicitly specified in legacy approaches. They are hard-coded in a control algorithm, and thus any change in the product or application is difficult. Therefore, the creation of the product agent with requirements for new production results in a compilation of variables from different relevant algorithms is necessary. On the other hand, a request for creating a new product agent consists of a

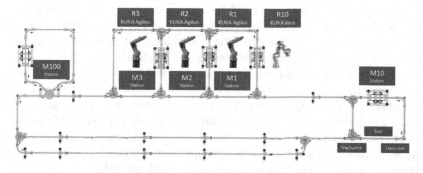

Fig. 6. Testbed for Industry 4.0

particular instance (specifying specific truck configuration) of the truck concept if PPR ontology is exploited. All of the entities from the ontology are uniquely identified, and therefore any mismatch is prevented.

The last important part is the utilization of OPC UA. All agents communicate to the lowest layer of the system via OPC UA. It means that every agent responsible for communication with a certain machine is implemented as an OPC UA client, and every machine to be controlled or monitored from the system represents an OPC UA server. This essential benefit of this approach is the easy and secure establishment of communication with the help of subscriptions. In the case of other communication standards to PLCs, it was required to implement such notifications for tag changes proprietarily.

The MAS control approach is demonstrated on the production line testbed for Industry 4.0 (see Fig. 6) composed of:

- Three Kuka Agilus Robots (R1, R2, R3);
- One Kuka iiwa Robot (R10);
- Five Stations (M1, M2, M3, M10, M100);
- Five Shuttles; and
- Passive components (Rails, Rail Switches, Rail Curves).

Each of these components (except the passive ones) is represented by its agent of a particular type and together provide services requested by a product agent that holds the description of the required product in the form of a recipe. The agents representing production resources are connected to their physical counterparts via OPC UA communication standard.

5   Conclusions

The concept of multi-agent systems is entering the scene of Industry 4.0 solutions. This is the only viable approach enabling to manage complex manufacturing systems, to handle difficult tasks of production planning, scheduling and assembling/manufacturing.

The main implementation issue is the lack of available SW integration platforms which would enable an efficient design, implementation and tuning of the MAS systems. Each platform should be accompanied by appropriate templates of agents which might be considered as specific types of digital twins of the physical manufacturing units. The other task is to have a tool for representing and exploring the semantic information/knowledge efficiently.

We have developed Cluster 4.0 Integration Platform as a vehicle for developing and running real-time agents at the testbed operated by CIIRC CTU. This SW testbed is linked with physical machines using the OPC UA technology and explores the PPR ontology written in OWL. The integration platform enables a really fast development of a new MAS solution for another use case as the agent templates (for each type of the designed agents) can be easily reused. The PPR-based ontology structure became also strongly reusable.

The particular use-case documenting the viability of the multi-agent app-roach to manufacturing tasks in combination with semantic description of man-ufacturing processes has been presented in this paper. It is aimed at flexible assembling of toy-trucks. Both the design of the solution as well the practical experiments have been carried out in the testbed facility located at CIIRC.

We will never forget that the CIIRC Institute was built leveraging the experi-ence from its successful direct predecessor, the Gerstner Lab as a Joint Research Lab of FAW Linz and CTU, which was co-directed by Prof. Roland R. Wagner. This Lab was aimed at knowledge handling, large complex distributed informa-tion and knowledge-based systems. Prof. Roland R. Wagner provided support to the research in these fields including that of MAS since 90's [12,13]. Both the FAW and Prof. Roland R. Wagner personally especially supported the indus-trial MAS community in the difficult period of the "MAS-winter" by helping to organize workshops and later conferences HoloMAS (Industrial Applications of Holonic and Multi-Agent Systems) within the frame of the DEXA events, bi-yearly since 1999. This unique line of conferences enabled to keep the MAS community ready for the today's Industry 4.0 needs.

Let us remember this significant contribution of Prof. Roland R. Wagner forever.

References

1. Cossentino, M., Hilaire, V., Molesini, A., Seidita, V. (eds.): Handbook on Agent-Oriented Design Processes. Springer, Heidelberg (2014). https://doi.org/10.1007/978-3-642-39975-6
2. Jirkovský, V.: Semantic integration in the context of cyber-physical systems (2017)
3. Jirkovský, V., Kadera, P.: Data exchange ontology for interoperability facilitation within industrial automation domain. In: Mařík, V., et al. (eds.) HoloMAS 2019. LNCS (LNAI), vol. 11710, pp. 145–158. Springer, Cham (2019). https://doi.org/10.1007/978-3-030-27878-6_12
4. Jirkovský, V., Šebek, O., Kadera, P., Burget, P., Knoch, S., Becker, T.: Facilitation of domain-specific data models design using semantic web technologies for man-ufacturing. In: Proceedings of the 21st International Conference on Information Integration and Web-Based Applications and Services, pp. 649–653 (2019)
5. Kadera, P., Tichy, P.: Plan, commit, execute protocol in multi-agent systems. In: Mařík, V., Strasser, T., Zoitl, A. (eds.) HoloMAS 2009. LNCS (LNAI), vol. 5696, pp. 155–164. Springer, Heidelberg (2009). https://doi.org/10.1007/978-3-642-03668-2_15
6. Kagermann, H., Wahlster, W., Helbig, J.: Recommendations for implementing the strategic initiative INDUSTRIE 4.0: Securing the future of German manufacturing industry; final report of the Industrie 4.0 Working Group. Forschungsunion (2013)
7. Karnouskos, S., Leitao, P., Ribeiro, L., Colombo, A.W.: Industrial agents as a key enabler for realizing industrial cyber-physical systems: multiagent systems entering industry 4.0. IEEE Ind. Electron. Mag. 14(3), 18–32 (2020)
8. Leitão, P., Mařík, V., Vrba, P.: Past, present, and future of industrial agent appli-cations. IEEE Trans. Ind. Inf. 9(4), 2360–2372 (2012)
9. Leitner, S.H., Mahnke, W.: OPC UA-service-oriented architecture for industrial applications. ABB Corporate Res. Center 48, 61–66 (2006)

10. Luck, M., McBurney, P., Shehory, O., Willmott, S.: Agent Technology: Computing as Interaction (A Roadmap for Agent Based Computing). University of Southampton (2005). https://eprints.soton.ac.uk/261788/
11. Mahnke, W., Leitner, S.H.: OPC Unified Architecture. Springer (2009). https://doi.org/10.1007/978-3-540-68899-0
12. Mařík, V., Lažanský, J., Wagner, R.R. (eds.): DEXA 1993. LNCS, vol. 720. Springer, Heidelberg (1993). https://doi.org/10.1007/3-540-57234-1
13. Mařík, V., Štěpánková, O., Flek, O., Kout, J.: Cooperative agents in DISCIM environment. In: Wagner, R.R., Thoma, H. (eds.) DEXA 1996. LNCS, vol. 1134, pp. 356–368. Springer, Heidelberg (1996). https://doi.org/10.1007/BFb0034694
14. Mendes, J.M., Leitão, P., Restivo, F., Colombo, A.W.: Service-oriented agents for collaborative industrial automation and production systems. In: Mařík, V., Strasser, T., Zoitl, A. (eds.) HoloMAS 2009. LNCS (LNAI), vol. 5696, pp. 13–24. Springer, Heidelberg (2009). https://doi.org/10.1007/978-3-642-03668-2_2
15. Müller, J.P., Fischer, K.: Application impact of multi-agent systems and technologies: a survey. In: Shehory, O., Sturm, A. (eds.) Agent-Oriented Software Engineering, pp. 27–53. Springer, Heidelberg (2014). https://doi.org/10.1007/978-3-642-54432-3_3
16. Skobelev, P.: Towards autonomous AI systems for resource management: applications in industry and lessons learned. In: Demazeau, Y., An, B., Bajo, J., Fernández-Caballero, A. (eds.) PAAMS 2018. LNCS (LNAI), vol. 10978, pp. 12–25. Springer, Cham (2018). https://doi.org/10.1007/978-3-319-94580-4_2
17. Tichý, P., Kadera, P., Staron, R.J., Vrba, P., MAříÂk, V.: Multi-agent system design and integration via agent development environment. Eng. Appl. Artif. Intell. **25**(4), 846–852 (2012). Special Section: Dependable System Modelling and Analysis. https://doi.org/10.1016/j.engappai.2011.09.021, https://www.sciencedirect.com/science/article/pii/S0952197611001746
18. Van Brussel, H., Wyns, J., Valckenaers, P., Bongaerts, L., Peeters, P.: Reference architecture for Holonic manufacturing systems: Prosa. Comput. Ind. **37**(3), 255–274 (1998)
19. Vrba, P., Radakovič, M., Obitko, M., Mařík, V.: Semantic extension of agent-based control: the packing cell case study. In: Mařík, V., Strasser, T., Zoitl, A. (eds.) HoloMAS 2009. LNCS (LNAI), vol. 5696, pp. 47–60. Springer, Heidelberg (2009). https://doi.org/10.1007/978-3-642-03668-2_5
20. Vrba, P., et al.: Rockwell automation's Holonic and multiagent control systems compendium. IEEE Trans. Syst. Man Cybern. Part C (Appl. Rev.) **41**(1), 14–30 (2010)

From Strategy to Code: Achieving Strategical Alignment in Software Development Projects Through Conceptual Modelling

Oscar Pastor[1(✉)], Rene Noel[1,2], and Ignacio Panach[3]

[1] PROS Research Centre, Universitat Politècnica de València, Valencia, Spain
{opastor,rnoel}@pros.upv.es
[2] Escuela de Ingeniería Informática, Universidad de Valparaíso, Valparaíso, Chile
rene.noel@uv.cl
[3] Escola Tècnica Superior d'Enginyeria, Universitat de València, Valencia, Spain
joigpana@uv.es

Abstract. In this article we propose S2C, a strategy-to-code methodological approach to integrate organisational, business process, and information system modelling levels to support strategic alignment in software development. Through a model-driven approach and under the Conceptual-Model Programming paradigm, the proposal supports the semi-automatic generation of working software, as well as traceability among the modelling levels. Via a working example, we illustrate how strategic definitions can be traced into specific software components by the integration of three modelling methods: Lite*, for modelling strategic reaction to external influences, Communication Analysis, for business process modelling, and the OO-Method, for modelling the conceptual schema of the information system. We discuss how this approach not only supports strategic alignment, but fosters the elicitation of business process performance measurement requirements, as well as its relevance considering the business and code alignment of the most recent enterprise architecture and agile software development initiatives.

Keywords: Requirements engineering · Model-driven development · Organisational modelling

1 Introduction

Bridging the gap between the strategic perspective of the organisation and information systems engineering has been studied since the late eighties [9]. From a top-down perspective, Enterprise Architecture (EA) has approached to model

This project has the support of the Spanish Ministry of Science and Innovation through the DATAME project (ref: TIN2016-80811-P) and PROMETEO/2018/176 and co-financed with ERDF and the National Agency for Research and Development (ANID)/ Scholarship Program/ Doctorado Becas Chile/ 2020-72210494.

A. Hameurlain and A Min Tjoa (Eds.): TLDKS XLVIII, LNCS 12670, pp. 145–164, 2021.
https://doi.org/10.1007/978-3-662-63519-3_7

business, information technology infrastructure, and information system perspectives in order to effectively enable and implement the enterprise strategy [17,26,29], to foster innovation and adaptation [13]. However, EA elements, thus high-level strategic definitions, are not usually considered for requirements engineering [11]. The more recent efforts on this track are focused on improving business strategy description [25,28].

A bottom-up perspective for the strategic alignment of information systems has been promoted by the requirements engineering and the model-driven engineering research community. By integrating software requirements with business process modelling, and business process modelling with organisational goals, several proposals aimed to trace business motivation and actors intentions information system requirements [7,12,21,23]. Nevertheless, the "working software over comprehensive documentation" principle of the widely adopted agile software development vision [8], hinders the bottom-up approach of connecting strategy and code through models.

The Conceptual-Model Programming (CMP) [3] paradigm allows to reconcile the model-based documentation with software production. CMP approach is comparable to Model-Driven Development (MDD, but with a special focus on automatic software production). CMP aims for modelling the information system with total independence of the technological requirements for its implementation, leaving this task to a conceptual-model program compiler that generates fully working software. CMP supports that different models with different languages and intentions can be connected in order to provide as much information as possible to the conceptual-model programs. Hence, the CMP paradigm allows to also include stakeholders that are relevant for the initial conception of the information system, though the modelling of business processes and organisational and organisational strategy [16].

Although traditionally EA and MDD initiatives have been considered in isolation, today's constantly changing world is daily influencing the organisations to quickly adapt their strategy to new market trends, competitors or regulations, with immediate impact on their business processes and over the information systems that support them. Hence, the integration of strategy with code is an open door for MDD, and in particular for CMP. However, EA has been criticized for not providing a cost-efficient answer for the strategic alignment of technology [2], so its integration with software production methods might be counterproductive.

Recently, we have proposed an alternative for heavy EA frameworks named Lite*: a lightweight organisational modeling method [15]. Lite* provides concepts and methodological guidance for representing how external influences affect the organisational goals, and to define strategies, tactics, and objectives for reacting to these influences, as well as the organisational structure to support it. In this article, we present a methodological approach to integrate Lite* with two modeling methods that have been already (partially) integrated: Communication Analysis [5] for business process modelling, and the OO-Method [18] for information systems modelling. The improvement goals of the proposal, namely S2C (strategy to code) aim to

- 1. provide traceability from strategic definitions to code of the information system
- 2. ensure that strategic requirements are considered into the development process, and
- 3. support, as much as possible, the automatic production of software from strategic conceptual models.

The rest of the article is structured a follows. In the next section, we present the related work, and in Sect. 3 we introduce the three modelling methods that will be considered in the proposal. In Sect. 4 we present in detail the methodological integration approach using a working example. Section 5 presents the perspectives of the proposal regarding the achievement of the improvement goals and the challenges considering recent EA and software development initiatives. Finally, Sect. 6 presents the conclusions and further work towards the materialization of the methodological proposal.

2 Related Work

The strategic alignment of technology and business has been tackled from different perspectives. From a top-down perspective, Enterprise Architecture initiatives such as TOGAF [29] and its modelling language ArchiMate [26] aims to model and align business, information technology, and information systems perspectives. From a bottom-up perspective, requirements engineering modelling methods and languages have attempted to connect model-driven software engineering with high-level organisational definitions through modelling methods.

Enterprise Architecture offers different approaches (or schools, as named by Lapalme in [13]) towards the conceptual modelling of business, technology infrastructure, and information systems. These different schools differ on the main aim: while the more high-level approaches exploit the models for organisational planning, and subverting the information technology concerns to the organisational goal, a few initiatives (under the Enterprise Ecological Adaptation school) aim for the system-in-environment coevolution. However, none of these three schools explicitly address the integration of EA into the software development process. Moreover, current research on business strategy modelling based on EA shows that there is no consideration on requirement analysis in most existing EA techniques [11].

From the bottom-up perspective, the related work towards the integration of strategic perspectives in requirements engineering is centered on goal-oriented modelling languages such as KAOS [30] and i* [32]. Goal-oriented languages have been integrated into business process models, providing alignment with information systems engineering. In [12], Koliades and Ghose propose the GoalBPM methodology, that supports the integration of KAOS with Business Processes modelled using Business Process Model Notation [24], while Ruiz et al. propose GoBIS [21] to integrate i* and business processes modelled using the Communication Analysis method [5].

Both i* and KAOS have been integrated with the highest level business models; for instance, the integration with the Dynamic Value Description method is presented by Soza et al. in [23]. Moreover, i* has been integrated with EA in several initiatives. In [4,19], the authors propose a modelling language named ARMOR, for linking intentionality and requirements. Other initiatives related to integrating intentionality to EA are also centered on organisational analysis. In the context of complex decision making, the integration of EA and goal modelling has been considered in [1] to allow the identification, modelling, and analysis of relevant information of organisational structure, goals, and operational processes. Here, i* concepts are applied to represent actors and goals. The proposal aims to simulate what scenarios are based on i* and other specific models. However, it does not provide guidelines for the identification of goals and for its top-down refinement, nor for its integration with operational process elements.

Although the before commented top-down and bottom-up approaches and initiatives aim to connect high-level organisational definitions with software development, recent initiatives both on EA frameworks and software development processes still aim to close this gap, and with special emphasis on agility. The Open Agile Architecture [27], published in September of 2020, focuses on the transit of enterprise architects to agile contexts, introducing software development frameworks, and practices such as Domain Driven Design, Hexagonal Architectures, and Non-Functional Requirements into an EA framework. On the other hand, from the software development processes perspective, the last version of the Scaled Agile Framework (SAFe), published in July of 2020, moves forward to the strategic level [20] by introducing Business Agility, thus, agile practices into the strategical management of the organisation to quickly react to market changes.

In summary, although several academic and industrial initiatives have been proposed and applied, the alignment between strategy and software development is still an ongoing effort.

3   Background

3.1   Organizational Modelling with Lite*

Lite* [15] is an Organizational Modelling method that allows the representation of the strategic reaction of an organization to external actors that influence the achievement of its goals. Lite* has been designed following the constructs from EA modelling frameworks for representing business motivation [17,25,25], and taking from i* the goal and agent-oriented modelling language. Lite* provides a systematic approach for organizational modelling through four steps, detailed below and depicted in Fig. 1

- Step 1 - Influence Modelling: identify external actors and its influence over the organization, as well as the organizational goal affected. The elements modelled in this stage are depicted in green in Fig. 1.

- Step 2 - Objectives and Roles Modelling: based on SWOT analysis, the organization defines the idea of how to achieve the organizational goal (strategy), as well as one or more specific actions to implement the strategy (tactics). Also, the organizational units responsible for implementing the tactics are defined. The elements from Stage 2 are depicted in yellow in Fig. 1.
- Step 3 - Objectives and Roles Modelling: the tactics are refined in one or many measurable and verifiable indicators (objectives), which are assigned to organizational roles. Objectives and Roles are depicted in pink in Fig. 1.
- Step 4 - Reaction and Secondary Influences modelling: the product of the implementation of tactics are value offers with which the organization aims to influence the environment (customers, competitors, etc.). Also, new influences from and to actors (both external or other organizational units) can be identified. These influences can be analyzed as separated scenarios using the same 4 stages. Stage 4 concepts are depicted in blue in Fig. 1.

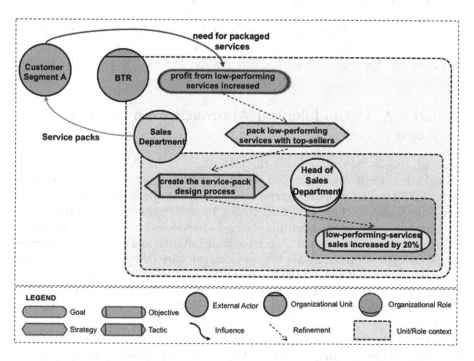

Fig. 1. An organizational model example- using Lite*. (Color figure online)

3.2 Business Process Modelling Using Communication Analysis

Communication Analysis (CA) [5] is a communication-oriented business process modelling method. It aims to graphically describe the communicative interactions among actors in terms of a flow of Communicative Events in the Communicative Event Diagram. Each one of the communicative events have input and output messages. These messages can be formally described using the Message Structure technique [6], that allows to represent the data fields and more complex date structures that are interchanged by the actors during the communicative event. Also, each CE can be textually described using a specification template, which guides the requirements specification for the contact among actors, the constraints regarding the message structures, and the reactions produced after the communication.

3.3   Information System Modelling Using the OO-Method

The OO-Method (OOM) [18] is an object-oriented software production method that, under the conceptual-model programming paradigm, allows the automatic generation of information systems from conceptual models. Using four conceptual models, OOM allows the structural definition of classes (Class Model), the dynamic representation of the classes (Behavior Model), the user interaction with the interface components (Presentation Model), and the internal logic of the classes services (Functional Model). OOM is currently supported by INTE-GRANOVA Model Execution System, an industrial tool that, by specifying the programming language, allows the compilation of OOM models into working software.

4   S2C: A Methodological Approach from Strategy to Code

Through this section, we present the integration of Lite*, CA, and OOM into a single, holistic method intended to cover the full "picture" from strategy to code (S2CM). The proposal purpose is to connect these three different modelling methods into three modelling stages, to incrementally go from the highest level business motivation definitions behind a software development initiative, to the more precise process and requirement definitions, and to conceptual-model programs that can be compiled into working software (through the use of a conceptual model compiler). Figure 2 presents the modelling methods for each level and the modelling activities and the contribution of the transformations.

In order to illustrate the application of the S2C method in detail, in Subsect. 4.1 we introduce the working example. In Subsect. 4.2 we represent the strategic elements of the example using Lite*. In Subsect. 4.3 we present the modelling elements that can be mapped to the Communication Analysis model, which is further presented in Subsect. 4.4. In Subsect. 4.5 we present the elements that can be mapped from the CA model to the OOM model, which is detailed in Subsect. 4.6. Finally, Subsect. 4.7 shows the transformation from the conceptual schema of the information system to code.

4.1   Working Example

As a working example, we introduce B-Bank, a bank that offers financial products to its customers, which are classified in different segments according to their

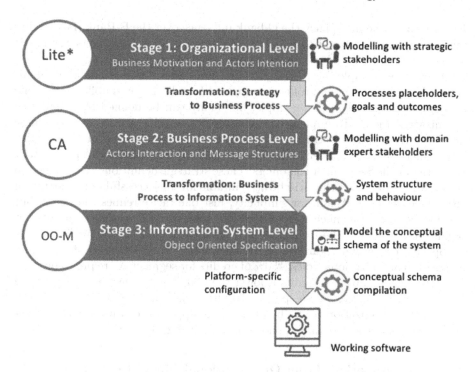

Fig. 2. Modelling stages of the Strategy-to-Code method.

financial risk. The Segment A customers are the more profitable for the B-Bank, however, a new competitor, the C-Bank, is attracting them by offering fast-approval credits. In order to prevent an exile of Segment A customers, B-Bank must define an organizational strategy, that will affect its business processes and the information systems that support them.

4.2   Stage 1: Organizational Modeling with Lite*

Goal: The first stage consist of eliciting the strategic requirements that motivate the software development endeavor, and that will allow assessing the performance of its organizational deployment from a business perspective.

Method: Using Lite* as modelling language and method, the analyst must elicit the strategic requirements from top executive stakeholders (such as CEOs COOs, and CPOs), in order to answer *why* the organization is facing a change endeavor, *how* will the organization approach such an endeavor, *who* will be accountable for the successful implementation of the approach, and how the results of the implementation will be measured.

Example: In the first place, the C-bank influence over the B-Bank (fast credits marketing campaign) and the goal affected (Segment A Customers Retained) are represented in the Lite* model, as presented in green in Fig. 3.

Then, after completing a strengths and weaknesses assessment, the organizational strategy is defined (offer pre-approved credits). For simplicity, just one strategy is presented in the example, but many can be defined to achieve the organizational goal. To implement the strategies, specific actions over the business processes (called tactics) are defined for the organizational units: the Risk Department must implement a new process in order to calculate a preliminary risk ratio for the Segment A customers. These strategic definitions are assigned to the organizational unit that will be accountable for its successful implementation (Risk Department). Again, for simplicity, just one tactic refines the tactic, but it could be many (as much as required) and they could be assigned to different organizational units. These elements are depicted in color yellow in Fig. 3.

Specific objectives regarding the verification of the tactics are defined and assigned to organizational roles: "50% of credits for segment A are pre-approved" and "risk of pre-approved credits is lower than 20%" are assigned to the Head of Risk Department role. These specific definitions are depicted in pink in Fig. 3. Finally, the organization reacts by offering pre-approved credits service to Customer Segment A as the target, shown in blue in Fig. 3.

4.3 Transformation: From Organizational Model to Business Process Model

Goal: As depicted in Fig. 2, the automatic transformation of a Lite* model into a CA can provide primitives for defining

- 1. the identification of the business processes to be modelled (namely "process placeholders"),
- 2. quantitative indicators to measure the performance of the business processes,
- 3. processes outcomes.

Method: Even though a formal specification of the transformation rules from Lite* to CA is still an ongoing endeavor, we illustrate the potential of the approach by transforming Lite* tactics into business processes placeholder. Lite* tactics represent actions towards the design or improvement of a business process [15]; while it is not possible to automatically generate the full business process (at least not from a Lite* model), it is possible to systematically trace and generate some key concepts and relationships that set the basis for the business process design.

Example: Following our working example, in Fig. 4 we present the transformation of the tactic "implement preliminary risk assessment process" introduced in the Lite* example (Fig. 3) into a process placeholder. It is worth noting that

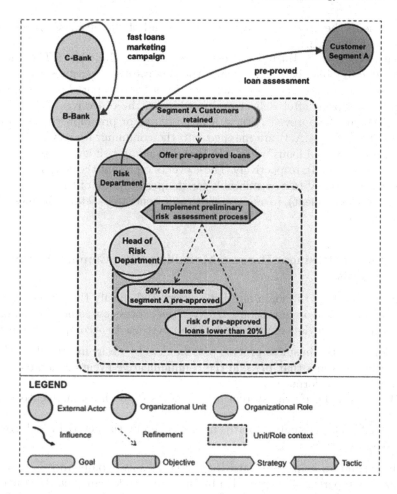

Fig. 3. An organizational model example using Lite*. (Color figure online)

if the strategy "Offer pre-approved loans" would have a second tactic, it would yield to a second process placeholder. These two process placeholders can be seen as different views of the same business process model.

As seen in Fig. 4.A, the tactic "implement preliminary risk assessment process" (Fig. 4.A.0) and its associated concepts yield to the business process placeholder depicted in Fig. 4.B. The transformation follows two rules:

– Organizational Unit Influence to Business Process Outcome: In order to accomplish the influence (Fig. 4.A.1) of the Organizational Unit holding the tactic under analysis ("Risk Department"), the influence is mapped into the communicative event "Deliver pre-approved loan assessment" (Fig. 4.B.1). Both the actor that delivers the assessment is automatically generated and named, and the business process analyst can modify its name when designing the whole business process. As this communicative event represents the main outcome of the process, it is placed at the end of the business process to be designed (Fig. 4.B.1).

– Role Objective to Business Process Performance Indicator: The tactic is refined into objectives, that define the quantitative measures towards the achievement of the organizational goal. In order to report how the business process performs after delivering its outcome, the objectives "50% of loans for Segment A approved" (Fig. 4.A.2) and "risk or pre-approved loans lower than 20%" (Fig. 4.A.3) are mapped into the communicative events "Update % of pre-approved loans" (Fig. 4.B.2) and "Update risk level of pre-approved loans" (Fig. 4.B.3), respectively. These events represent the communication of the organizational role accountable for the performance of the process (Head of Risk Department) to an automatically generated actor (Business Data Analyst).

4.4   Stage 2: Business Process Modelling with Communication Analysis

Goal: In this stage the main aim is to design and specify the business process that will enable the organization to deliver the process outcomes. Based on the transformations previously presented, the analyst has to accomplish three goals:

– 1. Complete the business process placeholders by designing the flow of communicative events that precede the communicative events generated by the automatic transformation,
– 2. Elicit and specify the system requirements for each communicative event, and
– 3. Specify the information that is interchanged by the actors in each communicative event.

It is important to emphasize how the methodological compliance between the organizational perspective (provided by the Lite* model) and the BPM perspective (provided by the Communication Analysis (CA) model) is an essential property of the solution presented in this paper, that is warrantied by its definition: the "conceptual bone" of the BPM in CA is got from the Lite* organizational model,

Method: For each business process placeholder, and using the CA method [5], the analyst must hold meetings with domain experts in order to elicit the as-is situation of the actual business process under analysis. Later, and considering the objectives, tactics, and goals that can be traced back to the Lite* model, the analyst must re-design the business process. For both models, as-is and to-be, the analyst must complete the three CA specification: 1. the communicative event diagram, to represent the flow of communicative events, 2. the communicative event template, for each communicative event in the diagram, in order to specify the system requirements to support the interaction, and 3. the message structure of each communicative interaction, to specify the structure of the information that is interchanged among the actors.

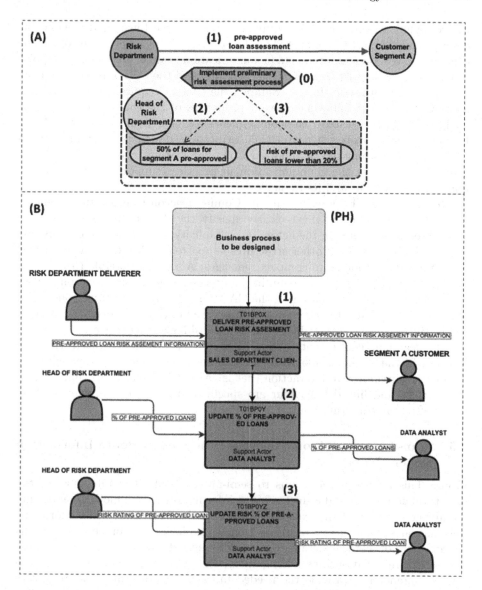

Fig. 4. Transformation of a Lite* tactic into a CA business process placeholder

Example: For brevity, the as-is and to-be designs for the business process placeholder presented in Fig. 4.B will not be exemplified. In Fig. 5 we present the CET (Communicative Event Template) for the communicative event "T01BP0Y - Update % of pre-approved loans", and the MS (Message Structure) for the interaction "% of pre-approved loans".

As seen in the example, the CET allows the specification of the contact, communication content, and reaction requirements. The goal field allows tracing the communicative event to its source objective in the Lite* model, while the description field must be completed by the analyst. The description, as well as the contact and reaction requirements (communication channel, frequency, temporal restrictions, etc.), must be specified depending on if the CET represents the as-is or the to-be situation. In the example, the contact requirements include the identification of the following relevant properties of the communication under analysis: its primary actor, the communication channel (in person, by phone, by mail... for an as-is situation, while in a to-be design this communication could be fully automated or reported using the system to be developed), the actor that supports the communication in practice (support actor), potential temporal restrictions and its frequency .

Regarding the MS described in the Communication Content Requirements of the CET, the analyst must clearly specify the data elements of the messages interchanged among the actors. For simplicity, the example considers just data fields, but there are other structures supported by MS (such as iterations and aggregations) for more complex messages. Also, it is possible to reference other MS already defined upstream in the process. The MS specification plays a basic role in the transformation of the CA model into an executable conceptual schema, as it contains the core data that are used in the transformation process to identify classes, their attributes and relationships among classes.

The reaction requirements allows to specify the business objects that are involved in the system response to a communicative event, together with the outgoing communicative interaction that is generated. Treatments, linked communications and linked behaviour are specified in order to characterize these pieces of relevant information.

4.5   Transformation: From Business Processes Model to Information System Model

Goal: This transformation aims to semi-automatically generate most of the structural and behavioral elements of the information system model. conforming an advanced sketch of the exectuable conceptual schema that will conform the information system model resulting from this phase, The process transforms the information entities detailed in the MSs into the classes (with attributes) and structural relationships among them, the actors and their messages into services intended to provide the needed functionalty to create, update, delete and query instances of the classes, together with characterizing the process flow to be followed to generate services and attributes for representing valid state and transitions for systems objects.

Method: The transformation takes as input a CA model, and using the guidelines presented by España in [7], generates the *skeleton* of an OO-Method model [18]. The transformation considers that the analyst must make decisions during the transformation process; also, the transformation technique considers three of the four OO-Method models (class, behavior, and functional model), leaving the user interaction aspects out of the transformation's scope.

T01BP0Y – Update % of pre-approved loans
Goals: Update the indicator of achievement of the objective "50% of loans for Segment-A are pre-approved" (1) **Description:** The Head of the Risk Department reports the percentage of loans for Segment A Customer that have been pre-approved, with respect to the total of approved loans for the Segment A customers.
Contact Requirements
Primary Actor: Head of Risk Department **Communication Channel:** In person, by phone, by e-mail. **Support actor:** Data Analyst **Temporal Restrictions:** Only working days (09:00-18:00) **Frequency:** Weekly.
Communication Content Requirements
Message Structure: % of pre-approved loans

Field	OP	Domain	Example
`<PRE_APPROVED_LOANS_UPDATE =`			
`  {update_id +`	g	number	99999
`   date +`	i	date	11-05-2020
`   week +`	i	date	04-05-2020
`   total segment a loans +`	i	number	10
`   pre approved segment a loans`	i	number	8
`  }>`			

Structural constraints: None of the fields can have null values. **Contextual constraints:** The date field is the day when the update is delivered, and the week field corresponds to the date of the Monday of the reported week.
Reaction Requirements
Treatments: The update is stored. **Linked Communications:** The data Analyst is notified of the new order. **Linked behavior:** no exceptional behaviors are considered.

Fig. 5. Communicative Event Template and Message Structure example.

Example: Following the transformation technique, the CET and the MS presented in Fig. 5 map into the class diagram presented in Fig. 6.C. The MS detailed in Fig. 6.B maps into the class "PreApprovedLoansUpdate", taking each data field as an attribute. Also, an instance creation service is generated, which is induced because the MS is defined for the first time in the process in this communicative event. The transformation also generates OOM agents, which are classes representing actors that can be associated with services. In the example, from the Head of Risk Department actor that inputs the message for the communicative event detailed in Fig. 6.A, the HeadRiskDepartment agent is generated. The dashed relationship line with the PreApprovedLoansUpdate is the OOM notation used to represent that the agent has access to the instance creation service of the class.

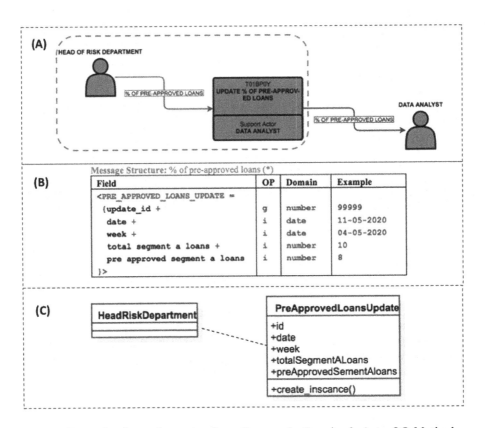

Fig. 6. Example of transformation from Communication Analysis to OO-Method.

4.6   Stage 3: Information System Modelling with OO-Method

Goal: In this final modelling stage, the information system model is completed. The analyst must complete the relevant information of the conceptual schema that has been generated in the transformation process described before, providing the required details that make possible to execute the code generation process (a conceptual model compilation process that the INTEGRANOVA tool performs).

Method: Starting from the solid basis that the intial, generated conceptual schema conforms, the OO-Method expressiveness must be used to let the analyst complete the detailed specification of the functionality of each service, including event pre/post conditions, transactions definition and integrity constraints declaration. Additionally specific parameters for classes, attributes, and services must

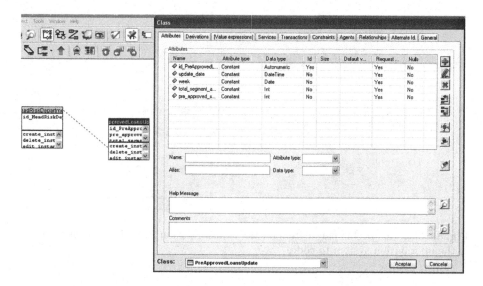

Fig. 7. Design view for OO-Method classes model.

be included, according to the method presented in [18]. OO-Method's tool support, INTEGRANOVA [10] allows the configuration of these parameters. The analyst must also design the presentation model, that defines the user interfaces and their connection to services. However, the OO-Method has a series of pre-defined patterns (which are implemented in INTEGRANOVA), that allows generating an archetypal presentation model based on the classes model.

Example: Figure 7 presents an sketch of the classes model design view of INTEGRANOVA, as well as the configuration interfaces for the class PreApprovedLoansUpdate.

4.7   Transformation: From Information System Model to Working Software

Goal: This final transformation is based on a conceptual model compilation process that deliver a working software product (the application code) from the conceptual schema of the information system provided by the previous phase. This what makes real the CMP goal of providing full traceability through the whole software production process, the main contribution of the approach presented in this paper.

Method: The method, linked to the OO-Method proposal and the INTEGRANOVA tool support, allows the specification of platform-specific requirements, such as the selected programming language for the generated code, together with significant software architectural decisions (for example, if the generated system

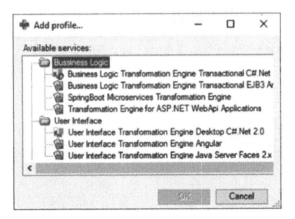

Fig. 8. Platform specific parameters for the transformation from the conceptual model of the information system to code.

will run in desktop mode or it will be a web application, with separated front end and back end components).

Example: In Fig. 8, the platform-specific components currently supported by INTEGRANOVA are depicted, showing that business logic and user interface are generated separately; the business logic component can be generated in c#, in java (using EJB or Microservices with Springboot architectures), or as an ASPNET service. The user interface component can be a desktop .NET application, an Angular application, or a Java Server Faces application. These are dimensions offered to the user to let her select the most appropriate software architecture.

5 Discussion

We have presented the S2C method, considering three modelling methods and stages to go from strategy to code that are properly integrated under a common, holistic perspective. The working example, even though it is necessarily limited in size and complexity, is intended to show as clearly as possible how the method meets the three main goals stated in Sect. 4.

Regarding traceability, looking at the class "PreApprovedLoansUpdate", depicted in Fig. 7, it is possible to trace it back to the business process level, to the communicative event where the actor must report the performance indicators of the pre-approved loans assessment process (Fig. 6), that, likewise, can be traced to the business objective of covering the 50% of the loans for Segment A Customers with pre-approved loans, modelled using Lite* (Fig. 4).

Regarding strategic requirements engineering, the working example also shows a strategic requirement that, otherwise, could be possible missing from the requirements analysis: while business process modelling would lead to a detailed requirements specification of the information system needed to perform the risk assessment for the loan pre-approval, the process performance measurement requirement is derived from the objectives defined at the organizational level. These strategic requirements could help to specify in advance process measurement functionalities that otherwise would require more sophisticated techniques to be automatically measured, such as process mining [14]. However, we are perfectly aware that many other process measurements are not evident at the strategic level [31], and shoud be incorporated to the model. This shoud not be seen at all as a limitation. On the contrary, having a solid model "conceptual bone" that is kept throughout the software development life cycle, the analyst must exploit the opportunity to add these requirements in the business process modelling level, making possible to fine tune the system according to specific, more detailed constraints.

In the third place, considering automatic code generation, the example shows how, with a small modelling effort, it is possible to deliver running software: just by identifying objectives in the Lite* model and adding the message structure detail in the Communication Analysis model, the class, service, and agent in the OO-Method model could be compiled into a working web application for the actor to report the performance indicator, or into a Microservice to receive the report from another software component. However it is worth noting that most of the message structures and the business logic for its creation, update, and deletion could be more complex and could require more effort at the business process and information system level. Nevertheless, the approach that we present here is scalable in its design, and it is ready to face complexity. A sound experimental work is an important immediate further work that we plan to accomplish in practical settings.

Finally, regarding the most recent initiatives on aligning organizational strategy and software development [20,27], it is worth noting that the method fosters a model-driven engineering environment and typical agile environments are mainly based on traditional programming. While the integration of model-driven engineering with the agile context has been explored, further work is needed to integrate the presented strategy-to-code method with the Open Group's agile enterprise architecture or with SAFe's business agility initiative.

6   Conclusions and Future Work

We have presented S2C, a strategy-to-code methodological approach to integrate organizational, business process, and information system modelling methods to support the strategic alignment of software development through the elicitation, traceability, and semi-automatic generation of strategic requirements. Via a working example, we have demonstrated the feasibility of

- 1. Transform high-level organizational definitions, such as tactics, into business process placeholders and concrete interactions to report the performance of the business process,

 – 2. connect these strategic elements with existing methodological integration of business process models and information system models.

We have discussed the limitations of the example, and how they do not prevent from showing that the proposal is suitable to achieve the improvement goals.

For the consolidation of the methodological approach, further work is needed to formalize and extend the integration of Lite* and Communication Analysis, in order to exploit all the advantages of the strategic definitions, for instance, for the automatic generation of business process performance dashboards. Tool support for the integration of all the three methods is an ongoing work, nevertheless, the maturity of INTEGRANOVA sets a solid cornerstone for the approach. Other research perspectives for the approach are its integration into business software processes, such as the Scaled Agile Framework [22].

References

1. Barat, S., Kulkarni, V., Clark, T., Barn, B.: A method for effective use of enterprise modelling techniques in complex dynamic decision making. In: Poels, G., Gailly, F., Serral Asensio, E., Snoeck, M. (eds.) PoEM 2017. LNBIP, vol. 305, pp. 319–330. Springer, Cham (2017). https://doi.org/10.1007/978-3-319-70241-4_21

2. Blosch, M., Burton, B.: Hype Cycle for Enterprise Architecture, 2017 (2017). https://www.gartner.com/en/documents/3772086/hype-cycle-for-enterprise-architecture-2017

3. Embley, D.W., Liddle, S.W., Pastor, O.: Conceptual-model programming: a manifesto. In: Embley, D., Thalheim, B. (eds.) Handbook of Conceptual Modeling, pp. 3–16. Springer, Berlin, Heidelberg (2011). https://doi.org/10.1007/978-3-642-15865-0_1

4. Engelsman, W., Quartel, D., Jonkers, H., van Sinderen, M.: Extending enterprise architecture modelling with business goals and requirements. Enterprise Inf. Syst. 5(1), 9–36 (2011)

5. España, S., González, A., Pastor, Ó.: Communication analysis: a requirements engineering method for information systems. In: van Eck, P., Gordijn, J., Wieringa, R. (eds.) CAiSE 2009. LNCS, vol. 5565, pp. 530–545. Springer, Heidelberg (2009). https://doi.org/10.1007/978-3-642-02144-2_41

6. España, S., González, A., Pastor, Ó., Ruiz, M.: A practical guide to message structures: a modelling technique for information systems analysis and design. arXiv preprint arXiv:1101.5341 (2011)

7. España Cubillo, S.: Methodological Integration of Communication Analysis into a Model-Driven Software Development Framework. Ph.D. thesis, Valencia (Spain), December 2011. https://riunet.upv.es/handle/10251/14572, https://doi.org/10.4995/Thesis/10251/14572

8. Fowler, M., Highsmith, J., et al.: The agile manifesto. Softw. Dev. 9(8), 28–35 (2001)

9. Gerber, A., le Roux, P., Kearney, C., van der Merwe, A.: The zachman framework for enterprise architecture: an explanatory is theory. In: Hattingh, M., Matthee, M., Smuts, H., Pappas, I., Dwivedi, Y.K., Mäntymäki, M. (eds.) I3E 2020. LNCS, vol. 12066, pp. 383–396. Springer, Cham (2020). https://doi.org/10.1007/978-3-030-44999-5_32

10. Integranova: Integranova Software Solutions. http://www.integranova.com/es/
11. Kitsios, F., Kamariotou, M.: Business strategy modelling based on enterprise architecture: a state of the art review. Bus. Process Manage. J. (2019)
12. Koliadis, G., Ghose, A.: Relating business process models to goal-oriented requirements models in KAOS. In: Hoffmann, A., Kang, B., Richards, D., Tsumoto, S. (eds.) PKAW 2006. LNCS (LNAI), vol. 4303, pp. 25–39. Springer, Heidelberg (2006). https://doi.org/10.1007/11961239_3
13. Lapalme, J.: Three schools of thought on enterprise architecture. IT Prof. **14**(6), 37–43 (2011)
14. Leyer, M., Heckl, D., Moormann, J.: Process performance measurement. In: vom Brocke, J., Rosemann, M. (eds.) Handbook on Business Process Management 2. IHIS, pp. 227–241. Springer, Heidelberg (2015). https://doi.org/10.1007/978-3-642-45103-4_9
15. Noel, R., Panach, I., Ruiz, M., Pastor, O.: Technical report: Lite* preliminary version. Tech. Rep. PROS-TR-02021-I, PROS Research Centre, Universitat Politecnica de Valencia (2020)
16. Noel, R., Panach, J., Pastor, O.: A model-to-program information systems engineering method. In: European Conference on Advances in Databases and Information Systems. Springer (2020)
17. Objetc Management Group: Business Motivation Model Specification Version 1.3. https://www.omg.org/spec/BMM/About-BMM/
18. Pastor, O., Molina, J.C.: Model-Driven Architecture in Practice: A Software Production Environment based on Conceptual Modeling. Springer Science & Business Media, Berlin (2007)
19. Quartel, D., Engelsman, W., Jonkers, H., Van Sinderen, M.: A goal-oriented requirements modelling language for enterprise architecture. In: 2009 IEEE International Enterprise Distributed Object Computing Conference, pp. 3–13 (2009)
20. Richard, K., Leffingwell, D.: SAFe 5.0 Distilled: Achieving Business Agility with the Scaled Agile Framework (2020)
21. Ruiz, M., Costal, D., España, S., Franch, X., Pastor, O.: GoBIS: an integrated framework to analyse the goal and business process perspectives in information systems. Inf. Syst. **53**, 330–345 (2015). https://doi.org/10.1016/j.is.2015.03.007
22. Scaled Agile: Scaled agile framework - what's new in safe 5.0. https://www.scaledagileframework.com/whats-new-in-safe-5-0/. Accessed 21 Jan 2021
23. Souza, E., Moreira, A., Araújo, J.: Aligning business models with requirements models. In: Themistocleous, M., Morabito, V. (eds.) EMCIS 2017. LNBIP, vol. 299, pp. 545–558. Springer, Cham (2017). https://doi.org/10.1007/978-3-319-65930-5_43
24. The Object Management Group: Business process model notation specification 2.0. https://www.omg.org/spec/BPMN/2.0/PDF. Accessed 20 Jan 2021
25. The Open Group: Archimate® 2.1 specification - motivation extension. https://pubs.opengroup.org/architecture/archimate2-doc/chap10.html. Accessed 11 Sept 2020
26. The Open Group: The archimate® enterprise architecture modeling language—the open group website. https://www.opengroup.org/archimate-forum/archimate-overview. Accessed 21 Dec 2020
27. The Open Group: The open agile architecture™ standard. https://publications.opengroup.org/standards/c208. Accessed 21 Jan 2021
28. The Open Group: Open business architecture. https://publications.opengroup.org/standards/business-architecture. Accessed 11 Sept 2020

29. The Open Group: The togaf® standard, version 9.2. https://publications. opengroup.org/c182. Accessed 11 Sept 2020

30. Van Lamsweerde, A.: Goal-oriented requirements engineering: a guided tour. In: Proceedings Fifth IEEE International Symposium on Requirements Engineering, pp. 249–262. IEEE (2001)

31. Van Looy, A., Shafagatova, A.: Business process performance measurement: a structured literature review of indicators, measures and metrics. Springerplus 5(1), 1–24 (2016). https://doi.org/10.1186/s40064-016-3498-1

32. Yu, E.S.K.: Modelling strategic relationships for process reengineering, p. 131

On State-Level Architecture of Digital Government Ecosystems: From ICT-Driven to Data-Centric

Dirk Draheim[1(✉)], Robert Krimmer[2], and Tanel Tammet[3]

[1] Information Systems Group, Tallinn University of Technology, Tallinn, Estonia
dirk.draheim@taltech.ee
[2] Johan Skytte Institute of Political Studies, University of Tartu, Tartu, Estonia
robert.krimmer@ut.ee
[3] Applied Artificial Intelligence Group,
Tallinn University of Technology, Tallinn, Estonia
tanel.tammet@ttu.ee

Abstract. The "digital transformation" is perceived as the key enabler for increasing wealth and well-being by politics, media and the citizens alike. In the same vein, digital government steadily receives more and more attention. Digital government gives rise to complex, large-scale *state-level* system landscapes consisting of many players and technological systems – and we call such system landscapes *digital government ecosystems*. In this paper, we systematically approach the state-level architecture of digital government ecosystems. We will discover the primacy of the state's institutional design in the architecture of digital government ecosystems, where Williamson's institutional analysis framework supports our considerations as theoretical background. Based on that insight, we will establish the notion of data governance architecture, which links data assets with accountable organizations. Our investigation results into a digital government architecture framework that can help in large-scale digital government design efforts through (i) separation of concerns in terms of appropriate categories, and (ii) a better assessment of the feasibility of envisioned digital transformations. With its focus on data, the proposed framework perfectly fits the current discussion on moving from ICT-driven to data-centric digital government.

Keywords: Digital government · e-government · e-governance · New institutional economics · Digital transformation · Data governance · Consent management · Data exchange layers · X-Road · GAIA-X

1 Introduction

The so-called "digital transformation" is currently perceived as a – or even *the* – key enabler for increasing wealth and well-being by many in politics, the media and among the citizens alike; and we find digital transformation initiatives as crucial building blocks in today's political agendas in all countries, recently, also

© Springer-Verlag GmbH Germany, part of Springer Nature 2021
A. Hameurlain and A Min Tjoa (Eds.): TLDKS XLVIII, LNCS 12670, pp. 165–195, 2021.
https://doi.org/10.1007/978-3-662-63519-3_8

under the keyword "smart city". In the same vein, digital government steadily receives more and more attention by governments, actually, ever since it became mainstream in the 1990s under the name e-Government [1]. From all over the world, we hear about many great success stories in digital government. At the same time, when we look into concrete digital government projects, we often see tremendous project expenditures (with millions or even billions of USDs, even for single projects, are not an exception). Over and over again, we see project failures with tremendous cost overruns (millions, billions) and time overruns (years), with results far below initial expectations or even complete project abortions. Note, that we are not even talking about massive digital government initiatives here, i.e., often, these problems already show in single digital government projects that aim at realizing a single digital administrative process or delivering a single e-service, e.g., a concrete e-health information system, a single e-court system, a tax declaration service etc. How come? Our hypotheses is that essential aspects of the *state-level* ecosystem, in which the several single digital government solutions are realized are neglected (or: unknown, overlooked, not addressed properly etc.) And indeed, digital government gives rise to complex-adaptive systems [46], which are, actually, large-scale, *state-level* system landscapes consisting of many players (authorities, companies, citizens) and technological systems – we call such system landscapes *digital government ecosystems*.

Therefore, the purpose of this paper is to systematically examine the state-level architecture of digital government ecosystems. As a crucial step, we will discover the primacy of the state's institutional design, which, as we argue, provides the core reference point for all system design efforts in digital government. Based on that insight, we will establish the notion of data governance architecture. A data governance architecture links data assets with accountable organizations and represents the essence of co-designing institutions and technological systems of a digital government ecosystem. In our endeavours, Williamson's institutional analysis framework will support us as a valuable theoretical background. Our investigation results into a digital government architecture framework that can help in large-scale digital government design efforts through (i) separation of concerns in terms of appropriate categories, and (ii) a better assessment of the feasibility of envisioned digital transformations.

Following the UN e-Government Survey 2020, a dominating theme in digital government is to reach the ideal of a data-centric digital government. In a data-centric digital government, data would be used pervasively in decision-masking at all organizational levels and, beyond this, would enable the continuous optimization and innovation of people-centric services. With current Big Data [31,47] and data science technologies [45], the necessary tools are available to realize such a data-centric digital government vision; however, yet, such data-centric digital government is far from becoming the standard. With its focus on data, the proposed architectural framework perfectly fits the current discussion on moving to data-centric digital government. In particular, it can help in identifying and understanding obstacles in the implementation of data-centric digital government.

The paper proceeds as follows. In Sect. 2, we briefly review the discussion of data in the current digital government discourse. We look into the UN e-Government Survey 2020 and what it tells us about the role of data in digital government. The section is meant to serve as background information and motivation. In Sect. 3 we explain, why institutions matter in the design of digital government architectures. We discuss Koppenjan and Groenewegen's systems design framework and briefly explain Oliver Williamson's institutional analysis framework. In Sect. 4 we establish the notion of data governance architecture and the notion of digital government solution architecture; we explain, how they relate to each other and to the state's institutional architecture. We arrange these components (data governance architecture, solution architecture, institutional architecture) into an architectural framework and aim at explaining the mutual dependent dynamics of changing these components. In Sect. 5, we review a series of digital government technologies against the background of the proposed architectural framework. Here, a digital government technology is a technology that have been explicitly designed for digital government or is otherwise relevant for building digital government systems. Among others, we look in the Estonian X-Road data exchange layer, the European federated data infrastructure initiative GAIA-X, and Tim Berner Lee's web-decentralization project Solid (Social Linked Data). The purpose of the section is, on the one hand, to reinforce the line of arguments embodied in the architectural framework and, on the other hand, to provide some confidence in the industrial-strength applicability of the framework. In Sect. 6 we further discuss the suggested digital government architecture framework. We discuss, in how far the framework can help in large-scale digital government design efforts. Also, we discuss how the framework is placed in the tension between e-democracy and e-administration. We finish the paper with a conclusion in Sect. 7.

2   From ICT-Driven to Data-Centric

In today's organizations, IT is about *data processing*, about the collection and manipulation of data in support of the business processes [15,17]. But it is also about reporting on the basis of available data, in service of decision making [28] and knowledge management [53]. It is similar – at a higher level – in digital government. In digital government, we have a great deal of ICT being used to make administrative processes in the authorities as well as in between authorities more efficient and effective, however, the huge potential is now in exploiting data for better decision making and leveraging innovations. In that vein, the UN Agenda for Sustainable Development 2030 has stated:

"Quality, accessible, timely and reliable disaggregated data will be needed to help with the measurement of progress and to ensure that no one is left behind." [69]   (1)

In the note [68], the Committee of Experts on Public Administration of the UN Economic and Social Council identifies three main principles of effective

Table 1. "Data as a key resource for Governments" [67]; literally compiled from the SOURCE: E-Government Survey 2020 [67], p. 150.

Approach	Description
ICT-driven	Where Governments are highly influenced by the use of new and existing information and communications technology (ICT)
Data-informed	Where Governments are guided by data; data play an inferential role in policymaking, with the understanding that data will inform rather than drive decision-making because there are rational, political and moral elements of decision-making and data are just one important aspect of the process [63]
Data-driven	Where Governments use analytics and algorithms in decision-making (elaborated in a recent OECD working paper on a data-driven public sector) [71]
Evidence-based	Where policy approaches reflect the practical application of the findings of the best and most current research available [...]
Data-centric	Where Governments place data and data science at the core of public administration; data are seen as a key asset and central to government functions and are leveraged for the provision, evaluation and modification of people-centric services [14]

governance for sustainable development: *effectiveness, accountability* and *inclusiveness*. The UN e-Government Survey 2020 [67] systematically has screened the indicators and strategies that are connected to these three principles for those that are directly or indirectly related to data. And it finds many of them; here, we list a selection of them (for the full list see Table 6.2 in [67], p. 149): "investment in e-government", "monitoring and evaluation", "strategic planning and foresight", "results-based management", "performance management", "financial management and control", "risk management frameworks", "science-policy interface", "network-based governance", "open government data", "budget transparency", "independent audit", "participatory budgeting", "long-term territorial planning and spatial development" [67,68]

All of this strongly indicates the relevance of data for digital government. Different countries utilize data following different approaches, with different attitudes. The UN e-Government Survey 2020 [67] distinguishes between five such approaches: (i) *ICT-driven*, (ii) *data-informed*, (iii) *data-driven*, (iv) *evidence-based*, and (v) *data-centric*, see Table 1. Those are not merely qualitative characterizations of different possible approaches, but, clearly, the UN survey wants to express a "ranking" with the sequence (i)–(v), as it states the following in regards to Table 1 (Table 6.3 in [67]): "Table 6.3 shows the different approaches countries take and reflects a progression of sorts, illustrating how government data are increasingly leveraged for effective governance." [67] In that sense, the data-centric digital government seems to be the ideal to be reached. The question remains, what such *data-centric digital government* should be. It is clear, as it is put at the top of the ranking imposed by (i)–(v), that data are used here most pervasively (as compared with (i)–(iv), and most strategically, i.e., as "key asset"). As eventual purpose, it is said that "data [...] are leveraged for the provision, evaluation and modification of *people-centric* services". Sure, *people-centric* sounds splendid – an eyecatcher. But what are *people-centric* services? Are they services to the citizens? Or to the government? Is people-centricity just a synonym for inclusiveness, which would be nice, or is it something else? Is it something that the citizens actually want? Without a definition, it is not possible to answer such and similar questions. The case study provided by the UN Survey is frightening in this regard, i.e., "The data-centric online-offline integration of digital government in Shanghai" (Box 6.1, p. 157 [67]). The digital government described in this success story incorporates the super-application [43] WeChat – a central building block of China's futuristic next-generation citizen surveillance programme, see the respective Human Rights Watch web page[1], compare also with, e.g., [2,49]. The Gartner Group Report of Andrea Di Maio [14], which is given as reference for the data-centric digital government by the UN survey, does not help clarifying the concept of people centricity – it does not mention the notion of *people-centric* at all.

There are still vast, yet unused, opportunities to exploit data at state level to better the government's effectiveness, accountability and inclusiveness. At the same time, there are huge risks that citizens' data are exploited for citizens' monitoring and control. The challenge is in getting the data governance structure right. And this challenge needs to be understood early in all digital government design issues and, therefore, needs to be reflected in each approach to digital government architecture.

3   On Large-Scale ICT Systems and Institutions

Digital government ecosystems need to be analyzed and designed as socio-technical systems. In analysis of digital government ecosystems, we can receive guidance from Bruno Latour's actor-network theory [40], which "treats the social and the technical as inseparable" [72]. When it comes to design, a digital government ecosystem needs to be *co-designed* with respect to its *institutional architecture* and its *technological assets*.

In [37], Koppenjan and Groenewegen have provided a framework for the co-design of technological assets and institutions of complex, large-scale, technological systems – with foundations in Williamson's *new institutional economics* [74]. The class of systems that are addressed by Koppenjan and Groenewegen can be characterized simply as exactly those systems that have institutions as part of their solution, in particular, with resp. organizations that are not merely consumers of the solution, but make essential contributions to the solution, and

---

[1] https://www.hrw.org/tag/mass-surveillance-china.

Table 2. Economics of institutions; literally compiled from SOURCE: Williamson 1998 [74].

Level	Purpose	Frequency
L1 (social theory) *Embeddedness*: informal institutions, customs, traditions, norms, religion	Often noncalculative; spontaneous	100–1000 years
L2 (economics of property rights) *Institutional Environment*: formal rules of the game – esp. property (polity, judiciary, bureaucracy)	Get the institutional environment right. 1st-order economizing	10–100 years
L3 (transaction cost economics) *Governance*: play of the game – esp. contract (aligning governance structures with transactions)	Get the governance structure right. 2nd-order economizing	1–10 years
L4 (Neo-classical economics/agency theory): resource allocation and employment (prices and quantities, incentive alignment)	Get the marginal conditions right. 3rd-order economizing	Continuous

that "have institutions" (i.e., have institutional setups) that matter. The class of these systems encompass systems such "energy networks, water management services (drinking water, sewage, protection, management), waste treatment, transport systems (rail, road, water, tube), industrial networks, information systems and telecommunication networks, city service [...]." [37]. Rather obvious, many digital government solutions would fall into this category. No later than when it comes to whole digital government ecosystems at the level of states, the whole system can be conceived as belonging to this system class. For example, we have successfully used Koppenjan and Groenewegen's framework to compare the digital government ecosystems of the Netherlands and Estonia [7].

Koppenjan and Groenewegen's (henceforth: KaG's) framework deals with the design process, and also with questions of the *design of the design process* (called 'process design' in [37]), and elaborates a four-level model for institutional analysis, which is ingrained in Williamson's institutional analysis framework (the details of differences between KaG's institutional model and Williamson's framework are not relevant to the discussions in this paper and we will not delve into them). KaG's framework fits scenarios, in which a solution is designed from scratch, as well as scenarios, in which some institutions already exist and need to become subject of re-design. The key insight (key takeaway) from KaG's framework for our framework in Sect. 4 is that, whenever the shape of institutions is crucial for a solution, it needs to be incorporated into the design efforts of the solution. However, beyond that, we do not want our framework in Sect. 4 to be understood as a specialization KaG's framework, and also not as an extension of Kag's framework. We step from considering the design of large-scale solutions to the design of ecosystems of solutions. Such an ecosystem consists of many solutions (in our case, typically, a phletora of solutions; each owned by a different organization). At the same time, we specialize to digital government, which means, in particular, that our architectural considerations are always at *state-level*, i.e., address the state as a whole. Furthermore, we can assume that digital government ecosystems are never build from scratch, as a result of the existing institutional backbone. Building digital government ecosystem is, in major chunks, about adjusting and re-designing institutions.

We want to choose Williamson's institutional analysis framework as a theoretical underpinning. In Table 2, we have compiled the "four levels of social analysis" of the framework (from Fig. 1 in [74]). In [74,75], the analysis framework is presented as part of wider discussions of *new institutional economics*. Institutions at the several levels, L1 trough L4, continuously evolve, at different pace and with different volatility; where they all influence each other (back and forth, even across several levels) in this evolvement. Level L1 is about culture at the societal level. Here, the level of analysis is about history and social science [29,52]. Level L2 is about laws, regulations, government, i.e., formal rules. The investigation of this level dates back to Ronald Coase's 'The Problem of Social Cost' [12]. Level L3 is about organizational governance, in particular, in so far it concerns inter-organizational transactions. It is the level of Coase's 'The Nature of the Firm' [13]. Level L4 is the level of neoclassical economics (price/output, supply/demand etc.) as well as agency theory [32].

An institution is a compound of informal rules (social norms, customs, traditions, commitments etc.) and formal rules (legislation, regulations, contracts etc.). An organization is an *organized* group of people. Organization adhere to institutions. Sometimes, *institution* is used to denote a group of people, for example, it might be that the "family" is called an institution. However, here we would usually not mean a particular group of people but rather the set of typical norms that shape families and that families adhere to, i.e., the notion of family. Similarly, in everyday language, some organizations are often called institutions, in particular, organization from the public sector: the police, a particular university etc. Douglass North defines institutions as "as humanly devised constraints that structure political, economic, and social interactions. They consist of both informal constraints (sanctions, taboos, customs, traditions, and codes of conduct), and formal rules (constitutions, laws, property rights!)" [54].

When we explain our digital government architecture framework in Sect. 4, we use the notions of

- state's institutions,
- (state's) institutional architecture,
- accountable organizations.

The *state's institutions* encompass all kinds of informal and formal rules existing in the society, in particular legislation, in so far they are relevant for government. We do not attempt a precise definition of "relevant for government" here. The notion of the state's institutional architecture is almost synonym to the state's institutions. It merely stresses the fact, that the state's institutions show mutually dependencies and interplay with each other. For the sake of the paper, the *accountable organizations* are deliberately formed, formal organizations and encompass all kinds of organizations from the public sector (agencies, authorities, offices, bureaus, commissions, chambers, chancelleries, public bodies, ministries, etc.) and organizations from the private sector (companies on behalf of public-private partnership, non-governmental organizations, associations etc.). Throughout the paper, we use also *state's organizations* for the organizations from the public sector for short.

4   Digital Government Architecture

This section aims at elaborating a digital government architecture framework, depicted in Fig. 1, that is, essentially, based on the following line of hypotheses:

- The state's institutions are formed following the state's functions. The entirety of the state's institutions, how they are shaped and the way how they interplay makes the state's *institutional architecture*. The institutional architecture usually changes slowly. More precise: substantial changes to the institutional architecture, i.e., those that are the result of societal change, usually occur non-disruptively and take significant time.
- The state's institutional architecture determines the state's *data governance architecture*. The data governance architecture links data assets with accountable organizations along two dimensions: the *interoperability* dimension and the *provisioning* dimension.
- The data governance architecture limits the design space of the *digital government solution architecture*, which consists of all *digital administrative processes* and delivered *e-services*, i.e., those assets that are eventually perceived as digital government by end-users and citizens. The digital government solution architecture can show small, ad-hoc and fast changes.
- Changes in the institutional architecture are so severe, that they can trigger immediate changes in the digital government solution architecture, whereas changes in digital government solution architecture (usually) can only have a long-term influence on changes in the institutional architecture.

In our framework, we say that the data governance architecture and the digital government solutions architecture together form the *digital government architecture*. The data governance architecture forms the backbone, or let us say, the core of the digital government architecture that deals with the necessary fulfilment of data governance; whereas the solutions architecture addresses all kinds of quality aspects of the offered solutions, i.e., usefulness, adherence to good service-design principles, maturity of processes etc.

It is important to note that the discussed architectural framework is not limited to transforming the classic services of public administration or what we would call *e-administration*. Our concept of e-service delivery in Fig. 1 definitely encompasses all e-services, also from the realm of what we would call *e-democracy* including initiatives such as open government data, e-participation, or i-voting. In the current section, we rather not delve into a discussion of the different kinds of state functions. This is deferred to Sect. 6, where we look into digital government architecture in the tension between e-democracy and e-administration.

We claim that a key to understand architecture of digital government ecosystems is in understanding *data governance*. In the context of digital government, data governance is an ultra large-scale, cross-organizational challenge. As a next step, we need to discuss the most important data governance principles in Sect. 4.1, before we can continue with a definition of data governance architecture in Sect. 4.2.

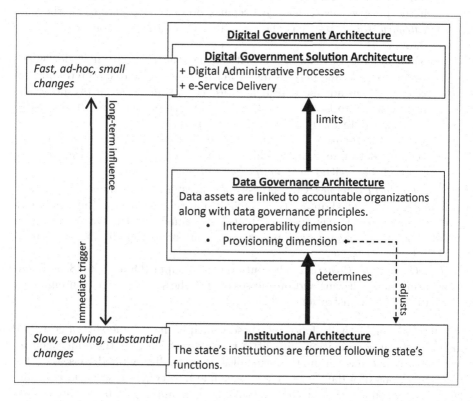

Fig. 1. A digital government architecture framework.

4.1   Data Governance Principles

When it comes to the single authority or organization, data governance is always about *responsibility* for adherence with *data governance principles*; often, it is about *accountability* for adherence with data governance principles. Accountability goes beyond responsibility, i.e., it is given whenever the relevant data governance principles are subject to laws and regulations. If data governance principles are merely recommendations or best practices, we call them *soft* data governance principles; if they are subject to laws or regulations, we call them *hard* or *strict* data governance principles.

In today's digital government initiatives, the following (partially overlapping and mutually dependent) categories of data governance principles can be identified:

- *Data Protection Principles.*
  - *Minimality Principles.* Citizens' data are collected, stored and processed only for *defined* purposes and for *defined* time periods. Data are deleted, if the purpose of its storage becomes obsolete. Depending on the *data category*, the citizen has the right to enforce the deletion of his or her data.
  - *Transparency Principles.* The citizen has the right to know, for which purposes and time periods his or her data are collected, stored and processed. As an advanced principle, for certain *data categories*, he or she has the right to know the data processing history, i.e., *who* has accessed his or her data *when* and for *which* purpose.
  - *Consent Principles.* Depending on the *data category*, the citizen has the right to determine whether his or her data are stored. Consent can be granted resp. withdrawn as *opt-in* or *opt-out*.
- *Data Quality Principles.* Correctness and consistency (resp. non-redundancy), including referential integrity (which is particularly challenging in cross-organizational settings such as digital government [64]). Or, in terms of ISO 25012 [30]: accuracy; completeness; consistency; creditability; currentness. Etc.
- *The Once-Only Principle.* The once-only principle (OOP) [36,38] is about ensuring that "citizens and businesses supply the same information *only once* to a public administration" [23].

Observe that actually following these principles may come with a cost, and higher costs in combination with little to no direct gain for the state agencies will make it less likely that the principles are actually followed. Assessing the costs and gains of a data governance principle in a concrete scenario is a difficult, complex endeavor. The cheapest among these appears to be the minimality principle: collecting less data is typically cheaper than collecting more. On the other hand, deleting data after a prescribed time period is already associated with a cost. Similarly, the data quality principles are important for the functioning of the e-administration and are thus expected to be followed. On the other hand, transparency, consent and the once-only principles provide rather few – if any – immediate benefits to the e-administration; and their implementation is associated with significant costs. Hence, these principles are always less likely to be followed.

On Data Consent. The relationship between the citizen and the state authorities is different from the relationship between a company and its customers, as it is again different between a company and their employees. This matters in so far, as the citizen has no consent right for all kind of data. In accordance with the minimality principle, the state can consider (and regulate) certain citizen data as critical; only beyond this, the consent principle applies. Following the minimality principle, we would expect that critical data are usually master data; whenever it comes, e.g., to log data, trajectory data, or any kind of aggregated personal data, we would expect that a consent principle is granted. Super-application such as Tencent's WeChat in China, as we have described in [43], are the counter-example. We would not count such an application as digital government. In the ideal world, each digital government initiative is expected to be in service of strengthening our democracies, independent of whether the concrete initiative follows a democratic or rather a technocratic narrative [19].

Data consent comes with several synonyms, each with different flavors and different, yet overlapping communities, such as MyData, Self Data, Internet of Me, or PIMS (Personal Information Management Services), compare with the MyData Declaration[2].

Consent Management. The first question of consent management is whether and how citizens can actually block or enable data collection and processing. We argue that building such mechanisms is complex, expensive and may lower the efficiency of e-administration, despite the positive aspects such as increased trust. For example, in the digital government system practiced in Estonia there are almost no consent management mechanisms for citizens. The first pilot project for managing consent (in the context of providing health data to insurers) will be launched in 2021. Instead, a specialized state authority acts as an overseer of digital government systems with the goal to block the unnecessary collection of citizen data, i.e., enforcing the minimality principle. As an additional mechanism, several digital government systems participate in a monitoring system enabling citizens to see when and why their personal data has been transferred from one organization to another. However, participation in this monitoring system is not obligatory and most state organizations do not participate in it, apparently in order to avoid related development costs.

Need for systematic consent management arises also as companies enter the scene. The players in a digital government ecosystem are not restricted to government authorities. Companies and other organization, that are no government authorities can be involved on behalf of public-private partnership (PPP) [55].

On the Once-Only Principle and Data Consistency. At a first sight, the once-only principle (OOP), looks rather like a *service design principle* than a data governance principle, as we have said that it is about not asking the same data from the citizen more than once. It becomes a data governance principle as it can only be resolved by joint coordination efforts of all authorities of the digital government ecosystem together. Sometimes, you can hear that the once-only principle is about not storing a data item in more than one location. But it is

---

[2] https://mydata.org/declaration/.

not. As an example, a simple act of transferring data from one system to another immediately yields a replication of data in different locations. It is also usual – and architecturally sensible – to cache some of the transferred data for longer time in order to avoid frequent requests for the same data items from external sources. Similarly, adherence to the once-only principle cannot help with *data consistency*, which is a data quality principle. Similarly, it can not help resolving lack of consistency in cross-organizational transactions (*long transactions*) [20]. All in all, the OOP appears to be beneficial to the citizens interacting with the e-services, but not so much to the efficiency of e-administration.

4.2   Data Governance Architecture Defined

Each digital government ecosystem has a data governance architecture. A data governance architecture links data assets to accountable organizations along with data governance principles.

First, there is a primary institutional design of the state authorities. This design follows the branches of the state's government with all its entities from the executive, judiciary, and legislature – embodying the entire public administration. The authorities are designed following the functions to be fulfilled by the state's government, following the principle of separation of powers, implementing checks and balances and targeting good governance principles. This primary institutional design is hierarchical and cannot, in general, be arbitrarily changed. Of course, we sometimes see that ministries are re-shaped, e.g., a super ministry might be formed by merging; a new ministry might appear in a legislation period and again disappear in the next etc. However, at the lower level, changing the primary institutional design amounts to major efforts or even reforms.

The state authorities need to collect citizen data to fulfill there functions. By collecting and processing citizen data they become accountable for the fulfillment of data governance principles. This is how data governance architecture is determined by the institutional design. Actually, we can see now that the data governance architecture is the architecture of the digital government ecosystem *per se*. Indeed, data governance may be determined by legislation. For example, in the case of Estonia, both the obligation and right to collect and store specific kinds of data are given to organizations by lower-level legislative acts. These acts then become a primary enforcer for the creation or modification of corresponding IT systems.

A data governance architecture achieves the following. It creates a correspondence between data assets and accountable organizations together with lists of specified data governance principles. More precisely:

A *data governance architecture* specifies for each data asset α, each accountable organization ω, and each data governance principle γ, in how far exactly ω is accountable for α in regards of γ.   (2)

The complete description of a data governance architecture as defined in (2) can quickly become quite complex, because there can be overlaps. Several different organizations might be accountable with respect to the same data asset and data governance principle. Then, it needs to be clarified, what there specific roles are with respect to this data asset in regards to the resp. data governance principle and how they interplay. Actually, we have used accountability as a rather broad term in (2). An accountability in (2) can come in various forms and need to be specified in each single case. In particular, accountability comes with different levels of strictness; a typical approach is, e.g., to distinguish accountabilities in a range from *accountable* (in a more narrow sense then) as the most strict notion (as hard legal accountability) over *responsible* to *consulted* [58]. We will make no attempt here to elaborate a concrete data governance specification approach.

We have seen that the data governance architecture *essentially* follows the primacy of the institutional design; but, at the same time there is some degree of freedom in how the concrete data governance architecture materializes. This degree of freedom shows in two dimensions:

- IT system interoperability
- IT service provision

the first dimension is about *IT system interoperability* (or just *interoperability* for short) and the second dimension is about *IT service provision* (or just *provisioning* for short). The distinction of these two dimension is crucial in design efforts for digital government solutions; we delve into the IT system interoperability dimension in Sect. 4.3 and the IT service provision dimension in Sect. 4.4.

4.3   IT System Interoperability

IT system interoperability and its objective, i.e., IT system *integration* [76], form a major strand of digital government efforts [25] and digital government research [41,42,62]. We explain interoperability via the transformation of data governance architecture in service of strengthening data governance principles as follows. In principle, there is no need for interoperability. Each authority of the primary institutional design could collect and hold all the citizen data it needs. In such a trivial, ad-hoc data governance architecture it is likely to have many data assets redundantly held in several authorities, resulting in significant issues: overall lower data quality, potential inconsistencies, violation of the once-only principle, higher risk of violation of data protection principles (minimality, transparency), difficulties in consent management; hand-in-hand with an increased amount of stakes/efforts in accountability. If an authority stops to collect and hold citizen data, it has to request the data it needs (as transactional data) from peer authorities that grant them access to these data assets, i.e., *interoperability* becomes necessary. The introduction of interoperability can change the data governance architecture to a better one. We see that interoperability cannot be simply explained as the result of *legacy system integration*, instead, it can be shaped along with the design space of the data governance architecture.

Interoperability has several key aspects:

- *Physical Access to Data.* For one organization/system, in order to access data of another organization/system, special parts of the IT systems have to be built. Typically, these come in the form of APIs (Application Programming Interfaces) enabling one system to query specific data from another.
- *Access Management.* Since the data to be transferred is typically not public, both systems must be able to verify the identity of the other system and the existence of actual rights or agreements for transferring data.
- *Semantic Interoperability.* Both the nomenclature, the meaning and the way data are encoded in one system may be different from how it is understood or encoded in another. To facilitate the use of external data, special translation systems have to be developed.

The Estonian governmental data exchange platform X-Road described later in Sect. 5.1 targets both the physical access and access management aspects, but not the semantic interoperability aspect. Indeed, as the number of different systems and their interconnections grows, the semantic interoperability is becoming the most expensive part of interoperability. Due to the immaturity of the technology devoted to semantic aspects of data, this component is typically implemented by non-automated programming, i.e., costly analysis and development work which is repeated anew for most new connections made between different systems.

4.4   IT Service Provision

Multi-tenancy, IT service provision, cloud computing: different terminology for almost the same thing (differences are in the decade, in which the terminologies have been used mostly; and in the technology stack usually connected to them). An IT service provider can increase resilience (this way decreasing risk) and take over responsibility, this way lowering the accountability stake. Often, IT service provision is assessed as the exact opposite by accountable stakeholders, i.e., as increasing risk. This is so, if the stakeholder does not trust or cannot trust the IT service provider (e.g., due to the lack of a sufficient regulatory framework – think of the "safe harbor" debate alone), i.e., if he or she needs to consider the IT service provider as the risk in itself. For example, it is common for governments to require that data managed by the state's organizations has to be stored in the servers physically located in the country. Even more, often government prefer to store data in data centres over which they have direct control: these data centers, on the other hand, may or may not be owned and managed by companies on behalf of public-private partnership.

The introduction of an IT service provider makes this provider a player in the digital government ecosystem. The introduction of an IT service provider changes the data governance architecture, but more fundamentally as in the *interoperability* dimension that we described in Sect. 4.3. The *interoperability* dimension is about shaping accountabilities only; the *provisioning* dimension is indeed about changing the institutional architecture, as indicated by the dashed arrow in Fig. 1. These changes are usually conservative changes, i.e., they extend the existing institutional architecture without changing roles of existing institutions and the interplay between existing institutions. For example, the establishment of a national central data center that hosts the data of the state agencies might not be considered a change to the institutional architecture, but it actually is. The role of the data center needs to be fixed and legally underpinned. The interplay of the data center with the other agencies need to be regulated and established. Now we are in a dilemma. Once the data center is fully established as an organization, provisioning turns out to be interoperability in our framework (and technically, i.e., disregarding the distinction in our framework, ICT provisioning is a form of interoperability anyhow). So, how can we distinguish ICT provision from interoperability any longer? And: should we distinguish ICT provision from interoperability at all? We could distinguish provisioning from interoperability by introducing a notion of *genuine* functions of the state as opposed to *digital-government*-related functions. Actually, it is fair to state, that provision of digital solutions itself is a distinguishable function of the state. With respect to the question, whether we should maintain the distinction between provisioning and interoperability; yes, we think it is important. Actually, it is a distinction that is of utmost importance in practice, for example, it shows in the distinction between *data controllers* and *data processors* in the European GDPR regulation (General Data Protection regulation), as we will explain in due course in Sect. 4.6. Also, the differences are often overlooked or neglected, when it comes to discussion of alternative architectural approaches and styles, in particular, in the analysis of centralization vs. decentralization – we will delve into a discussion of centralization vs. decentralization again in Sect. 4.6.

4.5   Evolving Digital Government

The digital government solution architecture shapes the digital administrative processes and the e-service delivery of the government authorities. Digital administrative processes run inside the authorities and inter-organizational, between the authorities. e-Services are delivered to citizens and companies and allow for triggering digital administrative processes. However, digital administrative processes need no e-service to be triggered. Administrative processes can be digitized (typically always for the sake of making them more efficient and effective) without re-shaping the interaction with the citizens and companies. In public perception and discussion, digital government is often identified with e-service delivery. However, many digital administrative processes actually run without being triggered through e-services. The ratio of administrative processes that are triggered by e-services is actually an interesting, however, often hard to assess or even hard to estimate, indicator for the maturity of digital government, compare with Sect. 5.1.

The state's institutional architecture does not change quickly. Despite smaller adjustments, changes to the institutional architecture are severe, as they reflect changes to the state's functions. A change to the institutional architecture can immediately trigger changes in the solution architecture. Often, in practice, we observe, that changes to the digital government architecture can then be very cost-intensive or even fail. The reason for this is, in general, in the efforts needed to adjust the interoperability and the provisioning dimension of the data governance architecture. Digital government projects that deal with administrative processes inside a single authority can be executed, in principle, without changing the data governance architecture. Still, those projects often fail. But the reason for such this is only in lack of ICT maturity, i.e., with respect to IT governance, IT management, used ICT technologies etc. These are practical problems that are not specific to digital government but can concern all large-scale ICT projects. The question, whether public organization typically rather have a lower ICT maturity (as compared to private companies) is independent of that.

Small, ad-hoc changes to the solution architecture are always possible – as long as these changes do not require changes to the data governance architecture. Such small changes do not lead to direct changes in the institutional architecture. They can contribute, in the long run, to a change of the state's functions (by changing people's awareness, attitudes, minds), and on behalf of that to the institutional architecture. Take participatory budgeting as an example. Surely, a single agency in a single municipality could easily realize some participatory budgeting. (At least, technically and organizationally they could easily; whether they are allowed in regards of the surrounding regulatory framework, i.e., the institutional environment, is exactly again a different question). But a single agency in a single municipality introducing participatory budgeting would make no huge difference at state level, not even at municipality level. Only a systematic, state-level participatory budgeting initiative would also lead to a change in the institutional architecture.

These considerations also set limits to the notion of *disruptive technology*. As soon as institutional architecture is critically involved, technology itself cannot be disruptive. A technology can disrupt a market, but only in the boundaries of the established "formal rules of the game" [74]. A technology can never disrupt a state or a society as a whole, as long as the respective state or society is *non-dysfunctional*.

4.6   Data Governance Architecture in Practice

The Case of the European GDPR Regulation. Understanding the *interoperability* dimension and the *provisioning* dimension as described in Sects. 4.3 and 4.4 is a key to architecture of digital government ecosystems. For example, the dimensions are also reflected in the European General Data Protection Regulation (GDPR) [24]. The GDPR introduces the notions of *data controller* and *data processor* as follows:

(i) "A data controller is a key decision makers [sic]. They have the overall say and control over the reason and purposes behind data collection and over the means and method of data processing."[3]

---

[3] https://www.gdpreu.org/the-regulation/key-concepts/data-controllers-and-proce ssors/.

(ii) "If two or more controllers have the control over purposes and processes, then they are joint controllers. However, this doesn't [sic] apply if they are using the same data for different purposes." (see Footnote 3)

(iii) "A data processor will act on behalf of the controller. They only operate via instructions from the controller. (see Footnote 3)

(iv) "Individual users can make claims for compensation and damages against both [-a] processors and [-b] controllers." (see Footnote 3)

In our context, the data controller (i) is an entity (authority, organization, company etc.) that collects/holds/uses data. (i) also assigns the accountability with respect to the *minimality principle* to the data controller, where the accountability emerges from (iv-b). (ii) is about the interoperability dimension; it clarifies the accountability of entities that exchange data; however, only for the case that the data are used for the same purpose. (iii) is about the *provisioning* dimension – we would call a data processor simply an IT service provider; and again, (iv-a) clarifies the accountability in the *provisioning* dimension.

From the GDPR example we also learn the following. It is important to understand that the *interoperability* dimension and the *provisioning* are crucial, in general. But then it is also crucial to understand their details when it comes to concrete regulatory frameworks.

Centralization vs. De-centralization. Often, in digital government system design efforts, it comes to a discussion of *centralization* vs. *decentralization*, e.g., in the implementation of data exchange solutions. In such discussions, arguments are often misleading, e.g., because they mix technical with organizational arguments at levels that do not fit, or neglect complex relationships between the technological design and institutional design of large-scale systems. A typical argument (that we heard occasionally) might be for example:

$$\text{``We cannot use an ESB (Enterprise Service Bus) implementation,} \atop \text{because citizens cannot trust a centralized government.''} \qquad (3)$$

In a practical project, we cannot ignore a statement such as (3) either, as it surely expresses an important concern.

The point in digital government ecosystem architecture is to systematically decouple considerations from each other along the described *interoperability* and *provisioning* dimension, always against the background of a well-understood data governance architecture. Meaning: when we discuss *centralization*, we first need to clarify and create awareness of the context of the discussion (the same with de-centralization). Are we discussing a centralization in the *institutional architecture* or are we discussing a centralization in the *digital government architecture*, compare again with Fig. 1? If we discuss a centralization in the digital government architecture, are we discussing it with respect to the *interoperability* dimension or with respect to the *provisioning* dimension? For example, a centralization of entities in the primary institutional design is completely different issue from nominating an organization as a *data steward* in the *interoperability* dimension of a data governance architecture. And this is again different from establishing an organization in the *provisioning* dimension, for example, an organization that hosts a message-oriented middleware component or that acts, as yet another example, as the certification authority (CA) of a public key infrastructure (PKI).

5   Established and Emerging e-Government Technologies

5.1   The X-Road Data Exchange Platform

X-Road [3,4,33–35,55,61,73][4,5,6,7] is the data exchange platform of the Estonian digital government ecosystem. X-Road is the only data exchange platform that is mentioned in the UN e-Government Survey 2020 [67]: "The data exchange platform in Estonia (X-Road) is administrated centrally to interconnect government information systems and databases and allow government authorities and citizens to securely send and receive information over the Internet within the limits of their authority."

The Estonian regulation on X-Road [59] defines: "1) the data exchange layer of information systems (hereinafter X-Road) is a technical infrastructure and instance between the members of X-Road, which enables secure online data exchange, ensuring evidential value".

X-Road is a peer-to-peer data exchange system teaming together

- a PKI (public key infrastructure),
- sophisticated software components for secure data exchange,
- a nomenclature of metadata items associated with each message along the core representation language and structure of messages,
- systematic (regulated [59]) organizational measures.

The main technical component of X-Road is the *security server*. An instance of the security server is installed by each authority and organization participating in X-Road (called X-Road members), i.e., there are many security servers running that together realize the secure data exchange in a decentralized manner. The security servers encrypt and decrypt messages, check the identity of other servers and their access rights and preserve a log of messages. Each member registers its e-services in a centrally administered directory. Each member grants access to its e-services itself via the access right management of the security server, i.e., access management remains with the member, determining which other members are allowed to access which of its services and data assets.

---

[4] X-tee in Estonian; in English: originally pronounced as 'crossroad', nowadays pronounced as 'x road'.

[5] https://x-road.global/.

[6] https://www.niis.org/.

[7] https://x-road.global/.

X-Road Usage Patterns. The official statistics page of X-Road[8] indicates, as of January 2021, that there are almost 3000 different services on X-Road, altogether answering approx. 162 million queries per month. Only approx. three percent of the X-Road queries were initiated by private persons for their own informational needs, whereas the absolute majority – 97% – were initiated by a small category of very specific businesses and service providers as well as a large number of the several state's organizations. To be more concrete, the five top data providers for queries during the last month (January 2021) are listed in Table 3. An important context information for these numbers is the population size of Estonia with approx. 1.3 million people.

Table 3. Top five Estonian data providers (X-Road) as of January 2021.

State authority	Queries per month
Employments Registry	≈40 million
System for Drug Prescriptions	≈10 million
e-Health System	≈10 million
Population Registry	≈10 million
Medical Insurance System	≈10 million

In our understanding, almost all the queries to the Employments Registry and the Population Registry are expected to be made for the functioning of e-administration, i.e., intra-organizational data exchange. However, the rest of the top queries (drug prescriptions and health information) are mostly generated by pharmacies selling prescription drugs and doctors writing, storing and using personal medical data and prescribing drugs. Almost all the drug prescriptions in Estonia are electronic and use the X-Road for data exchange. Soon after the introduction of the system in 2010, it has been one of the most frequent sources for X-Road queries.

Looking at the more detailed query statistics along with the X-Road visualization tool[9], we see that the next most active groups of X-Road users after the ones listed in Table 3 are:

– Bailiffs: mainly querying the information from the tax and customs board.
– The Police: mainly querying information from the police databases and car insurances.
– Ridango (a private company managing the sales of most of the public transport e-tickets): querying information about student status, age and similar information directly influencing the price of tickets.

---

[8] https://www.x-tee.ee/factsheets/EE/.
[9] https://logs.x-tee.ee/visualizer/EE/.

Is X-Road De-centralized? The technical basis of X-Road is decentralized. In the actual data exchange, i.e., in sending messages, there is no middleware component involved, as we would find, e.g., in ESB (enterprise service bus) technology, see [16]. In the actual data exchange, there is no man-in-the-middle involved, as we know it, e.g., from the value-add networks (VAN) back in the days of EDI (electronic data exchange), again see [16]. The messages are sent directly between members; but sending of messages is streamlined by the joint protocol of X-Road, which is enforced through the obligatory usage of the security server (either the available implementation, or an own implementation that adheres to the X-Road security server specification). This does not mean, that there is no *centralization* at all in X-Road. First, there is a state-managed central organization and the certification authority (CA) for establishing the PKI (public key infrastructure) [26,65]. Also, the information systems of members (that are accessed then via the e-services of the members) have to be published and confirmed by a registry maintained by the central authority, see the Estonian "X-Road regulation" [59]. This registration process aims to enforce the *minimality principle*, the *data quality* principles and the *once-only* principle, compare with Sects. 4.1. Enforcement of these principles is carried out by different state authorities who have been assigned the task of auditing these aspects of all the information systems registered as users of the X-Road system.

All of this concerns the basic data exchange mechanism provided by X-Road, i.e., the X-Road platform. It does not mean that X-Road prevents *centralized services*. Centralized services can be implemented on top of X-Road. The Estonian *Document Exchange Center* (DEC) resp. Dokumendivahetuskeskuse (DVK) [18,21,57], was a perfect example for this – interestingly, the document exchange center has been deprecated and supersesed by a *de-centralized* document exchange protocol, i.e., DHX (Dokumendivahetusprotokoll)[10]. As another example for adding a centralized service, it is interesting to look at the concept of X-Rooms, which is described in the vision document of Estonia's Government CIO Office on the next generation of digital government architecture [70]. An X-Room is a publish-subscribe service, a standard pattern in message-oriented middleware. If it is just a recommended architectural pattern for realizing e-services, it is not necessarily about adding a centralized service; whereas, if it comes with provisioning, it leads to a centralized service. Adding message-oriented middleware components to a decentralized IT system architecture is standard in enterprise computing. When adding a centralized component, this amounts to adjusting the data governance architecture along the *provisioning* dimension as described in Sect. 4.4.

Is X-Road Based on Blockchain? X-Road is not based on blockchain. The fact that the X-Road security server might exploit cryptographic data structures and algorithms that are also used by blockchain technology [51] (such as Merkle trees [48] for implementing audit logs) does not make it a blockchain. A blockchain – as introduced with the cryptocurrency Bitcoin by Satoshi Nakamoto

---

[10] https://www.ria.ee/dhx/EN.html.

in 2019 [50] – is a peer-to-peer network that implements a distributed, replicated database that achieves consensus via an entirely de-centralized consensus protocol [5,9]. X-Road makes no efforts to achieve consensus, except for authentication, despite there is no centralized ledger. Although X-Road is not based on blockchain technology, it has been sometimes perceived as such by the media. Therefore, in 2018, NIIS (the official product owner of X-Road) launched an official statement[11] that "there is no blockchain technology in the X-Road". What is true however (and what might have contributed to the fact that X-Road has been perceived as blockchain-enabled or even as blockchain) is the fact, that many of the Estonian state registries are secured by a so-called KSI blockchain (keyless signature infrastructure) that we will describe further in due course in Sect. 5.3.

X-Road Federation. In 2014, Finland and Estonia decided to cooperate tightly in developing further their digital government ecosystems. The Nordic Institute for Interoperability Solutions NIIS[12] was founded as a joint agency of Finland and Estonia and was made the official product owner of the X-Road code base [27,60]. In the sequel, X-Road was deployed as a data exchange platform also in Finland and joint efforts were started to realize cross-border, federated digital government services. For a discussion of challenges of and approaches to federation of digital government ecosystem in the context of the case Finland-Estonia, see [27].

Impact of X-Road. The data exchange platform X-Road is mentioned in the UN e-Government Surveys 2016, 2018 and 2020. The UN e-Government Survey 2018 uses X-Road to explain the concept of what they call "Government as an API" [66], as follows:

"Estonia created X-Road, an application network for exchanging data among agency systems so that all government services are effectively available in one spot. In addition to offering querying mechanisms across multiple databases and supporting the secure exchange of documents, X-Road seamlessly integrates different government portals and applications.

The private sector can also connect with X-Road to make queries and benefit from access to a secure data exchange layer.

X-Road has made it possible to bring 99 per cent of public services online. On average, 500 million queries per year are made annually using X-Road. Indeed, its use has been estimated to save as many as 800 years of working time. The solution has been equally successful in its roll-out to Finland, Azerbaijan, Namibia, as well as the Faroe Islands. Furthermore, cross-border digital data exchanges have been set up between Estonia and Finland, making X-Road the first cross-border data exchange platform. " ([66], Box 8.2. Government as an API, p. 184)

---

[11] https://www.niis.org/blog/2018/4/26/there-is-no-blockchain-technology-in-the-x-road.

[12] https://www.niis.org/.

It is important to note, however, that X-Road is used primarily as a tool of e-administration: it is not meant for nor is it used for directly providing e-services or increasing citizen participation. The "public services" mentioned in the last quote should be understood as either inter-organizational data exchange services or information services for citizens, the software of which uses X-Road for obtaining necessary data from other organizations.

Additionally, dozens of countries have used X-Road to implement digital government data exchange[13].

5.2   Other Data Exchange Platforms

Cybernetica UXP. Cybernetica[14] is a spin-off from the Estonian research institute Küberneetika (see Footnote 14) (1969–2006, since 2007: Department of Cybernetics and Department of Software Science of Tallinn University of Technology). Cybernetica designed and implemented crucial parts of the first versions of X-Road in 2001, including architecture, protocols, security solutions, security server. Nowadays, Cybernetica offers its own data exchange platform UXP as a product[15], which is partly based on the same prototype as X-Road version 6.

NLX. NLX[16] is a data exchange platform that is implemented on behalf of an initiative of municipalities in the Netherlands. "NLX is an open source peer-to-peer system facilitating federated authentication, secure connecting and proto-colling in a large-scale, dynamic API ecosystem with many organizations."[17]. The system architecture of NLX is oriented towards X-Road, see Sect. 5.1.

GAIA-X. In September 2020, GAIA-X has been founded as a non-profit organization by eleven companies from Germany plus eleven companies from France under the aegis of the German Federal Ministry for Economic Affairs and Energy (BMWi). According to GAIA-X, it wants "to create the next generation of data infrastructure for Europe, its states, its companies and its citizens."[18]. GAIA-X targets federation; consequentially, *semantic representation* is among its architectural principles [22]. Semantic interoperability is the key to cross-border digital government solutions. A similar institutional design can be found in the digital government ecosystems of several countries (several states of a federal country). Where, e.g., the format of data assets of municipalities can be centrally standardized respectively prescribed, this is not any more possible in federated scenarios. Here, the differences in data format are a major obstacle to successful digital transformation. A key success is in systematic efforts in semantic description and semantic mapping of data assets.

---

[13] https://x-road.global/xroad-world-map.
[14] https://cyber.ee/.
[15] https://cyber.ee/products/secure-data-exchange/.
[16] https://nlx.io/.
[17] https://docs.nlx.io/understanding-the-basics/introduction/.
[18] https://www.data-infrastructure.eu/.

5.3   Auxiliary Technologies for Digital Government

Keyless Signature Infrastructure. Document timestamping solutions are mission-critical in many organizational contexts. Organizations want to have tamper-proof and provable document logs not only in the communications with other organizations; they also want to be safe against failure (accidental or intentional) of their own members/employees. Equally, the state wants to trust the operations of its authorities and, again, the authorities want to trust the operations of their employees. Since 2007, Guardtime offers a document time stamping solution as a service, i.e., the so called KSI blockchain (keyless signature infrastructure blockchain). In the Estonian digital government ecosytem, the solution is successfully used to secure the healthcare registry, the property registry, the succession registry, the digital court system and the state gazette [44].

The KSI blockchain achieves a practical implementation of an idea that goes back to Stornetta et al. in 1993 [6], i.e., it stores timestamped document hashes in a Merkle tree [48] and publishes the root hash of the tree *periodically* (e.g., once a month) in a newspaper (e.g., in the Financial Times, among others, in case of the Guardtime solution) [8, 10], see also [9].

Solid. Solid[19] (Social Linked Data) is a technology originally designed and advocated by Tim Berners Lee. Given the frustration over the state of data sovereignty in the World Wide Web – with players such as Facebook and Alphabet and data scandals such Cambridge-Analytica, Solid targets to free data from applications: to reconnect people to their data, so to speak. The key concept of Solid is the *pod* (personal online data store). A user stores his or her data in a *pod* and grants applications access to these. The user decides where the *pod* is stored and who can access it. In [11], Solid has been used in a pilot study of local and regional governments of Flanders (one of the federated states of Belgium) to "empower citizens in reusing their personal information online in different contexts such as public services, banking, health insurance, and telecom providers." [11]. As such, this project provides a rigorous consent management approach. Therefore, in the context of digital government ecosystems, the limits to such approach are in the limits of consent management *itself*, as described in Sect. 4.1.

6   Discussion

6.1   On Step-by-Step Emergence of Digital Government Solutions

Despite the formulation of all the digital government strategies, visions, agendas, and declarations, today's digital governments are rather *arbitrarily emerging* instead of *systematically evolving*. See Fig. 2. A first digital solution is built. During the design of the solution, the project learns, step-by-step, about the limitations imposed by the underlying institutional architecture. The resulting data

---

[19] https://solidproject.org/.

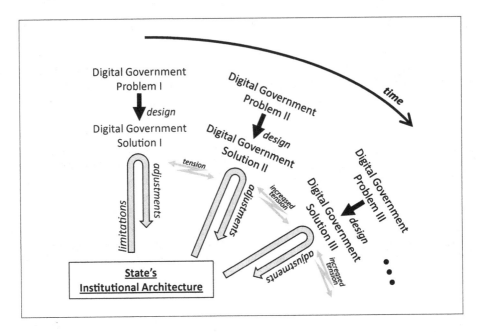

Fig. 2. Step-by-step emergence of digital government solutions in a digital government ecosystem.

governance architecture has the scope of the solution, it is a sub-architecture encompassing only those organizations involved in the solution. A lot of effort is usually invested into provisioning decisions, with the many different stakeholders developing ad-hoc opinions on-the-fly. Slight adjustments are made to the institutional architecture on behalf of provisioning, that seem to have little impact, but actually embody new unpredictable constraints and limitations on future digital government solutions. Next, a further solution project is started for a next digital government problem (problem/solution II in Fig. 2). All problems in shaping the data governance architecture are approached from scratch. Overall, in this process, there is no learning curve. In general, the stakeholders in the second project are different from those in the first; and there is no knowledge transfer from the first to the second project, as there is no systematic *state-level* knowledge management process. This means that the project needs more efforts (is more costly) as it needed to be. A more severe problem is that the design decision in the new project usually follow different design rationales leading to different kinds of decision. The latter creates tension with in between the projects; on the one hand, indirectly via the adjustments to the institutional architecture and, one the other hand, directly – if the projects continue to run in parallel (in future maintenance, follow-up projects etc.). The more digital solutions emerge, the higher rise the tension and, actually, the project costs of new projects.

It can be hoped, that the described frictional losses can be mitigated with a deliberate state-level approach to systematically manage the emergence of the single digital government solutions, this way turning this arbitrary process into a systematic evolvement of digital government. We are convinced, that the elaboration of an architectural framework (such as ours in Sect. 4.2) would be a crucial step towards such systematically evolving digital government.

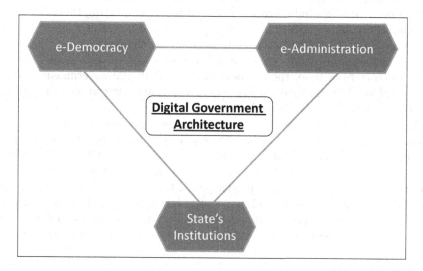

Fig. 3. Digital government architecture in the tension between e-democracy and e-administration.

6.2   On e-Democracy and e-Administration

The field of digital government has always been dominated by two major, well distinguishable strands that we have called *democratic* and *technocratic* narrative in [19]. In the technocratic strand, digital government is about increasing the *efficiency* and *effectiveness* of e-services offered to the *citizen as a customer*. In the democratic strand, digital government is about strengthening our democracies embracing the *citizen as a citizen* with enabling participation and fostering transparency. However, we should not assume that these narratives are a perfect reflection of the underlying forces and motivation driving the development of digital government. Indeed, a strong motivational force is automation of work – similar to industrial automation – even if no e-services are offered or participation encouraged. We will start using the notion of *e-administration*, defined as the automation aspect of digital government. Now, e-administration can be opposed to *e-democracy* with typical digital initiatives such as open government data[20], e-consultation, participatory budgeting, and i-voting [39], see Fig. 3.

---

[20] https://opengovdata.org/.

We have to understand the evolutionary forces behind the development of digital government. Following Bruno Latour, we can look at the modern government authorities as a network of people and automated software systems (e-administration), with the e-democracy component enabling feedback. Since administrations have a tendency to grow [56], but the financial and personnel limits are severe, the growth is naturally channeled into the development of more and more software systems, i.e., a more elaborate e-administration. That is, the motivation behind e-administration is not so much simplifying the work of people working in the organization, as it is growing the power of the organization via automation. We speculate that it is easier to channel regularly necessary change into e-administration than it is to change the traditional human part of the organization. If so, then a more automated digital government could be more flexible while the pace of organizational change would slow down. This hypothesis needs to be confirmed yet.

As the e-administration component grows, so does the need for data: first, automated systems manage to handle practically unlimited amounts of data, second, machine learning and A.I. create a possibility to predict risks in various spheres and thus to both optimize organizational processes and to take a more proactive stance. As examples, consider public transport and road network optimizations, distribution of firefighting and police resources, selecting tax audit targets etc. Since more power needs more feedback for stability, we might expect the e-democracy component to be driven by the growth of e-administration.

7   Conclusion

Currently, the level of digital government implementation, i.e., the pervasiveness of digital government, is discussed prominently in terms of data, i.e., as proceeding form ICT-driven to data-centric digital government. This comes as no surprise, given the substantial developments in the data technology sector, with Big data and data science. Indeed, there are still vast opportunities to exploit data at state level to better the government's effectiveness, accountability and inclusiveness. At the same time, the risk that citizens' data are misused for citizens' surveillance and control will never vanish. The challenge is in getting the data governance structure right. And this challenge needs to be understood early in all digital government design issues and, therefore, needs to be reflected in each approach to digital government architecture.

Technologies come and go. Emerging technologies drive change. Emerging ICT technologies drive digital transformation. In three decades now, the field of digital government has always shown a particularly optimistic approach to be determined by emerging technologies. Digital government has always been ICT-driven. But what is the *function* of digital government? It should be more than making public administration more efficient and effective. It should be in *connecting* governments with citizens. And what is the *form* of digital government? Government has an institutional design. This institutional design gains primacy in the architecture of digital government ecosystems. We argue that the architecture of any digital government ecosystem can be identified, essentially, with its data governance architecture, which links data assets with accountable organizations, supporting a range of data governance principles. We are convinced, that such viewpoint not only helps to analyze existing digital government ecosystems, solutions and technologies alike; but is also a key to shaping the next generation of digital government.

Acknowledgements. The work of Robert Krimmer was supported in parts by European Union's Horizon 2020 research and innovation programme under grant agreements 857622 (ECEPS) and 959027 (mGov4EU).

References

1. Al Gore: Access America: Reengineering Through Information Technology - Report of the National Performance Review and the Government Information Technology Services Board. Vice President of the United States (1997)
2. Andersen, R.: The panopticon is already here. The Atlantic September (2020)
3. Ansper, A.: E-State From a Data Security Perspective. Tallinn University of Technology, Faculty of Systems Engineering, Department of Automation, Tallinn (2001)
4. Ansper, A., Buldas, A., Freudenthal, M., Willemson, J.: High-performance qualified digital signatures for X-Road. In: Riis Nielson, H., Gollmann, D. (eds.) NordSec 2013. LNCS, vol. 8208, pp. 123–138. Springer, Heidelberg (2013). https://doi.org/10.1007/978-3-642-41488-6_9
5. Antonopoulos, A.M.: Mastering Bitcoin: Programming the Open Blockchain. O'Reilly (2017)
6. Bayer, D., Haber, S., Stornetta, W.: Improving the efficiency and reliability of digital time-stamping. In: Capocelli, R., De Santis, A., Vaccaro, U. (eds.) Sequences II, pp. 329–334. Springer, New York (1993). https://doi.org/10.1007/978-1-4613-9323-8_24
7. Bharosa, N., Lips, S., Draheim, D.: Making e-government work: learning from the Netherlands and Estonia. In: Hofmann, S., et al. (eds.) ePart 2020. LNCS, vol. 12220, pp. 41–53. Springer, Cham (2020). https://doi.org/10.1007/978-3-030-58141-1_4
8. Buldas, A., Kroonmaa, A., Laanoja, R.: Keyless signatures' infrastructure: how to build global distributed hash-trees. In: Riis Nielson, H., Gollmann, D. (eds.) NordSec 2013. LNCS, vol. 8208, pp. 313–320. Springer, Heidelberg (2013). https://doi.org/10.1007/978-3-642-41488-6_21
9. Buldas, A., Draheim, D., Nagumo, T., Vedeshin, A.: Blockchain technology: intrinsic technological and socio-economic barriers. In: Dang, T.K., Küng, J., Takizawa, M., Chung, T.M. (eds.) FDSE 2020. LNCS, vol. 12466, pp. 3–27. Springer, Cham (2020). https://doi.org/10.1007/978-3-030-63924-2_1
10. Buldas, A., Saarepera, M.: Document Verification with Distributed Calendar Infrastructure. US Patent Application Publication No.: US 2013/0276058 A1 (2013)
11. Buyle, R., et al.: Streamlining governmental processes by putting citizens in control of their personal data. In: Chugunov, A., Khodachek, I., Misnikov, Y., Trutnev, D. (eds.) EGOSE 2019. CCIS, vol. 1135, pp. 346–359. Springer, Cham (2020). https://doi.org/10.1007/978-3-030-39296-3_26
12. Coase, R.H.: The problem of social cost. Economia November, pp. 386–405 (1937)
13. Coase, R.H.: The nature of the firm. Law Econ. **3**, 1–44 (1960)

192 D. Draheim et al.

14. Di Maio, A.: Moving Toward Data-Centric Government. Gartner Group Report G00248186. Gartner (2014)
15. Draheim, D.: Business Process Technology - A Unified View on Business Processes. Workflows and Enterprise Applications. Springer, Heidelberg (2010). https://doi. org/10.1007/978-3-642-01588-5
16. Draheim, D.: The service-oriented metaphor deciphered. J. Comput. Sci. Eng. **4**(4), 253–275 (2010)
17. Draheim, D.: Smart business process management. In: 2011 BPM and Workflow Handbook, Digital Edition: Social BPM - Work, Planning and Collaboration under the Influence of Social Technology, pp. 207–223. Workflow Management Coalition (2012)
18. Draheim, D., Koosapoeg, K., Lauk, M., Pappel, I., Pappel, I., Tepandi, J.: The design of the Estonian governmental document exchange classification framework. In: Kő, A., Francesconi, E. (eds.) EGOVIS 2016. LNCS, vol. 9831, pp. 33–47. Springer, Cham (2016). https://doi.org/10.1007/978-3-319-44159-7_3
19. Draheim, D., et al.: On the narratives and background narratives of e-Government. In: Proceedings of HICSS 2020 - The 53rd Hawaii International Conference on System Sciences, pp. 2114–2122. AIS (2020)
20. Draheim, D., Nathschläger, C.: A context-oriented synchronization approach. In: Proceedings of PersDB 200 - the 2nd International Workshop in Personalized Access, Profile Management, and Context Awareness: in Conjunction with the 34th VLDB Conference, pp. 20–27. ACM (2008)
21. Äriarhiivi, E.: Requirements for electronic document management systems' functionality (Nõuded elektrooniliste dokumendihaldussüstemide funktsionaalsusele). Eesti Äriarhiivi (2002)
22. Eggers, G., et al.: GAIA-X: Technical Architecture. Federal Ministry for Economic Affairs and Energy (BMWi) Public Relations Division, Berlin (2020)
23. European Commission: EU eGovernment Action Plan 2016–2020: Accelerating the Digital Transformation of Government - COM(2016) 179 final. European Commission (2016)
24. European Commission: Regulation 2016/679 of the European Parliament and of the Council of 27 April 2016 on the protection of natural persons with regard to the processing of personal data and on the free movement of such data, and repealing Directive 95/46/EC (General Data Protection Regulation). European Commission (2016)
25. European Commission: New European Interoperability Framework: Promoting Seamless Services and Data Flows for European Public Administrations. Publications Office of the European Union, Luxembourg (2017)
26. Felt, S., Pappel, I., Pappel, I.: An overview of digital signing and the influencing factors in Estonian local governments. In: Dang, T.K., Wagner, R., Küng, J., Thoai, N., Takizawa, M., Neuhold, E. (eds.) FDSE 2016. LNCS, vol. 10018, pp. 371–384. Springer, Cham (2016). https://doi.org/10.1007/978-3-319-48057-2_26
27. Freudenthal, M., Willemson, J.: Challenges of federating national data access infrastructures. In: Farshim, P., Simion, E. (eds.) SecITC 2017. LNCS, vol. 10543, pp. 104–114. Springer, Cham (2017). https://doi.org/10.1007/978-3-319-69284-5_8
28. Holsapple, C., Whinston, A.B. (eds.): Decision Support Systems: Theory and Application. Springer, Heidelberg (1995). https://doi.org/10.1007/978-3-642-83088-4
29. Huntington, S.P.: The Clash of Civilizations and the Remaking of World Order. Simon & Schuster (1996)

30. ISO/IEC JTC 1/SC 7: ISO/IEC 25012:2008: Software engineering - Software product Quality Requirements and Evaluation (SQuaRE) - Data quality model. International Organization for Standardization (2008)
31. Janssen, M., Kuk, G.: The challenges and limits of big data algorithms in technocratic governance. Gov. Inf. Q. **33**(3), 371–377 (2016)
32. Jensen, M.C., Meckling, W.H.: Theory of the firm: managerial behavior, agency costs and ownership structure. J. Financ. Econ. **3**(4), 305–360 (1976)
33. Kalja, A.: The X-Road: a key interoperability component within the state information system. In: Information Technology in Public Administration of Estonia - Yearbook 2007, pp. 19–20. Ministry of Economic Affairs and Communications Estonia (2008)
34. Kalja, A.: The first ten years of X-Road. In: Kastehein, K. (ed.) Information Technology In Public Administration of Estonia - Yearbook 2011/2012, pp. 78–80. Ministry of Economic Affairs and Communications Estonia (2012)
35. Kalja, A., Robal, T., Vallner, U.: New generations of Estonian eGovernment components. In: Proceedings of PICMET 2015 - the 15th Portland International Conference on Management of Engineering and Technology, pp. 625–631. IEEE (2015)
36. Kalvet, T., Toots, M., Krimmer, R.: Contributing to a digital single market for Europe: barriers and drivers of an EU-wide once-only principle. In: Proceedings of DG.O'2018 - The 19th Annual International Conference on Digital Government Research, pp. 45:1–45:8. ACM (2018)
37. Koppenjan, J., Groenewegen, J.: Institutional design for complex technological systems. Int. J. Technol. Policy Manage. **5**(3), 240–257 (2005)
38. Krimmer, R., Kalvet, T., Toots, M., Cepilovs, A., Tambouris, E.: Exploring and demonstrating the once-only principle: a European perspective. In: Proceedings of DG.O 2017 - The 18th Annual International Conference on Digital Government Research, pp. 546–551. ACM (2017)
39. Krimmer, R., Volkamer, M., Duenas-Cid, D.: E-voting – an overview of the development in the past 15 years and current discussions. In: Krimmer, R., Volkamer, M., Cortier, V., Beckert, B., Küsters, R., Serdült, U., Duenas-Cid, D. (eds.) E-Vote-ID 2019. LNCS, vol. 11759, pp. 1–13. Springer, Cham (2019). https://doi.org/10.1007/978-3-030-30625-0_1
40. Latour, B.: Reassembling the Social - An Introduction to Actor-Network-Theory. Oxford University Press, Oxford (2005)
41. Layne, K., Lee, J.: Developing fully functional e-government: a four stage model. Gov. Inf. Q. **18**(2), 122–136 (2001)
42. Lee, J.: 10year retrospect on stage models of e-government: a qualitative metasynthesis. Gov. Inf. Q. **27**(3), 220–230 (2010)
43. Lemke, F., Taveter, K., Erlenheim, R., Pappel, I., Draheim, D., Janssen, M.: Stage models for moving from e-government to smart government. In: Chugunov, A., Khodachek, I., Misnikov, Y., Trutnev, D. (eds.) EGOSE 2019. CCIS, vol. 1135, pp. 152–164. Springer, Cham (2020). https://doi.org/10.1007/978-3-030-39296-3_12
44. Martinson, P.: Estonia - The Digital Republic Secured by Blockchain. PricewaterhouseCoopers (2019)
45. Matheus, R., Janssen, M., Maheshwari, D.: Data science empowering the public: Data-driven dashboards for transparent and accountable decision-making in smart cities. Gov. Inf. Q. **37**(3), 1–9 (2020)
46. McBride, K., Draheim, D.: On complex adaptive systems and electronic government - a proposed theoretical approach for electronic government studies. Electron. J. e-Gov. **18**(1), 43–53 (2020)

47. McNeely, C.L., Hahm, J.: The big (data) bang: policy, prospects, and challenges. Rev. Policy Res. **4**, 304–310 (2014)
48. Merkle, R.: Protocols for public key cryptosystems. In: Proceedings of S&P'1980 - The 1st IEEE Symposium on Security and Privacy, pp. 122–122 (1980)
49. Mozur, P.: Inside China's dystopian dreams: A.I., shame and lots of cameras. The New York Times 8 (2019)
50. Nakamoto, S.: Bitcoin: A Peer-to-Peer Electronic Cash System (2008). https:// bitcoin.org/bitcoin.pdf
51. Narayanan, A., Clark, J.: Bitcoin's academic pedigree. Commun. ACM **60**(12), 36–45 (2017)
52. Nee, V., Ingram, P.: Embeddedness and beyond. In: Brinton, M., Nee, V. (eds.) The New Institutionalism in Sociology, pp. 2–45. Russell Sage Foundations (1997)
53. Nonaka, I., Takeuchi, H.: The Knowledge-Creating Company: How Japanese Companies Create the Dynamics of Innovation. Oxford University Press, Oxford (1995)
54. North, D.: Institutions. J. Econ. Perspect. **5**, 97–112 (1991)
55. Paide, K., Pappel, I., Vainsalu, H., Draheim, D.: On the systematic exploitation of the Estonian data exchange layer X-Road for strengthening public private partnerships. In: Proceedings of ICEGOV 2018 - The 11th International Conference on Theory and Practice of Electronic Governance, pp. 34–41. ACM (2018)
56. Parkinson, C.N.: Parkinson's law. Economist (1955)
57. PricewaterhouseCoopers: Public Services Uniform Document Management - Final Report (Lõpparuanne Avalike teenuste ühtne portfellijuhtimine). Pricewaterhouse-Coopers (2014)
58. Project Management Institute: Organization Charts and Position Descriptions. In: A Guide to the Project Management Body of Knowledge (PMBOK Guide), 5th edn., pp. 260–261. Project Management Institute (2013)
59. Regulation no. 105: The Data Exchange layer of Information Systems. Government of the Republic of Estonia (2016)
60. Robles, G., Gamalielsson, J., Lundell, B.: Setting up government 3.0 solutions based on open source software: the case of X-Road. In: Lindgren, I., et al. (eds.) EGOV 2019. LNCS, vol. 11685, pp. 69–81. Springer, Cham (2019). https://doi.org/10.1007/978-3-030-27325-5_6
61. Saputro, R., Pappel, I., Vainsalu, H., Lips, S., Draheim, D.: Prerequisites for the adoption of the X-Road interoperability and data exchange framework: a comparative study. In: Proceedings of ICEDEG 2020 - The 7th International Conference on eDemocracy & eGovernment pp. 216–222, IEEE (2020)
62. Scholl, H.J., Klischewski, R.: E-government integration and interoperability: framing the research agenda. Int. J. Public Adm. **30**(8–9), 889–920 (2007)
63. Shen, J., et al.: Data-informed decision making on high-impact strategies: developing and validating an instrument for principals. J. Exp. Educ. **80**(1) (2012)
64. Tepandi, J., et al.: The data quality framework for the Estonian public sector and its evaluation. Trans. Large-Scale Data Knowl. Center. Syst. **35**, 1–26 (2017)
65. Tsap, V., Pappel, I., Draheim, D.: Key success factors in introducing national e-identification systems. In: Dang, T.K., Wagner, R., Küng, J., Thoai, N., Takizawa, M., Neuhold, E.J. (eds.) FDSE 2017. LNCS, vol. 10646, pp. 455–471. Springer, Cham (2017). https://doi.org/10.1007/978-3-319-70004-5_33
66. UN Department of Economic and Social Affairs: United Nations E-Government Survey 2018 - Gearing e-Government to Support Transformation Towards Sustainable and Resilient Societies. United Nations, New York (2018)

67. UN Department of Economic and Social Affairs: E-Government Survey 2020 - Digital Government in the Decade of Action for Sustainable Development. United Nations, New York (2020)

68. UN Economic and Social Council: Relating the Principles of Effective Governance for Sustainable Development to Practices and Results - Note by the Secretariat, E/C.16/2019/4. United Nations (2019)

69. United Nations General Assembly: Transforming Our World: the 2030 Agenda for Sustainable Development - Resolution A /RES/70/1. United Nations (2015)

70. Vaher, K.: Next Generation Digital Government Architecture. Republic of Estonia GCIO Office (2020)

71. van Ooijen, C., Ubaldi, B., Welby, B.: A Data-Driven Public Sector: Enabling the Strategic Use of Data for Productive, Inclusive and Trustworthy Governance. OECD Working Papers on Public Governance No. 33. OECD (2019)

72. Walsham, G.: Actor-network theory and IS research: current status and future prospects. In: Lee, A.S., Liebenau, J., DeGross, J.I. (eds.) Information Systems and Qualitative Research. ITIFIP, pp. 466–480. Springer, Boston, MA (1997). https://doi.org/10.1007/978-0-387-35309-8_23

73. Willemson, J., Ansper, A.: A secure and scalable infrastructure for inter-organizational data exchange and eGovernment applications. In: Proceedings of the Third International Conference on Availability, Reliability and Security 2008, pp. 572–577 (2008)

74. Williamson, O.E.: Transaction cost economics: how it works; where it is headed. De Economist **146**, 23–58 (1998)

75. Williamson, O.E.: The new institutional economics: taking stock, looking ahead. J. Econ. Lit. **38**(3), 595–613 (2000)

76. Wimmer, M., Traunmüller, R.: Integration - the next challenge in e-government. In: Proceedings of EurAsia-ICT 2002: 1st EurAsian Conference Information and Communication Technology, pp. 213–218. LNCS 2510, Springer (2002)

Correction to: pygrametl: A Powerful Programming Framework for Easy Creation and Testing of ETL Flows

Søren Kejser Jensen (D), Christian Thomsen (D),
Torben Bach Pedersen (D), and Ove Andersen (D)

Correction to:
**Chapter "pygrametl: A Powerful Programming Framework
for Easy Creation and Testing of ETL Flows" in:**
A. Hameurlain and A Min Tjoa (Eds.):
*Transactions on Large-Scale Data- and Knowledge-Centered
Systems XLVIII*, **LNCS 12670,**
https://doi.org/10.1007/978-3-662-63519-3_3

In the originally published version of chapter 3, there was an error in the affiliation and email address of the author Ove Andersen, as well as in reference 17. This has been corrected.

The updated version of this chapter can be found at
https://doi.org/10.1007/978-3-662-63519-3_3

Author Index

Printed in the United States
by Baker & Taylor Publisher Services